Titles include:

Pascale Aebischer, Edward J. Esche and Nigel Wheale (*editors*)
REMAKING SHAKESPEARE
Performance across Media, Genres and Cultures

James P. Bednarz
SHAKESPEARE AND THE TRUTH OF LOVE
The Mystery of 'The Phoenix and Turtle'

Mark Thornton Burnett
FILMING SHAKESPEARE IN THE GLOBAL MARKETPLACE

Lowell Gallagher and Shankar Raman (*editors*)
KNOWING SHAKESPEARE
Senses, Embodiment and Cognition

Stefan Herbrechter and Ivan Callus (*editors*)
POSTHUMANIST SHAKESPEARES

David Hillman
SHAKESPEARE'S ENTRAILS
Belief, Scepticism and the Interior of the Body

Jane Kingsley-Smith
SHAKESPEARE'S DRAMA OF EXILE

Stephen Purcell
POPULAR SHAKESPEARE
Simulation and Subversion on the Modern Stage

Erica Sheen
SHAKESPEARE AND THE INSTITUTION OF THEATRE

Paul Yachnin and Jessica Slights
SHAKESPEARE AND CHARACTER
Theory, History, Performance, and Theatrical Persons

Palgrave Shakespeare Studies
Series Standing Order ISBN 978–1–403–91164–3 (hardback)
978–1–403–91165–0 (paperback)
(*outside North America only*)

You can receive future titles in this series as they are published by placing a standing order. Please contact your bookseller or, in case of difficulty, write to us at the address below with your name and address, the title of the series and the ISBN quoted above.

Customer Services Department, Macmillan Distribution Ltd, Houndmills, Basingstoke, Hampshire RG21 6XS, England, UK

Posthumanist Shakespeares

Edited by

Stefan Herbrechter
Coventry University, UK

and

Ivan Callus
University of Malta, Malta

First published 2012 by
PALGRAVE MACMILLAN

Palgrave Macmillan in the UK is an imprint of Macmillan Publishers Limited,
registered in England, company number 785998, of Houndmills, Basingstoke,
Hampshire RG21 6XS.

Palgrave Macmillan in the US is a division of St Martin's Press LLC,
175 Fifth Avenue, New York, NY 10010.

Palgrave Macmillan is the global academic imprint of the above companies
and has companies and representatives throughout the world.

Palgrave® and Macmillan® are registered trademarks in the United States,
the United Kingdom, Europe and other countries.

ISBN 978–0–230–36090–7

This book is printed on paper suitable for recycling and made from fully
managed and sustained forest sources. Logging, pulping and manufacturing
processes are expected to conform to the environmental regulations of the
country of origin.

A catalogue record for this book is available from the British Library.

A catalog record for this book is available from the Library of Congress.

10   9   8   7   6   5   4   3   2   1
21 20 19 18 17 16 15 14 13 12

Printed and bound in Great Britain by
CPI Antony Rowe, Chippenham and Eastbourne

To the memory of Adam Max Cohen (1971–2010)

Contents

Illustrations   x

Acknowledgements   xi

Contributors   xii

Introduction – Shakespeare ever after   1
Stefan Herbrechter
Shakespeare 'after' Shakespeare   1
Shakespeare 'after' theory   4
Shakespeare 'after' humanism   7
Life 'after' Shakespeare   9
Shakespeare 'after' technology   11
Shakespeare 'after' the human   12
We have never been human   14
The contributions   15
Works cited   17

Part I   Reading Shakespeare 'after' Humanism

1 **The Science of the Heart: Shakespeare, Kames and the
   Eighteenth-Century Invention of the Human**   23
   Neil Rhodes
   Notes   38
   Works cited   39

2 **'a passion so strange, outrageous, and so variable':
   The Invention of the Inhuman in *The Merchant of Venice***   41
   Stefan Herbrechter
   When did we become posthuman?   41
   Shylock's humanism   46
   The Merchant of Venice: posthumanism and misanthropy   51
   Notes   55
   Works cited   56

3 **Shakespeare and the Character of Sheep**   58
   Bruce Boehrer
   Notes   73
   Works cited   74

4 **Homeostasis in Shakespeare**   77
   Gabriel Egan
   Notes   92
   Works cited   92

Part II 'Posthumanist' Readings

5 **Care, Scepticism and Speaking in the Plural:**
   Posthumanisms and Humanisms in *King Lear*   97
   Andy Mousley
   Notes   112
   Works cited   112

6 **Cyborg *Coriolanus* / Monster Body Politic**   114
   Mareile Pfannebecker
   Notes   129
   Works cited   130

7 **Renaissance Self-Unfashioning: Shakespeare's Late**
   Plays as Exercises in Unravelling the Human   133
   Rainer Emig
   Introduction   133
   Humanism's alterities   134
   Timon of Athens – unravelling humanism's premature
      success story   135
   Pericles, Prince of Tyre – alien encounters   145
   Working through / with / against humanism from within   153
   Notes   155
   Works cited   157

8 **Surviving Truth (*Measure for Measure*)**   160
   Mark Robson
   Notes   174
   Works cited   175

Part III *Hamlet*, 'Posthumanist'?

9 **(Post-)Heideggerian *Hamlet***   181
   Laurent Milesi
   Who's there? A thing or nothing?   181
   Untimeliness revisited   184
   From ek-sistence to desistance   185
   Post-scriptum: posthumous, posthuman Hamlet   188
   Notes   190
   Works cited   192

10 **Loam, Moles and *l'homme*: Reversible *Hamlet*** 194
   Marie-Dominique Garnier
   Becoming Gilles Shakespeare 194
   Touching ground 196
   Between who? 197
   Letters without post: from Chronos to Aion 199
   Imp, impersonal, imp/post/hume 202
   Your rats your rations your rats rations 204
   To M.E.L.T., to T.H.A.W. 205
   Hamlet on a plateau 207
   L'homme into loam 208
   Posts and stops: from *Hamlet* to Henry Miller 209
   Notes 210
   Works cited 211

11 **'This?': Posthumanism and the Graveyard Scene
   in *Hamlet*** 213
   Ivan Callus
   'The Shakespearean Collection': novelty, posthumanism
      and death 213
   Truncation, beheading, recognition, (mis)identification:
      the graveyard scene reread 220
   Posthumanism and the graveyard scene in *Hamlet* 229
   Notes 234
   Works cited 236

Afterword

12 **Post-Posthumanist Me – An Illiterate Reads Shakespeare** 241
   Adam Max Cohen and David B. King
   Works cited 255

Index 256

Illustrations

11.1 Toby Jug, *Hamlet*, Royal Doulton Number D6672,
photograph Joseph Mangion   215

11.2 Théodore Géricault, *Severed Heads*, © The Nationalmuseum
Stockholm, reproduced with permission   222

x

Acknowledgements

An earlier version of the 'Introduction' was first published in Andreas Höfele and Stephan Laqué (eds), *Humankinds: The Renaissance and Its Anthropologies*, Berlin: De Gruyter, 2011, pp. 261–78, as 'Shakespeare ever after: Posthumanism and Shakespeare', which can be obtained at <http://www.degruyter.com/>. Reproduced with permission.

Chapter 3, 'Shakespeare and the Character of Sheep', first appeared in Bruce Boehrer, *Animal Characters: Nonhuman Beings in Early Modern Literature*, Philadelphia: University of Pennsylvania Press, 2010, pp. 175–82. Reprinted by permission of University of Pennsylvania Press.

Contributors

Bruce Boehrer is author of five books, most recently *Animal Characters: Nonhuman Beings in Early Modern Literature* (2010). He is also editor of *A Cultural History of Animals in The Renaissance* (2007) and co-editor of the *Journal for Early Modern Cultural Studies*. He lives in Florida.

Ivan Callus is Associate Professor and Head of the Department of English at the University of Malta, where he teaches courses in contemporary narrative and in literary theory. Together with Stefan Herbrechter, he is the co-editor of Rodopi's monograph series, Critical Posthumanisms, and also of *Discipline and Practice: The (Ir)resistibility of Theory* (2004), *Post-Theory/Culture/Criticism* (2004) and *Cy-Borges: Memories of Posthumanism in the Work of Jorge Luis Borges* (2009). He is the author of papers and book chapters on poststructuralism and deconstruction, on contemporary fiction, and on posthumanism. He is currently completing a monograph on the anagram notebooks of Ferdinand de Saussure.

Adam Max Cohen was Associate Professor of English at the University of Massachusetts Dartmouth, where he specialized in Shakespeare, early modern literature and early modern cultural studies. He explored the intersections between early modern literature and the history of science and technology. He was the author of *Shakespeare and Technology: Dramatizing Early Modern Technological Revolutions* (2006), *Technology and the Early Modern Self* (2009) and *The Wonderful Worlds of William Shakespeare* (forthcoming 2012). At age 38, Adam succumbed to brain cancer on 2 January 2010.

Gabriel Egan is the author of *Shakespeare and Marx* (2004), *Green Shakespeare: From Ecopolitics to Ecocriticism* (2006) and *The Struggle for Shakespeare's Text: Twentieth-Century Editorial Theory and Practice* (2010). He has edited Richard Brome and Thomas Heywood's play *The Witches of Lancashire* (2002) and a collection of essays called *Electronic Publishing: Politics and Pragmatics* (2011) and co-edits the journals *Theatre Notebook* and *Shakespeare*. He is currently writing a book called 'Shakespeare and Ecocritical Theory'.

Rainer Emig is Chair of English Literature and Culture at Leibniz University in Hanover, Germany. He was educated at Frankfurt am Main, Warwick and Oxford, and has taught at Cardiff and Regensburg, Germany. He is especially interested in the link between literature and the media and in Literary, Critical and Cultural Theory, especially theories of identity, power, gender and sexuality. His publications include the monographs *Modernism in Poetry* (1995), *W. H. Auden* (1999) and *Krieg als Metapher im zwanzigsten Jahrhundert* (2001), as well as edited collections on *Stereotypes in Contemporary Anglo-German Relations* (2000), *Ulysses* (2004), *Gender ↔ Religion* (with Sabine Demel, 2008), *Hybrid Humour* (with Graeme Dunphy, 2010), *Performing Masculinity* (with Antony Rowland, 2010) and *Commodifying (Post-) Colonialism* (with Oliver Lindner, 2010). He is one of the three editors of the *Journal for the Study of British Cultures*.

Marie-Dominique Garnier is Professor of English literature and Gender studies at the University of Paris 8-Vincennes, France, where she teaches Shakespeare, modernism and gender. She co-edited a volume on Hélène Cixous, *Cixous sous X* (2010). Her main field of research is on the intersection of philosophy, literature and gender. Publications include articles on Derrida and the animal, on Cixous and haecceities, and on the poetry of James Joyce (forthcoming). She is currently working on the translation of American poets and architects Madeline Gins and Arakawa, with a translation of Madeline Gins's *Helen Keller or Arakawa* (1994).

Stefan Herbrechter is Reader in Cultural Theory at Coventry University. He is the author of *Critical Posthumanisms* (with Ivan Callus; 2012), *Posthumanismus – Eine kritische Einführung* (2009) and a number of books, edited volumes and articles on literature, film, media and critical and cultural theory.

David B. King co-authored the screenplay *Halsted* that won the silver medal at the Maryland Film Festival and is currently under option by Nine Dot Entertainment. He served as Creative Advisor for PBS station WETA's documentary *Halsted* and PBS American Experience's *Apollo 8: Race to the Moon*, assisted the news-writers of ABC-News, and taught English Literature and Creative Writing at Colorado State University, where he earned his MFA.

Laurent Milesi is Reader in Twentieth-Century English/American Literature and Critical Theory at Cardiff University and is a member of the ITEM-CNRS Research Group on James Joyce's manuscripts in Paris. He has written numerous essays on Joyce and related aspects of modernism, nineteenth- and twentieth-century (American) poetry, postmodernism and poststructuralism, with a particular emphasis on Jacques Derrida and Hélène Cixous. His edited collection, *James Joyce and the Difference of Language*, was published in 2003 (digitally reprinted in 2007), and his annotated translation (together with Stefan Herbrechter) of Jacques Derrida's *H. C. pour la vie, c'est à dire ...* came out in 2006. His annotated translations of Cixous's study of Beckett, *Le Voisin de zéro*, as well as of *Philippines* were both published in 2011, and his translation of her novel *Tombe* will be published in 2012. He is also preparing a collection of her shorter essays on Jacques Derrida as well as completing a long-term monograph on the sense of '(non-)place' in Derrida's works.

Andy Mousley is Reader in Critical Theory and Renaissance Literature at De Montfort University, Leicester. He is the author of *Re-Humanising Shakespeare: Literary Humanism, Wisdom and Modernity* (2007), *Critical Humanisms* (2003, with Martin Halliwell) and *Renaissance Drama and Contemporary Literary Theory* (2000). He is the editor of *Towards a New Literary Humanism* (2011) and *New Casebooks: John Donne* (1999). He has had articles published on new literary humanism in *Textual Practice* (2010), on posthumanism in *Postmedieval* (2010) and on 'Shakespeare and the Meaning of Life' in *Shakespeare* (2009). He is also the series co-editor of the Edinburgh Critical Guides to Literature.

Mareile Pfannebecker completed her PhD thesis on humanisms of travel in early modern drama and travel writing at the Centre for Critical and Cultural Theory, Cardiff University. She is now working on a project on posthumanist politics in Ben Jonson's and William Shakespeare's drama.

Neil Rhodes is Professor of English Literature and Cultural History at the University of St Andrews. He is co-General Editor, with Andrew Hadfield, of the MHRA Tudor and Stuart Translations. He is the author of *Shakespeare and the Origins of English* (2004) and his other publications include the edited collections (with Stuart Gillespie) *Shakespeare and Elizabethan Popular Culture* (2006) and (with Jonathan Sawday) *The Renaissance Computer: Knowledge Technology in the First Age of Print* (2000).

Mark Robson is Associate Professor of Modern English Literature at the University of Nottingham. In addition to having written many essays on Shakespeare, early modern culture and critical theory, he is the author of *Stephen Greenblatt* (2008) and *The Sense of Early Modern Writing* (2006), co-author of *Language in Theory* (2005), editor of *Jacques Rancière: Aesthetics, Politics, Philosophy* (2005) and co-editor of *The Limits of Death: Between Philosophy and Psychoanalysis* (2000). Forthcoming publications include *Shakespeare, Jonson and the Claims of the Performative* (with James Loxley), *What Is Literature?* and a book on the poetics and politics of suicide.

Introduction – Shakespeare ever after

Stefan Herbrechter

Shakespeare 'after' Shakespeare

> Shakespeare, like the sun, is a metaphor; he always
> means something other than he is.
>
> (Wilson, 1996, p. 128)

Edward Pechter's *What Was Shakespeare* (1995) set out to evaluate
Shakespeare Studies after the so-called 'Theory Wars' and concluded
that, at the turn of the millennium at least, there was no 'end of
Shakespeare Studies as We Know It' in sight, rather a 'transformation'
(Pechter, 1995, p. 14). This transformation – the result of ideological battles over the role of literature, history, politics and aesthetic
value – seemed to have shattered a kind of previous consensus, or,
as Pechter calls it, a 'unified discourse' (p. 18) in Shakespeare criticism. The unified discourse was that of 'formalist humanism' (p. 30),
which collapsed as a result of the combined attack of poststructuralist
theory, postmodernism, feminism, postcolonialism, new historicism
and cultural materialism. At the centre of this 'alternative' and
'political' Shakespeare were 'questions about textuality and history, and
about subjectivity, agency, and political effectiveness' (p. 38). Where the
self-stylized radicalism of the new dissidents saw discontinuity, however,
Pechter in his critique sees nothing but continuity – since dissidence and
radical critique are the very backbone of the humanities and humanism
itself. This is a tenet that has become quite strong in recent years: the
anti-humanism of theory and new historicism often relies in fact on a
caricature of ('liberal') humanism and detracts from the idea that the
humanities have always depended and thrived on dissensus, rather than
a kind of enforced ideological consensus, as their fundamental form of

1

knowledge production – an argument most forcefully made in Edward Said's *Humanism and Democratic Criticism* (2004).

There is of course something utterly disarming about the idea of the humanities – the core of the venerable humanist institution called 'University' – as thriving on dissensus rather than agreement. And it is true that some of the antihumanism of theory today, upon rereading, appears somewhat 'naff' and its use of politicized 'jargon', at times sounds almost like 'agit-prop'. But the idea that a return to some form of idealized 'radical humanism' might be possible is equally unconvincing, simply because the cherished idea of a humanist university ceased to exist at the same time as theory, cultural studies and the new interdisciplinarity apparently came to rule over it. The university (and the humanities) has been 'in ruins' ever since (Readings, 1997) and merely survives in its neoliberal, managerialized, 'posthistorical' and 'postcultural' form. With it ceased not only the consensus of a 'unified discourse' (e.g., in Shakespeare criticism) but also, in a sense, 'Shakespeare' himself. As Scott Wislon explains, Shakespeare has become a mere icon, an empty metaphor, a commodity and an 'object of an institutionally channelled desire' (Wilson, 1996, p. 129). Hence Wilson's conclusion that whatever remains of Shakespeare must be subject to 'heterology'. Shakespeare criticism 'after' Shakespeare has been looking for what remains 'other' and 'utterly heterogeneous to his homogenized cultural body' (p. 129). As Wilson rightly points out, even this heterology can still be recuperated by a new form of humanism – this volume is certainly not immune to this danger ('posthumanism' is still some form of humanism, after all). Shakespeare may have become a 'collapsing star' and a 'black hole' (Taylor, 1990), or a 'dense, retentive abyss reflecting nothing but the horror, the impotent plight of the would-be uniquely clever, honest and above all disciplined Shakespeare scholar faced with over 4,000 items lodged by the World Shakespeare Bibliography every year and the certain knowledge that any and every interpretation evaporates the instant it is written' (Wilson, 1996, pp. 130–1); but the human and humanist urge of the Shakespeare scholar past, present and to come should not be underestimated. Shakespeare's 'solar unassailability' will not stop engulfing humanistic scholarly labour. So, what to do when humanism in its most antihumanist, political and theoretical form becomes a cynical 'reflex'? If this sounds like an almost existentialist dilemma it probably is, and hence the call for 'authentic' action cannot be far off. We know, since Sartre, that existentialism is also a humanism, a 'dogged' and desperate humanism '*malgré tout*'. Wilson's proposed 'authentic' action, in fact, follows Bataille's logic in 'putting [Shakespeare] back into the use circuit *as* shit' and 'putting all of Shakespeare's shit, all that is remote, revolting, terrible, Other and so on back into play' (p. 136). Shakespeare's texts thus become the 'resident evil', that which cannot be recuperated by any humanism, simply because it is not (entirely) human. Investigations into the 'inhuman' in Shakespeare are what has been proliferating ever since and while these readings are not immune to a recuperation by humanism they are nevertheless no longer entirely humanist. We would suggest, they are, for want of a better word, 'posthumanist', and thus constitute a new approach within Shakespeare studies.

However, posthumanist does not imply a simple turning away, either from humanism or from theory, but rather a continued 'working through' or a 'deconstruction' of humanism for which something like theory is needed more than ever. It also is no turning away from historicism and materialism, but it is a historicism and materialism adapted to the changed, 'posthuman' condition. One aspect of this condition 'after' humanism is the lost consensus and the lost universalism concerning history and culture. The relevance of Shakespeare after humanism lies in a combination of the 'presentism', the strategic anachronism, even futurism, as expressed in Linda Charnes's well-known essay 'We Were Never Early Modern' (2006), in which she claims that Shakespeare in contemporary culture stands for 'Historicity itself' (p. 42). It is not so much 'calendar time' as the intensity of 'subjective time' outside the dialectic between early and late modernity that resonates in Shakespearean characters like Hamlet. They are 'always already postmodern, or rather, *amodern* – since ... one cannot "post" something that has not yet happened' (p. 47). This is not to say, however, that their value lies in a timeless aestheticist human essence, or that they speak to the 'heart of human feeling', but that they highlight – in analogy with Bruno Latour's argument in *We Have Never Been Modern* (1993) – that modernity (and we would claim humanism) remains a 'virtuality' or an impossible task:

> If Latour is correct that we have never been modern, then Hamlet has never been early modern, we have never been postmodern, and we are all, along with the pesky Prince, stuck in the same boat with regard to what, exactly, 'being historicist' means ... Hamlet continues to speak to us because he continues to be 'timeless': not because he 'transcends' history but because *we were never early modern*. (Charnes, 2006, pp. 48, 52)

Shakespeare 'after' theory

> A conjunction between tradition and novelty in Shakespeare's plays
> exercises an enchantment at once renewable and altogether singular.
> (Belsey, 2007, p. 20)

It seems thus that after several decades of heated ideological debates,
theory, canon and culture wars, if not settled, have petered out in the
general crisis and decline of the humanities. Hardened ideological
positions on historicist and cultural relativism and the role of truth,
politics, ethics and aesthetic value in literature and culture have mel-
lowed. However, the role of the early modern period, the Renaissance
and Shakespeare after having been hotly contested by new historicists,
cultural materialists, traditionalists and humanists, remains as unclear and
ambiguous as ever. As a result there is a new uncertainty in Shakespeare
and early modern studies. The uncertainty this time, however, seems
more profound – too pressing are the 'future of the humanities' and the
'role of literature' questions to allow for a simple return to business as
usual in the post-theoretical English department. What returns instead is
a new kind of pluralism, precisely around the notion of the human and
humanism, and around the relationship between literature and life, and
between mind, body and technology. Humanism, having been one of
the main targets of theory, continues to be the main battleground, arguably this time in its pluralized form: that is, humanism*s*. A new dissensus
about the past, present and future of humanism and its subject – that
is, the human – emerges, as a result of a number of new threats. The
'posthuman' and 'posthumanism' are starting to take shape, but just
like the fragmentation of humanism into mainstream or liberal humanism, existentialist humanism, radical humanism etc., the uncertainty
and pluralization spills over into that which is supposed to supersede
it. Posthumans promise and threaten in many familiar and sometimes
less familiar forms. Posthumanisms revaluate, reject, extend, rewrite
many aspects of real or invented humanisms. There is no surprise in this,
because that is what the prefix 'post-' does. This is its rhetorical essence: it
ambiguates. It plays with supersedence, crisis, deconstruction, regression
and progression at once. Its main virtue, if one chooses to take it seriously,
is to defamiliarize, detach and surprise. 'Posthumanist Shakespeares' does
not want to be dogmatic about the resurfacing of the human and humanism in their fragile forms. It wants not only to show 'care' for the human,
humanness, humanity but also to embrace the new plurality and the new
questions that are put to humanism, anti-humanism, posthumanism, even

transhumanism alike: questions of human survival in late modern, global, techno-scientific hypercapitalist societies with their technocultures. Above all, it wants to confront humanism with its 'specters' – the inhuman, the superhuman, the nonhuman in all its invented, constructed or actual forms. It is a strategic move away from anthropocentric premises: the human can no longer be taken for granted; humanity as a universal value is no longer self-legitimating; humanism as a reflex or self-reflex cannot be trusted. To stay 'critical' (in a humanistic or 'philological' [cf. Said, 2004] sense) in these times of plurality and global risk means to reread, to read carefully but also differently. This is what combines the contributions to this volume despite their obvious differences in their respective interpretation of what needs to be done and what role Shakespeare (and literature) can play in the face of this uncertainty. We would like to suggest the label 'critically posthumanist' as a compromise that shows the care, the scepticism and the openness towards Shakespeare 'after' Shakespeare, or Shakespeare after humanism. Some of the guiding questions are as follows. Is there life beyond Shakespeare? What is Shakespeare's importance for the age of 'life sciences'? What does Shakespeare have to tell us about our post-anthropocentric or even post-biological times? Can we still make him our contemporary?

It must be clear, however, that this kind of question cannot be answered without theory. But it is theory no longer entrenched in ideological dogmatism but a much more relaxed and open-minded theoretical approach that values the lessons learned from the theory and other wars. Theory that puts its ear to the ground and listens to the new sounds, which, it is true, mostly come from the sciences these days – bio-, info-, cogno-, neuro- etc. sciences to be precise. It is no wonder that, in the face of the challenges that these new sciences, after the so-called 'science wars', the question of the human and the question of the relationship between literature and life, come back to haunt the humanities. *Posthumanist Shakespeares* would therefore like to signal to everyone interested in literature, culture and the sciences that, by referring to the current climate as posthumanist, we do not mean dehumanizing but simply that the human and humanity are in radical transition or transformation. Humanism – the discourse about what it means to be human – is in the process of transformation and hence the object of this discourse – the human (who is also its subject, but maybe no longer exclusively so) – is being rewritten. The anxiety and desires that this change and uncertainty cause reopen, for Shakespeare studies, the question of the bard's (or by now also the 'CyberBard's' [Charnes, 1996, p. 142]) role within the history of humanism.

The argument as to what exactly Shakespeare's humanism entails and what function it plays in his work is far from being settled, and remains to be pursued in all its complexity. It goes beyond critiques of the positioning of Shakespeare as a mainstay of a 'liberal' education or the temptation to read decadence or 'anarchy' (as Matthew Arnold might have had it) in any of the related counter-positions. It is in any case not a question of polarization between pro- and anti-humanists that is needed in order to continue to make Shakespeare and the early modern period relevant to our so-called 'posthumanist' moment. What is at stake, instead, is a historically and textually informed clarification of the privileged relationship between the early modern on the one hand and the late modern, or even postmodern, on the other: between early humanism and a humanism that may be on its last legs, awaiting either its renewal or, indeed, its end. This opens onto what we mean by posthumanism. Posthumanism, as we understand it here, is a critical stance that is at one and the same time aware of at least three choices for a contemporary literary criticism mindful of the interdisciplinary temper of our time. The first of these choices reacts to the consequences of what is most canonical within the canon becoming increasingly detached from any of the assumptions that consolidated a humanist paradigm. The second choice responds to outlooks that distance themselves even further from those assumptions, and recognizes that the implications of bio-, nano-, cogno- and info-technology on body, mind, culture and epistemology have now become part of mainstream debate within the humanities and within interdisciplinary explorations of the integrity of the human. It should therefore be possible to read Shakespeare according to reconceptualizations influenced by these outlooks – among them the possibility that Shakespeare may actually have 'invented' the posthuman as well as the human. The third choice remains doggedly insistent that nothing much substantially has changed, that Shakespeare has survived far worse upheavals than these, and that it continues to be perfectly feasible to read him as if there were no hint of a brave new world that has such posthumanists in it.

It is with all this in the background that the contributions to *Posthumanist Shakespeares* revisit the humanist/anti-humanist debate in the light of current thinking, cultural practices and reorientations towards the posthuman. In practical terms, this involves recognizing that at present the question of what it means to be human is being asked in the context of dramatic technological change. Rereading Shakespeare within this present therefore takes on a new and exciting relevance. To discuss whether Shakespeare's work coincides with the invention of the human is surely to question also his understanding of the inhuman, the non-human, the more-than-human, the less-than-human. Above all, it involves exploring whether the posthuman, too, finds itself there already. Is it prefigured, represented, contested in Shakespeare? If so, is it possible to come up with a posthumanist approach to Shakespeare that would be able to respond to his work in the light of critical perspectives that retain the memory of humanism but which also seek to exemplify what posthumanist interpretation might entail?

Shakespeare 'after' humanism

> Life itself has become a naturalistic unreality, partly, because of Shakespeare's prevalence ... To have invented our feelings is to have gone beyond psychologizing us: Shakespeare made us theatrical ... (Bloom, 1999, p. 13)

The question of Shakespeare's humanism has created a vast amount of controversy and heated debate between self-proclaimed humanists and proponents of a politicized new historicist and cultural materialist Shakespeare. The argument has mostly been fought at an ideological level and has involved some strategic misrepresentations of the other camp. New Historicists and cultural materialists have been reduced to 'postmodernists' or 'constructivist anti-essentialists', while all too often defenders of Shakespeare's presumed 'humanism' have themselves been caricatured as politically naive, reactionary or idealist-*cum*-aestheticist. Those who seek a ready point of reference for this debate need go no further than reactions to Harold Bloom's notorious equation of Shakespeare with the 'invention of the human' and Bloom's idea that we were 'pragmatically invented' by Shakespeare.

Indeed, Harold Bloom's *Shakespeare: The Invention of the Human* (1999) insists on explaining Shakespeare's pervasiveness through his apparent universalism. It is of course a very Western universalism Bloom has in mind because he equates it with the invention of (modern) personality, which, in turn, is taken to be, as the subtitle professes, the 'invention of the human':

> More even than all the other Shakesperean prodigies – Rosalind, Shylock, Iago, Lear, Macbeth, Cleopatra – Falstaff and Hamlet are the invention of the human, the inauguration of personality as we have come to recognize it. The Idea of Western character, of the self as a moral agent, has many sources: Homer and Plato, Aristotle and

Sophocles, the Bible and St. Augustine, Dante and Kant, and all you might care to add. Personality, in our sense, is a Shakespearean invention, and is not only Shakespeare's greatest originality but also the authentic cause of his perpetual pervasiveness. (Bloom, 1999, p. 4)

For Bloom, Shakespeare *is* the Western and *therefore* the universal canon, and thus the only defence against the 'anti-elitist swamp of Cultural Studies' (p. 17) which has presumably led to the current identity crisis within the humanities. Quite obviously, Bloom represents all that has been discredited in 'mainstream' humanism: an aestheticism that makes moral political (i.e. liberal) judgements on the basis of an apparent 'empirical supremacy' (p. 16).

While Bloom defends the universalism and meliorism of the humanistic project against postmodern cultural relativism, others, like Robin Headlam Wells, in their defence of humanism and their attack on theory's anti-essentialism and cultural constructivism turn to quite unlikely allies, like evolution, biology and genetics. Quite ironically, the idea that there may be a human 'essence', after all, even if it is not cultural but genetic, is seen as somehow 'liberating'. Humanity is not a construct but a 'predisposition', the self not an invention but a neuropsychologically explicable effect of hard-wired evolution-driven brain activity. As a result, literature (including criticism), strictly speaking, becomes a branch of 'cognitive poetics' and neuroscience. We would certainly agree – and some of the contributions in this volume actually take on the cognitive and neuroscientific challenge – that in the light of technoscientific change literary criticism cannot stand still. But, from our point of view, it is precisely because of this change that a straight-forwardly humanist understanding of literature is no longer possible. Replacing theoretical anti-essentialism and constructivism with a new bioscientific essentialism cannot repair humanism, and using genetic notions of human 'nature' to defend oneself against antihumanist theory only accelerates the proliferation of a rather uncritical form of posthumanism. Wells's project in *Shakespeare's Humanism* (2005) to show 'the centrality of human nature in Shakespeare's universe', 'by listening to what other disciplines have to say about human nature', in order for criticism to 'move on from an outdated anti-humanism' (p. 5), might turn out to be rather counter-productive. The anti-anti-essentialism directed against new historicism and theory is bought at the price of a new 'naturalism' and techno-idealism. Instead, there is a new and, we would claim, critically posthumanist, materialism at work in the contributions to this volume, which does engage with technological challenges not by comparing concepts of human nature but, precisely, by denaturing the human as such. One simply does not need the mystification of a phrase like 'human nature' to explain what constitutes our species's biological and cultural characteristics once evolution is no longer confused with teleology. This does not invalidate the theory of evolution, it merely helps to 'de-anthropocentre' it. It is important not to confuse or freely slide between universalism and essentialism in terms of human nature. The fact that members of the species *homo sapiens* (*sapiens*) share genetic and cultural characteristics that, at a basic non-normative level, are undoubtedly universal does not *automatically* lead to moral aesthetic values about human nature since the concept of nature just like all the concepts used in science (from 'life' to 'gene') are first and foremost linguistically and culturally mediated entities. A *critical* posthumanism is turning its back neither on constructivism nor on materialism and historicism, nor on the idea that universal *meaning* like truth is not given but *made*. A statement such as Wells's 'If there were no universal passions and humors, we would have no means of evaluating literature from another age or another culture: a text would have value only for the community in which it was produced' (Wells, 2005, p. 192) is not an argument against a presumed theoretical 'presentism', because it neglects the fundamentally hermeneutic condition of all human and maybe also non-human knowledge, namely, that meaning, including historical and scientific meaning, always needs to be appropriated and interpreted by a materially, historically and radically contextualized subject. This is, in fact, precisely what Wells is doing in attempting to redress what he thinks is an imbalance. What else does it prove to show that Shakespeare and his historical Renaissance or early modern context were already in many ways anti-essentialist than to increase (and construct) Shakespeare's continued, renewed, intensified, modulated etc. relevance to our own, equally constructed, stance regarding *our* present time? We regard the opening up of literature and criticism 'after' humanism, following on from and thus inheriting postmodern theory, towards what appear to be fundamental technoscientific challenges, towards a constructed human nature, as inevitable but not as unproblematic – hence our appeal for a *critical* posthumanism.

Life 'after' Shakespeare

Can Shakespeare help us with the question of how to live? (Mousley, 2007, p. 1)

For Andy Mousley, in *Re-Humanising Shakespeare* (2007), Shakespeare's greatness undoubtedly lies in his 'humanity'. He tries to revive the idea of 'Shakespeare as sage' or of the great writer's wisdom as that part of Arnoldian criticism that looks upon literature as a 'coherent criticism of life'. Mousley sees a resurgence of 'literary humanism' after anti-humanist theory that reaffirms literature as an 'antidote to dehumanisation, alienation and instrumentalism' (p. 8). Shakespeare's ethics and the 'existential significance' of his writings for living an 'authentically human' life should not, however, do away with anti-humanist theory's 'scepticism' (p. 12). Mousley tackles this seemingly impossible task by differentiating between what he calls 'mainstream humanism' ('individualism ... sovereignty, unbridled freedom, autonomy and a magnified image of humanity'; pp. 16, 17) – which was and continues to be the justified target of theoretical scepticism – and 'other humanisms' that do not depart from a 'transcendent' human 'nature' but see the essence of humanness as an exploration of its limits – or, as Jean Paul Sartre famously explained, in defending existentialism against what he called '*les naturalistes*', that it, existentialism, is a humanism, because it starts from a radicalized idea of freedom (namely, as responsibility and task) and from the lack of determination in anything human, captured in the phrase 'l'existence précède l'essence'. For Mousley, however, we cannot be just anything. Having examined the various scepticisms and nihilisms staged by Shakespeare in Part 1 of his book, Mousley turns in Part 2 to plays which indicate the persistence of certain bodily and emotional needs or affects, and explores the implications of these needs for questions of value and ethics. In short, Shakespeare was both a sceptic and a sage, a kind of ironic humanist. Mousley thus puts his trust in Shakespeare to achieve a 'better humanism' (p. 23), one that constitutes an attempt 'to answer the question of what remains of the human, when "the human" like all else is liable to evaporate' (p. 25). Shakespeare, he hopes, may help us to 'become human' (p. 30), after all.

Mousley, in what we would call his 'yearning for the human' (paraphrasing Akeel Bilgrami's 'Foreword' (Said, 2004, p. x), is following in the footsteps of eminent and critical humanists like Edward Said, for whom humanism is first of all, literally speaking, self-criticism, while the foremost task of every humanist scholar or 'philologist' is to be critical of humanism itself. As admirable and noble as this existential, almost desperately hopeful, yearning for our 'promised' humanity is, the radical openness of the human and thinking the human 'at the limits' are part of a risky strategy. Humanism has never been able to guarantee anything, and even Shakespeare as 'life coach' cannot perform miracles. There have always been humans who yearn for something entirely other than (being) human – and currently their number seems on the rise again. One can yearn for God, the machine, artificial intelligence, transhuman successor species, in short, transcendence in any form. This is why we have no confidence in merely radicalizing the critical potential that undoubtedly lies in some forms of humanism (cf. Halliwell and Mousley, 2003) and instead insist on using the strategically ambiguous 'posthumanist' label, at the risk of being mistaken for 'techno-enthusiasts' ourselves. But the historical-material imperative compels us to take the newness of the posthuman challenge seriously and, to a certain extent, literally. Shakespeare 'after' humanism is still humanist – maybe. But the challenge to the humanist tradition does not just stem from anti-humanist theory, it also lies in 'post-, de-, super-, trans-' etc. humanizing tendencies *within* technoscience and late capitalist humanity itself. In this sense, Shakespeare is not only 'after' humanism but also 'after' technology and, ultimately, 'after' the human as such.

Shakespeare 'after' technology

In many ways, the posthuman gestures towards technology and cultural change that, if not driven by, at least is inseparable from technological and scientific development. However, that this is no one-way street is demonstrated by a number of the contributions to this volume, which take their cue from inspiring and provocative works such as Neil Rhodes and Jonathan Sawday's *The Renaissance Computer* (2000b) or Arthur F. Kinney's *Shakespeare's Webs* (2004) or Adam Max Cohen's *Shakespeare and Technology* (2006). Shakespeare's own awareness of technological change in early modern culture takes place at a time when modern knowledge partitioning was not yet in place and thus interdisciplinarity or rather 'transdisciplinarity' made a dialogue between early scientific investigation and humanistic study relatively simple. There was also no modern sense of technology but merely mechanical practices, tools, new instruments, machines and artefacts or 'techniques'. That technical and machinic metaphors are present in Shakespeare's works is no secret; but their ambiguity is also a reflection of a developing general cultural ambiguity towards the machinic human 'other'. Especially in such a mechanical environment as the theatre the mixing of human and machine, and thus early modern forms of 'cyborgization', is never far away – a process that Cohen names 'turning tech', by which he means the 'description of the individual as a machine' (Cohen, 2006, p. 17). If the early modern age is the beginning of the *homo mechanicus*, and if early modern literature gives rise to something like the literary cyborg (cf. Sawday, 1999), there is also ambiguity about the distinction between nature and culture, the boundaries of the body, biology and spirituality, materialism and idealism, emotion and cognition and the role and nature of affect. No wonder that cognitive and neurosciences are increasingly called upon to explain the cognitive cultural 'map' of the early modern mind and 'Shakespeare's brain' (cf. Crane, 2000). All these are attempts to demonstrate the continued if not increasing relevance of Shakespeare and the privileged relationship between early and late modern culture. One useful analogy here might be the image of 'retrofitting', in the sense of creating an adaptability between old and new (technologies, and by analogy cultures and their readings) which thus represent a kind of reinforcing and bridging continuity. *Posthumanist Shakespeares* is therefore also about 'retrofitting' the early modern in this sense – combining technological change with continuity and cultural 'ecology'. Links are forged between the 'first age of print' and that which presents itself as maybe the last age of print with its transition to digital and digitalized cultures and their respective major conceptual reorientations. As Rhodes and Sawday put it:

> The computer, through its possibilities for interactivity, 'play' and the creativity of hypertext, is now rapidly undoing that idealization of stability [underpinning the age of print], and returning us to a kind of textuality which may have more in common with the pre-print era. (2000a, pp. 11–12)

Even though the Shakespearean text will undoubtedly survive into the digital age, the idea and the available technologies relating to text and textuality (cf. the wonderful French phrase *traitement de texte*) – text, which itself, as Graham Holderness reminds us, is in its irreducible multiplicity a piece of technology (2003) – will change, have already changed the practice of textual editing and literary criticism. It is thus becoming increasingly difficult to disentangle 'pastism' (historicism), 'presentism' and 'futurism' in Shakespeare studies after technology.

Shakespeare 'after' the human

Ultimately, the effect of the collapsing of the humanist tradition and the radical opening of the human and its meaning is motivated ethically, hence the major focus on not only non-human others, the inhuman, the subhuman, but also the superhuman. On the one hand, there is the 'greening' of Shakespeare through various forms of ecocriticism; on the other hand, the postanthropocentric thrust of posthumanist theory that concerns itself with all kinds of nonhuman others also radicalizes the so-called 'animal question'. Gabriel Egan explains his motives in writing *Green Shakespeare* as an attempt to 'show that our understanding of Shakespeare and our understanding of Green politics have overlapping concerns' (Egan, 2006, p. 1). The increasing and concretizing threat of environmental disaster, questions of sustainability and the contemporary critique of 'speciesism' actually go hand in hand. What do early modern forms of 'ecology' and attitudes towards nature and animals have to teach late modern Green politics and animal rights movements? There is a new organicism, vitalism and ideas of interconnectedness between nature and culture, humans and their environment, networks and nodes, that promises new forms of interdisciplinarity between the sciences and the humanities outside or 'after' the humanist tradition, producing new, posthuman(ist) forms of subjectivity. To what extent can the beginning of modernity and humanism be helpful in making choices for us who find ourselves at the other end of five hundred years of modernity and humanism? Again, the notion of retrofitting seems appropriate here:

> Shakespeare's plays show an abiding interest in what we now identify as positive-negative-feedback loops, cellular structures, the uses and abuses of analogies between natural and social order, and in the available models for community. Characters in Shakespeare display an interest in aspects of this natural world that are relevant for us, and if we take that interest seriously we find that there is nothing childlike or naïve about their concerns. (Egan, 2006, p. 50)

In analogy with the indeterminacy of nature and culture in early modern times, there is also a 'space of ontological indeterminacy' between humans and animals, according to Bruce Boehrer (2002, p. 1). It is worth studying the 'distinctions between human and animal nature', which are 'central to western cultural organization ... help to license particular forms of material and economic relations to the natural world ... help to suggest and reinforce parallel social distinctions on the levels of gender, ethnicity, race, and so on' historically (p. 3), but it is also necessary to draw parallels with contemporary forms of anthropomorphism, anthropocentrism and speciesism. In *Perceiving Animals* (2000), Erica Fudge argues for this kind of continuity, this retrofitting of early modern and late modern speciesism. The 'degradation of humanity in the face of the beast in early modern thought is a recurring theme,' she explains (Fudge, 2000, p. 10); but anthropomorphism allows for both sentimental humanization of animals and animalization of humans. If this mutual dependence of the violent and speciesist process of 'becoming human' and 'becoming animal' is a major concern in early modern culture and in early modern humanism, then it increasingly comes back to haunt a late modern, posthumanist culture, in which the boundaries between human and animal (including all those between humans and their other related significant others which have played and continue to play a role in the process of shoring up and guaranteeing the humanity of the human: the monster, the machine etc.) once again, this time through bio- and other technologies, have become, to use Donna Haraway's word, 'leaky'. 'Thinking with animals' becomes thus a major task, since 'ignoring the presence of animals in the past [as in the present or the future one might add] is ignoring a significant feature of human life' (Fudge, 2004, p. 3). Nonhuman animals can be both agents in human culture and also subjects: 'humans cannot think about themselves – their cultures, societies, and political structures – without recognizing the importance of nonhumans to themselves, their cultures, societies, and political structures' (p. 4). *Posthumanist Shakespeares* means therefore also sharing in this 'dislocation of the human' brought about by the return of its nonhuman others and the possible parallel between the challenges to early modern and late modern humanism, where, as Donna Haraway (1985 [2004]) puts it, the distinctions between human and animal, and human and machine have become blurred (Haraway, 1985 [2004], p. 10).

We have never been human

Posthumanist Shakespeares – the phrase thus ultimately opens up several lines of questioning: what would it mean to read Shakespeare no longer 'as' humanist – neither as a humanist author nor from a humanist (reader's) standpoint? Who, in fact, is the 'real' posthumanist, Shakespeare or 'we'? Two humanisms are thus in doubt – Shakespeare's and ours. Doubting, after a period of prolonged theoretical anti-humanism, can also mean several things. On the one hand, it can simply be a rather stubborn confirmation of humanism, a return to 'common sense' in seemingly post-theoretical times (cf. Bloom, Wells). On the other, it can also lead to a revaluation of humanism, in the form of a critical return to and an affirmation of the radical potential within humanism itself (cf. Said, Mousley). But it may also be understood as an attempt to read Shakespeare through all sorts of figurations of the 'inhuman' (either in its late modern, technological forms, like cyborgs, machines, computers etc., or in its more timeless, even premodern or 'amodern' appearances, like ghosts, monsters, animals etc.). Finally, critical post-humanism can also work its way back to Shakespeare and construct genealogies between his work and a perceived or real current shift away from a humanist knowledge paradigm, the possible advent of a new 'episteme', in which the human again becomes a radically open category, for the promise of a postanthropocentric, posthumanist future.

The contributions

The contributions to this volume take up this variety of angles in their respective rereadings of Shakespeare's plays and Shakespeare criticism. While the first part ('Reading Shakespeare "after" Humanism') groups four essays that reflect on the legacy of humanist and anti-humanist criticism, the four essays in the second part ('"Posthumanist" Readings') contain readings of individual plays that at the same time critically engage with some 'clichés' found in posthumanist theory.

It is of course no surprise that some Shakespearean plays figure more prominently than others. Inevitably, *Hamlet* with its insistent questioning of 'man' takes centrestage, and we have therefore grouped the three essays on *Hamlet* in this volume in a separate section ('*Hamlet*, Posthumanist?') to emphasize the specific affinity between posthumanist approaches and both Hamlet the character and *Hamlet* the play. The volume concludes with a 'post-posthumanist' afterword, co-written by Adam Max Cohen and David B. King. Sadly, this after-word has by now indeed become a posthumous contribution. Adam Max Cohen here first narrates his experience of 'forced illiteracy' due to the blindness induced by a brain tumour. This tumour has since claimed his life.

The first chapter by Neil Rhodes helps to contextualize the shift from humanist to anti-humanist and posthumanist Shakespeare criticism by redrawing the discussion around the 'invention' of 'human nature' and the 'science of man' in the eighteenth century (and the Scottish Enlightenment in particular). It highlights the importance of Henry Kames's role in establishing a 'humanist' Shakespeare at the heart of English Studies. Stefan Herbrechter's detailed critique of Harold Bloom's *Shakespeare: The Invention of the Human* argues against the opposition of humanism and anti-humanism and, instead, proposes a 'critical posthumanism' which would 'need to overcome the ideological confrontation between liberal humanists and cultural materialists mindful of both the historical context and current cultural change' (p. 44).

Shakespeare's work in general, and *The Merchant of Venice* in particular, can thus be understood to be formally and historically located 'at a certain turning point within the process of "post/humanization"' in which Shakespeare is both 'the possible starting point of a certain humanism' and already anticipates 'its decline and ultimate ruin' (p. 45). Bruce Boehrer builds on his influential work on early modern animal studies and demonstrates 'the role played by the species divide in the development of sixteenth- and seventeenth-century models of literary character' (p. 58). He thus approaches 'Shakespearean posthumanism from the perspective of animal-studies'. Shakespeare's hinge-like position at the threshold of modernity preserves a privileged relation to the 'prehuman' which forms a point of contact with the 'post-anthropocentric' posthuman. Gabriel Egan, in his contribution, shows that the anti-cartesianism of the 'cognitive revolution' in the twentieth and twenty-first centuries had been anticipated by Shakespeare in a complication of the distinction between the inanimate, the merely living ('machine-matter') and the 'immaterial' mind, the 'hard distinction' between 'mechanical' and 'living' processes, which, according to Egan, favours an eco-critical reading of the 'dramatizations of self-regulation' (homeostasis) in Shakespeare and early modern culture.

Part II starts with Andy Mousley's contribution, which represents an account of 'the humanisms and versions of the human in contention in *King Lear*' (p. 98) and argues against the excesses of posthumanist scepticism and its lack of 'care' for the human.

Even though the tragedies and the problem plays figure prominently in this volume, there are also some less predictable choices. Mareile Pfannebecker's discussion of the 'early modern cyborg' theme is an example. While Coriolanus' character might look like an obvious choice for this form of reading, the essay breaks new ground by addressing 'how the theme of obstinacy in *Coriolanus* is relevant to human politics and a politics of the human' (p. 115). Rainer Emig uses Shakespeare's late plays (*Timon of Athens* and *Pericles* in particular) to problematize Greenblatt's notion of (Renaissance) self-fashioning by focusing on the complexity of Timon and Pericles as characters who turn themselves into 'aliens' and 'disappointed' humanists. Their misanthropy unsettles the foundations of humanist sociality and shows that 'a thinking through and thinking beyond the supposed essentials of an emerging humanism already and exactly at the time when these were first formulated' (p. 155). Mark Robson's revaluation of *Measure for Measure* focuses on the potential within the phrase 'measure for measure' for a posthumanist politics as, for example, in Derrida, Rancière and Nancy.

Part III, '*Hamlet*, "Posthumanist"?', contains three essays that re-engage with the philosophical problematics of ontology 'after' the 'ends of man' debate provoked by Jacques Derrida, Jean-Luc Nancy, Gilles Deleuze and others in the 1980s. Laurent Milesi uses Derrida's reading of *Hamlet* to show that posthumanist theory under-estimates the extent of Heidegger's and Derrida's (and by implication Shakespeare's) earlier critique of humanism and anthropocentrism. Hamlet's '"posthumanity" (both posthumous and posthuman) stems from the "non-contemporaneity with itself of the living present"', Milesi argues, slightly repositioning Derrida's well-known verdict on Hamlet's 'hauntology' (pp. 180, 184).

Marie-Dominique Garnier's essay is a questioning of the human/ posthuman pair in the context of a fireworks of seriously playful trans-formations of Hamlet's 'name' and the play's 'lexical encounters'. Ivan Callus focuses on the graveyard scene in *Hamlet* and argues against the dangers of the repression of death and finitude in some posthumanist (or 'transhumanist') scenarios. As Callus explains: 'The graveyard scene seems to predestine the reminder that as we move towards the post-human death pulls us back' (p. 232). To the extent that arguably the 'most clichéd scene' in Hamlet, maybe in all of Shakespeare, reminds us, 'humans', of our 'familiarity with death', it is almost enough to 'allay posthumanism's fondest hopes' (p. 232). What *Posthumanist Shakespeares* thus reminds us of is this curious 'yearning for the human' that always anticipates but never reaches its very essence of being 'posthum(an)ous' – a theme that is echoed in Adam Max Cohen's and David King's Afterword, 'Post-posthumanist Me – an Illiterate Reads Shakespeare'.

Works cited

Belsey, Catherine (2007) *Why Shakespeare?* Basingstoke: Palgrave.
Bloom, Harold (1999) *Shakespeare: The Invention of the Human*, London: Fourth Estate.
Boehrer, Bruce (2002) *Shakespeare among the Animals: Nature and Society in the Drama of Early Modern England*, Basingstoke: Palgrave, now Palgrave Macmillan.

Bruster, Douglas (2003) *Shakespeare and the Question of Culture: Early Modern Literature and the Cultural Turn*, Basingstoke: Palgrave, now Palgrave Macmillan.

Chambers, Iain (2001) *Culture after Humanism: History, Culture, Subjectivity*, London: Routledge.

Charnes, Linda (1996) 'Styles That Matter: On the Discursive Limits of Ideology Critique', *Shakespeare Studies* 24, pp. 118–47.

Charnes, Linda (2006) *Hamlet's Heirs: Shakespeare and the Politics of a New Millennium*, New York: Routledge.

Cohen, Adam Max (2006) *Shakespeare and Technology: Dramatizing Early Modern Technological Revolutions*, Basingstoke: Palgrave, now Palgrave Macmillan.

Crane, Mary Thomas (2000) *Shakespeare's Brain: Reading with Cognitive Theory*, Princeton: Princeton University Press.

Dollimore, Jonathan (2004) *Radical Tragedy: Religion, Ideology and Power in the Drama of Shakespeare and His Contemporaries*, 3rd edn, Basingstoke: Palgrave, now Palgrave Macmillan.

Egan, Gabriel (2006) *Green Shakespeare: From Ecopolitics to Ecocriticism*, London: Routledge.

Fudge, Erica (2000) *Perceiving Animals: Humans and Beasts in Early Modern English Culture*, Basingstoke: Macmillan, now Palgrave Macmillan.

Fudge, Erica (ed.) (2004) *Renaissance Beasts: Of Animals, Humans, and Other Wonderful Creatures*, Urbana: University of Illinois Press.

Fudge, Erica, Ruth Gilbert and Susan Wiseman (eds) (1999) *At the Borders of the Human: Beasts, Bodies and Natural Philosophy in the Early Modern Period*, Basingstoke: Palgrave, now Palgrave Macmillan.

Halliwell, Martin, and Andy Mousley (2003) *Critical Humanisms: Humanist/ Anti-Humanist Dialogues*, Edinburgh: Edinburgh University Press.

Haraway, Donna ([1985] 2004) 'A Manifesto for Cyborgs: Science, Technology, and Socialist Feminism in the 1980s', *The Haraway Reader*, London: Routledge, pp. 7–45.

Holderness, Graham (2003) *Textual Shakespeare: Writing and the Word*, Hatfield: University of Hertfordshire Press.

Joughin, John J. (ed.) (2000) *Philosophical Shakespeare*, London: Routledge.

Kinney, Arthur F. (2004) *Shakespeare's Webs: Networks of Meaning in Renaissance Drama*, New York: Routledge.

Latour, Bruno (1993) *We Have Never Been Modern*, Cambridge: Harvard University Press.

Mousley, Andy (2007) *Re-Humanising Shakespeare: Literary Humanism, Wisdom and Modernity*, Edinburgh: Edinburgh University Press.

Pechter, Edward (1995) *What Was Shakespeare? Renaissance Plays and Changing Critical Practice*, Ithaca: Cornell University Press.

Readings, Bill (1997) *The University in Ruins*, Cambridge: Harvard University Press.

Rhodes, Neil, and Jonathan Sawday (2000a), 'Introduction – Paperworlds: Imagining the Renaissance Computer', in Rhodes and Sawday, 2000b, pp. 11–12.

Rhodes, Neil, and Jonathan Sawday (eds) (2000b) *The Renaissance Computer: Knowledge Technology in the First Age of Print*, London: Routledge.

Said, Edward W. (2004) *Humanism and Democratic Criticism*, Basingstoke: Palgrave, now Palgrave Macmillan.

Sawday, Jonathan (1999) '"Forms Such as Never Were in Nature": The Renaissance Cyborg', in Fudge, Gilbert and Wiseman, 1999, pp. 171–95.

Taylor, Gary (1990) *Reinventing Shakespeare*, London: Hogarth Press.

Wells, Robin Headlam (2005) *Shakespeare's Humanism*, Cambridge: Cambridge University Press.

Wilson, Scott (1996) 'Heterology', in Nigel Wood (ed.), *The Merchant of Venice*, Buckingham: Open University Press, pp. 124–63.

Part I
Reading Shakespeare 'after' Humanism

1

The Science of the Heart: Shakespeare, Kames and the Eighteenth-Century Invention of the Human

Neil Rhodes

During the 1980s and for much of the 1990s a great deal of intellectual effort was devoted to showing that traditional critical readings of literary texts were based on an uninspected 'essentialist humanism'. As the principal location of traditional humanist values, Shakespeare in particular was subject to a complete historical, political and theoretical makeover as those values were reappraised and discredited. Shakespeare was, in a sense, dehumanized, at least in the academy. In the early twenty-first century, however, the idea of an essential human nature, either in the living species itself or as encoded by Shakespeare, would seem to be under increasing pressure not so much from literary theory as from science and technology. Computers and biotechnology have both invaded and destabilized our distinct sense of selfhood and eroded the boundaries between human and machine. Literary theory might well feel that contemporary scientific developments simply confirm its own contention that we have entered the posthumanist era.

The reality, however, is rather more complex, since scientists themselves have by no means given up on the possibility of identifying essential human-ness, as a recent essay collection shows (Pasternak, 2007).[1] And while they disagree about what these essential elements might be, many of the identifying characteristics proposed are of striking relevance to literary criticism. They include language ability, of course, while the geneticist Walter Bodmer adds that the role of English as a lingua franca could be interpreted as an example of group selection based on British colonialism over the last few hundred years. For the neuroscientists Michael Corballis and Thomas Suddendorf language is linked to storytelling and time travel, in the sense of being able to imagine past and future scenarios, which are their proposals for uniquely human capacities. For Susan Blackmore it is imitation, the key doctrine of literary theory in the age of Shakespeare, that makes us human. But it is the evolutionary psychologist Robin Dunbar who addresses Shakespeare directly. He argues that the defining characteristic of humans is 'capacity to live in an imagined world', an advanced cognitive ability that he illustrates by describing the multiple layers of intentionality that the audience of *Othello* is required to accept. For Dunbar, literature and religion, both products of 'the world of the imagination', are 'perhaps the two most central aspects of culture that define our humanity' (Dunbar, 2007, pp. 38, 48). Scientists working in different fields, then, are offering a variety of essentially human characteristics that could usefully interact with literary criticism. But attempts at cross-fertilization between criticism and science are nonetheless fraught with danger, as recent strictures about criticism's enthusiasm for neuroscience suggest. And from the other side, many literary scholars would question Dunbar's implicit contention that Shakespeare's degree of sophistication as a writer can be measured by his deployment of sixth-order intentionality, even if this does provide a useful illustration of an essentially human characteristic. It is not the intention of the present chapter to attempt a fusion between contemporary criticism and science, but rather to return to a time and place where these two intellectual spheres worked more obviously in harmony, and did so in order to produce the concept of human nature that was to underpin Shakespeare's position as the supreme literary genius. This is essentially an Enlightenment construction and one that was pursued with particular energy in eighteenth-century Scotland where intellectuals were engaged in producing a 'science of man' (the seminal work here is of course David Hume, *Treatise of Human Nature* [1739–40]). It is now widely accepted that Scotland is also where English Studies began as an academic discipline, with the founding of the Regius Chair of Rhetoric and Belles Lettres in Edinburgh in 1762 (cf. Crawford, 1998). But what is less well understood is how the institutionalization of criticism in eighteenth-century Edinburgh is intimately connected both with the formulation of a concept of human nature and with the elevation of Shakespeare to the position of pre-eminent literary genius. These three themes converge in the figure of Henry Home, Lord Kames, sponsor of the Edinburgh Chair and patron of Hugh Blair, its first holder. It was Kames who asserted that 'the science of criticism' was a vital element in 'the science of man' in his *Elements of Criticism* (1762; Kames, 2002, p. xi), and he used Shakespeare to provide the main evidence for his case. The importance of Kames's *Elements* in the construction of a humanist Shakespeare will be the main focus of this chapter.

The central subject here is human emotion, or the 'passions', to use the older term, since these form the basis on which Shakespeare's reputation was originally built and also lie at the heart of Kames's own argument in *Elements of Criticism*. Dramatic poetry had long been recognized as the principal cultural vehicle for the expression of the human passions and Shakespeare was seen as having a particular genius in this respect. This happened very early on in the development of his reputation and it is actually a more precise and informative rendering of the much vaguer designation of Shakespeare as 'the poet of nature'. The earliest published critical essay on Shakespeare, by Margaret Cavendish, Duchess of Newcastle, claims that Shakespeare 'Presents Passions so Naturally, and Misfortunes so Probably, as he Peirces the Souls of his Readers with such a True Sense and Feeling thereof, that it Forces Tears through their Eyes' (Cavendish, 1974, p. 40). John Dennis, whose *Grounds of Criticism in Poetry* (1704) made a significant contribution to the emerging concept of 'criticism' in the eighteenth century, wrote in his essay on Shakespeare that:

> He had so fine a Talent for touching the Passions, and they are so lively in him and so truly in Nature, that they often touch us more without their due Preparations than those of other Tragick Poets, who have all the Beauty of Design and all the Advantage of Incidents. (in Vickers, 1974–81, II, p. 282)

Pope's edition of 1723–5 contained an index of 'Manners, Passions and their External Effects' and his preface establishes Shakespeare's claim to greatness on the grounds that 'The *Power* over the *Passions* was never possess'd in a more eminent degree, or display'd in so many different instances' (Pope, 1723–5, I, p. 1). By the mid-eighteenth century this kind of observation had become commonplace.

Late seventeenth- and eighteenth-century tributes to Shakespeare's genius in representing the passions may disguise the fact that the way in which the passions were conceptualized had changed since the Elizabethan era. Eighteenth-century valuations of his achievement are based on a slightly different reading of his drama from the one experienced by Shakespeare's original audiences. This new account of the passions is part of a wider appropriation and rereading of Shakespeare in the period, which is reflected most obviously in the re*writing* of his plays to suit modern taste. In the sixteenth century the passions were still understood primarily in physiological terms. When Othello says 'My blood begins my safer guides to rule' (II.3.188) he can be understood literally as well as metaphorically (cf. Paster, 2004a; and Paster, 2004b, esp. pp. 17–18). There are many other examples of the humoral theory underlying Elizabethan conceptions of the passions, which are too familiar to be repeated here. This physiological model was located within a wider cosmology in which the human and natural worlds reciprocated each other. In *King Lear* the delicate balance of love, grief and pity that Cordelia feels for her wrecked father is captured in the exchange between Kent and the Gentleman in Act IV:

KENT.   O, then it moved her.
GENTLEMAN.   Not to a rage. Patience and sorrow strove
                             Who should express her goodliest. You have seen
                             Sunshine and rain at once: her smiles and tears
                             Were like a better way. (IV.3.34–8)

Throughout the play human emotion is expressed both physiologically and in terms of wider, cosmological activity, most obviously in the storm of Lear's personal disintegration which precedes Cordelia's sunshine and rain. This entire system, often referred to as the Book of Nature, was described perhaps most memorably by Michel Foucault in the section of *The Order of Things* called 'The Prose of the World'. Here, Foucault writes about the elaborate network of sympathies at work in the world, which is responsible for a universal interconnectedness. This analogical view of the order of things offers a wonderful resource for poetry and drama – one that is literally full of wonder – but it is also based on a pre-social concept of sympathy. In this model, sympathy is less a matter of being moved to fellow-feeling for other individuals as it is an experience of a condition of being in the world. The distinction is important because our definition of sympathy, our understanding of how this principle might operate, must also affect our understanding of how audiences and readers respond to the representation of human passions in drama and, in particular, to their experience of tragedy.

In the eighteenth century, the older physiological model was replaced by a social theory of the passions which is also a distinctive feature of the Scottish Enlightenment. The work of Francis Hutcheson and David Hume is central here. But as far as literary criticism is concerned the important figure is Kames, and it was Kames, working under the influence of Hutcheson and Hume, who made Shakespeare's mastery in representing the human passions central to his exposition of the principles of literary criticism in the *Elements of Criticism*. Kames's starting point is that the true source of criticism is human nature and it is this that enables criticism 'to be studied as a rational science' (Kames, 2002, p. xii). This is what makes criticism central to an arts and humanities curriculum, as Kames implies when he claims that 'the science of criticism may be considered as a middle link, connecting the different parts of education in a regular chain' (p. xii). But Kames's premise means that his project must also involve a discussion of the elements of human nature, which he acknowledges later in the Introduction when he admits that 'though criticism is thus his only declared aim, he will not disown, that all along it has been his view to explain the nature of man' (p. xv). He repeats this intention much later in the *Elements* when he says that 'the object of [the present work] is human nature in general, and what is common to the species' (p. 375). As a result, after a brief first chapter on the association of ideas and images, he devotes almost a hundred pages to a discussion of the 'emotions and passions', for it is these that criticism recognizes as the fundamental elements of human nature. It is, in fact, the function of criticism to educate the human heart ('The science of rational criticism tends to improve the heart no less than the understanding' [p. xiii]) and, in the first edition of the *Elements*, Kames goes so far as to say that 'the genuine rules of criticism are all of them derived from the human heart' (Kames, 1762, I, p. 16). What Kames offers the reader in the *Elements of Criticism*, then, is a science of criticism founded upon the psychology of emotional response, something that we might abbreviate simply as a science of the heart: 'Every subject must be important that tends to unfold the human heart; for what other science is of greater use to human beings' (Kames, 2002, p. 235).

Kames begins his long second chapter by attempting to distinguish between emotions and passions and between selfish and sociable passions. The superseding of the early modern term 'passions' by the modern term 'emotions' in the early nineteenth century has been ably discussed by Thomas Dixon (2003, pp. 101–4) and it is perhaps not surprising, given the point at which he was writing, that Kames had some difficulty in separating the two. After considering whether the terms may actually be synonymous, he proposes the 'solution' that a feeling which is unaccompanied by desire may be described as an emotion and, when followed by desire, as a passion. This is 'of considerable importance in the science of human nature' (Kames,

2002, p. 11) because it distinguishes between those feelings that lead to actions (passions) and those that do not (emotions). Pity is an example of the first because it brings with it a desire to help those in distress. This naturally leads Kames to make the further distinction between selfish and sociable passions:

> It is the end in view that ascertains the class to which they belong: where the end in view is my own good, they are selfish; where the end in view is the good of another, they are social ... If charity be given with the single view of relieving a person from distress, the action is purely social: but if it be partly in view to enjoy the pleasure of a virtuous act, the action is so far selfish. (pp. 14–15)

At this point Kames allows the possibility that some passions, such as the desire for revenge, may be so all-consuming that they can be described neither as social nor as selfish, since the object in view is simply the destruction of another person. For these he invents the term 'dissocial'. Here Kames seems to gesture, perhaps unwittingly, to an older (ultimately Stoic) view of the passions as disruptive and pathological, a view summed up by the modern critic, Philip Fisher, when he writes that 'The crux of many arguments against the passions lies in the recognition of their hostility to any genuinely social world ... they assert a world in which there is only a single person against all others.' By way of illustration Fisher cites Shakespeare's tragedies, which show 'the displacement of a social world by one passion and the will of one impassioned man' (Fisher, 2002, p. 64).[2] But this is not a point that Kames wishes to develop, even though his primary source of illustration is also Shakespeare. He travels in an entirely different direction, presenting the passions as a vehicle for the extension of human sympathy.

This is apparent from the start, when he explains in the Introduction that 'delicacy of taste tends no less to invigorate the social affections,than to moderate those that are selfish', adding that 'delicacy of taste heightens our feeling of pain and pleasure; and of course our sympathy, which is the capital branch of every social passion' (Kames, 2002, p. xiii). Since it is the function of criticism to educate taste, criticism is also therefore a means of eliciting human sympathy. Kames goes on to develop this argument in the section on 'Emotions caused by Fiction', where he associates sympathy with refinement: 'The social affections are conceived by all to be more refined than the selfish. Sympathy and humanity are universally esteemed the finest temper of mind; and for that reason, the prevalence of the social affections in the progress of society, is held to be a refinement in our nature' (p. 44). Sympathy is an instance of the fact that the social affections may be painful as well as pleasurable, but painful in a way that is 'yet in its nature attractive' and we will 'feel a secret charm in every passion that tends to the good of others' (p. 78). While malevolent passions are liable to be communicated by savages, in a more refined society, 'the progress of passion along related objects, by spreading the kindly affections through a multitude of individuals, hath a glorious effect' (p. 81). Whether sympathy itself is a passion is perhaps less clear (cf. e.g. Campbell, 1776, I, p. 320). Kames refers to 'the painful passion of sympathy', which is consistent with his earlier distinction between passions and emotions because he refers at the same time to 'the desire involved in it' (Kames, 2002, p. 195), but in other respects it would make more sense to see sympathy as the social affection aroused by certain passions rather than as a passion itself. What *is* clear, however, is the chain of reasoning that links the science of criticism to the refinement of human nature through an appeal to the passions and through a stimulation of the social rather than the selfish passions. This is a very different view of the passions from either the one based on the physiological principle of sympathy or the one that sees them as turbulent, 'dissocial' illnesses. It is also one in which Shakespeare plays a vital role.

Kames's observations on sympathy are interspersed with eulogies on and quotations from Shakespeare. 'Nothing can be more entertaining to a rational mind than the economy of human passions' (p. 81), he asserts, and nobody is more capable of demonstrating this than Shakespeare. He 'shows more knowledge of human nature than any of our philosophers' and he 'exhibits beautiful examples of the irregular influence of passion in making us believe things to be otherwise than they are' (pp. 67, 76). Shakespeare is 'an author who is acquainted with every maze of the human heart, and who bestows ineffable grace and ornament upon every subject he handles' and an author 'whom no particle of human nature hath escaped' (pp. 70, 82). Later, in the important chapter on 'Language of Passion', Kames again emphasizes the point that an understanding of human nature is dependent upon an ability to represent the passions. Shakespeare, he says, 'is superior to all other writers in delineating passion' and 'One thing must be evident to the meanest capacity, that wherever passion is to be displayed, Nature shows herself mighty in him, and is conspicuous by the most delicate propriety of sentiment and expression' (pp. 220–1). He then becomes grandly dismissive of critics less perceptive than himself:

> The critics seem not perfectly to comprehend the genius of Shakespeare. His plays are defective in the mechanical part: which is less the work of genius than of experience, and is not otherwise

brought to perfection but by diligently observing the errors of former compositions. Shakespear [*sic*] excels all the ancients and moderns in knowledge of human nature, and in unfolding even the most obscure and refined emotions. This is a rare faculty, and of the greatest importance in a dramatic author; and it is that faculty which makes him surpass all other writers in the comic as well as the tragic vein. (p. 221)

This is in part a familiar defence of Shakespeare in terms of the art/nature antithesis. What is new about it is the philosophical support that enables an earlier negative evaluation of Shakespeare based on the rules of criticism to be precisely reversed. If the rules of criticism are all to be derived from human nature, then criticism will place greatest importance on the ability of artists to reveal human nature through their delineation of the passions. If criticism is responsible for the education and refinement of human nature by developing sympathy in response to the arousal of the passions, then it has a social function that derives from its basis in human psychology rather than formal rules. This is what makes criticism central to the science of man and, for Kames, it finds its most perfect illustration in Shakespeare's science of the heart.

The most effective medium for the arousing of the passions is dramatic poetry, and for Kames Shakespeare is the supreme exponent of the natural language of passion. He adds: 'It is difficult to say in what part he most excels, whether in moulding every passion to peculiarity of character, in discovering the sentiments that proceed from various tones of passion, or in expressing properly every different sentiment' (p. 220). One aspect of dramatic speech in which Shakespeare certainly did excel, in Kames's view, was the soliloquy, and he claims that 'Shakespeare's soliloquies may be justly established as a model; for it is not easy to conceive of a model more perfect' (p. 223). This is the cue for a second round of assaults on Corneille, whom he had attacked along with Racine in the previous chapter. There he had written that 'the pronunciation of the genuine language of a passion is necessarily directed by the nature of the passion ... the French have formed their tone of pronunciation upon Corneille's declamatory tragedies, and the English upon the more natural language of Shakespeare' (p. 201). Now Kames pits Hamlet against the French neoclassical writers and quotes the entire first soliloquy ('Oh, that this too too solid flesh') in order to demonstrate how frigid, declamatory and pompous the French style is by comparison with the natural and impassioned speech of Shakespeare's character.

Kames's disparagement of French tragedy is indicative of a wider shift in cultural values that led to Shakespeare's being characterized as the supreme literary genius in many parts of Europe, especially Germany, in the second half of the eighteenth century. In France itself Voltaire fought hopelessly to stem the tide of literary barbarism washing across the Channel. Reviewing the *Elements* for the *Gazette littéraire* in 1764, he poured scorn on Kames's appraisal of Hamlet's soliloquies, claiming that the prince expressed himself like a clown at a rustic fair, without propriety or nobility. 'Le fond du discours d'Hamlet est dans la nature: cela suffit aux Anglais' was his dismissive summing up (Voltaire, 1877, XXIV, p. 161). But Voltaire was defending a lost cause, for 'la nature' was about to be adopted as an aesthetic touchstone throughout Europe in the age of Romanticism.

It is a short step from soliloquy to the question of the psychologically realistic representation of character. If Kames's account of the elements of criticism is based upon his identification of the elements of human nature with the passions in general, it is an account that nonetheless moves from the general to the particular, and from a social vision of human nature to the expression of human nature in individual characters. Shakespeare's soliloquies especially, which for obvious reasons are not ideally suited to expressing the *sociable* passions, are a vehicle not just for realizing the elements of human nature but also for realizing distinctive personality in drama. This is what Kames recognizes throughout Shakespeare's dramatic language, monologue or dialogue, when he refers to his 'moulding every passion to peculiarity of character' and, with regard to performance, in his stipulation that 'the pronunciation of the genuine language of passion is necessarily dictated by the nature of the passion' (Kames, 2002, pp. 220, 201). It is also a short step from soliloquy to questions of personal identity and the essential self. Kames had touched on these in the essay on 'Personal Identity' in *Essays on the Principles of Morality and Natural Religion* (1751) where he writes, in the third edition, that 'The knowledge I have of my personal identity, is what constitutes me a moral agent, accountable to God and to man for every action of my life. Were I kept ignorant of my personal identity, it would not be in my power to connect any of my past actions with myself' (Kames, (1762, p. 202).[3] The emergence of a concept of the individual and of the autonomous human self during the seventeenth and eighteenth centuries is a huge topic, which can only be glanced at here, though it is of obvious relevance to the issue of 'posthumanism'. Kames's own comment on this is significant here on account of its relevance to Shakespeare's dramatic construction of characters as individuals, which he celebrates as a central aspect of Shakespeare's achievement in the *Elements of Criticism*. While Kames's *Elements* has a philosophical and psychological basis which enables him to describe it as a science, it is precisely those aspects of it that lead him towards the kind of character criticism associated with the Romantics and, ultimately, with the humanist criticism of A. C. Bradley. What Kames presents the reader with in the *Elements*, then, is an account of criticism that grounds it in human nature; that sees its task as refining human nature through the nurturing of sympathy, expressed through the language of the passions; and that places as much value on the construction of psychologically realistic individual characters as it does on the representation of universal human nature. This wide and ambitious brief for criticism finds its most responsive subject in Shakespeare.

1

The importance of Kames's *Elements of Criticism* has not been widely appreciated in recent years, though it has had at least one distinguished modern advocate. There is certainly no doubt of the impact that it made both in its own day and in the following century. There were a dozen British editions between 1762 and 1840, and in the USA it enjoyed even greater longevity, with 32 editions appearing between 1796 and 1968. In Germany, where it provided a support system for the extraordinary Shakespeare cult of the 1760s and 1770s led by Goethe and Herder, a translation was begun the year after the book's British publication, completed in 1776 and reissued 4 times before the end of the century (cf. Rogers, 1997). Where Voltaire had remarked (in his *Gazette littéraire* review) that Shakespeare was hardly Sophocles, Herder claimed not only that Shakespeare was indeed the British Sophocles but also that Kames was his Aristotle (Herder, 1985, p. 75; see also Paulin, 2003, pp. 94–9). In Scotland itself, Kames's biographer, Alexander Fraser Tytler, summed up his achievement by saying that 'he is justly entitled to the praise of being the inventor of a science; I mean that which has with propriety been termed *Philosophical Criticism*' (Tytler, 1807). Aristotle is lined up alongside Kames and censured because he made 'not the slightest attempt' in the *Poetics* to deduce the laws of criticism 'from the nature of man, or from any analysis of the human passions'. He does a bit better in the *Art of Rhetoric*, Fraser Tytler concedes, but, since he was not trying to teach the art of criticism, 'we find not in that work any application of the passions to the works of taste and genius'. He then outlines Kames's method by quoting extensively from his Shakespeare criticism, concluding that he is 'the first writer who has raised philosophical criticism to the rank of a science'. The key to this achievement is Kames's locating the source of authority for criticism not in 'mechanical rules' but in human nature (Tytler, 1807, pp. 273–9, 286).

Fraser Tytler identifies the leading members of this school of 'philosophical criticism' as George Campbell, William Richardson and James Beattie. Their significance for us here lies in the way in which they propagate different aspects of the science of human nature. Richardson, a professor of Humanity at Glasgow University, was the only one of the three who was principally interested in Shakespeare, and his book *A Philosophical Analysis and Illustration of Some of Shakespeare's Remarkable Characters* appeared to enthusiastic reviews in 1774. The work consists of a long introduction followed by chapters on Macbeth, Hamlet, Jaques and Imogen. Richardson makes it clear at the start of the introduction that his approach to character will be directed to a moral end through an analysis of the passions: 'the genuine and original Poet, peculiarly favoured by nature ... displays the workings of every affection, detects the origins of every passion, traceth its progress, and delineates its character. Thus, he teaches us to know ourselves' (Richardson, 1774, p. 1). It is the task of criticism to reveal how this is done. He then makes a distinction between the imitation and the mere description of a passion which he claims that 'the author of *The Elements of Criticism*' was the first to recognize: 'Shakespeare imitates, Corneille describes', he says, following Kames (Richardson, 1774, pp. 39, 26). He goes on to explain that imitation requires 'every passion be naturally expressed ... Shakespeare, inventing the characters of Hamlet, Macbeth, or Othello, actually felt the passions, and contending emotions ascribed to them' (p. 23). The terms 'imitation' and 'invention' reveal the rhetorical outlines beneath the new philosophical criticism and the insistence on engagement, not detachment, has its origins in Quintilian. Here, though, it leads to one of the central tenets of Romantic Shakespeare criticism, adopted by Bradley, namely, that Shakespeare was uniquely capable of inventing individual characters from within: 'The genius of Shakespeare is unlimited. Possessing extreme sensibility, and uncommonly susceptible, he is the Proteus of the drama: he changes himself into every character, and enters easily into every condition of human nature' (Richardson, 1774, p. 40). Here is the model for Coleridge's much more famous 'the one Proteus of the fire and the flood' and Keats's 'chameleon poet' (cf. Bate, 1992, pp. 151, 199). Here too is a view of Shakespeare that credits him with an unrivalled power of recreating the elements of human nature through the dramatic construction of personal identity.

The influence of Campbell's *Philosophy of Rhetoric* (1776) is also unmistakeable and acknowledged. Although he persists with the older term, 'rhetoric', his premise that rhetoric is founded in 'the science of human nature' makes it indistinguishable from Kames's philosophic criticism (Campbell, 1776, I, p. vii). Like Kames, Campbell is also fond of the term 'science' and he does in fact refer to what he calls 'the critical science' (I, p. 17). Little of the book is devoted to discussions of literary authors, however, and, while Shakespeare is duly praised for his incomparable vitality and 'transcendent genius', the *practice* of criticism is not really part of Campbell's project. What he is more concerned to do is to construct a theory of communication where rhetoric is to be understood in relation to the principles of human nature and where human nature is to be understood in relation to the principles of rhetoric. This reciprocal arrangement inevitably leads Campbell to the watchword of 'sympathy'. 'Sympathy is one main engine by which the author operates on the passions', he says, quoting Horace:

With them who laugh, our social joy appears;
With them who mourn, we sympathize in tears ...

and adds, 'Whatever, therefore, weakens that principle of sympathy, must do the speaker unutterable prejudice in respect of his power over the passions of his audience' (Campbell, 1776, I, pp. 242–3). He writes that 'sympathy may be greatly strengthened or weakened by the influence of connected passions' and that 'we, as it were, participate by sympathy, in the known vivid perceptions of the speaker or the writer' (I, p. 320; II, p. 168). Richardson's *Shakespeare* and Campbell's *Rhetoric* are very different kinds of books, but they come from the same source and share many of the same assumptions.[4] They are equally concerned with the elements of human nature and the science of the heart.

Kames's *Elements* extended its life well into the nineteenth century as an educational textbook, as the study of literature in English began to develop outside Scotland. In the early twentieth century it also found an advocate in the seminal figure of I. A. Richards, who was particularly interested in Kames's account of metaphor. While Richards agreed that we have to get beyond the associationist theories to which Kames was attached, he also regarded Kames's ideas as 'first steps in a great and novel venture, the attempt to explain in detail how language works and with it to improve communication' (Richards, 1936, pp. 17–18). Kames's fundamental premise, however, that the science of criticism should be founded on the science of human nature, did not fare so well in the twentieth century. In the last quarter of the century especially, the elements of criticism established in the Scottish Enlightenment, which enable connections to be made between Kames, the Romantics and A. C. Bradley, began to unravel as English Studies (where criticism was now institutionalized) took an anti-humanist turn. The principles that came under attack were precisely those that are fundamental to Kames's *Elements* and to 'philosophic criticism', namely, a belief in the autonomous human subject and an essential human nature. Traditionalists would therefore have felt hopeful when a book appeared in 1998 called *Shakespeare: The Invention of the Human* by the veteran critic Harold Bloom. Bloom had originally been part of the Yale School which did so much to promote theory in the 1970s and 1980s, but had now become a staunch defender of humane literary values and a somewhat isolated figure. So isolated, in fact, that the book was met with almost universal scorn. It is indeed a self-indulgent (and very long) book, heavy on assertion and light on analysis, but there are glimpses of what might have been. He starts by claiming that he brings nothing but the 'aesthetic' to the work, which 'is an affair of perceptions and sensations. Shakespeare teaches us how and what to perceive, and he also instructs us how and what to sense and then to experience as sensation' (Bloom, 1999, p. 9). This sounds remarkably similar to eighteenth-century associationism and to Kames's own first chapter on 'Perceptions and Ideas in a Train', but the point is left completely undeveloped. Later we are told that 'The internalization of the self is one of Shakespeare's greatest inventions, particularly because it came before anyone else was ready for it. There is a growing inner self in Protestantism, but nothing in Luther prepares us for Hamlet's mystery' (p. 409). Again there is no contextualization, no historical or philosophical underpinning. Yet Bloom's subject and his title are not absurd. They could have made absolute sense if they had been explained in terms of the eighteenth-century science of man.

The hostile reception of *Shakespeare: The Invention of the Human* was certainly not unmerited, but one wonders how much of the hostility was directed towards the project itself rather than the achievement. If that were so it would have been short-sighted for, even if some academic criticism has already decided to dispense with it, human nature remains as much at the centre of intellectual debate as it was in the Scottish Enlightenment, and the terms of the debate are frequently those that we have seen in Kames and in his circle. In his introduction to the book cited at the start of this chapter, Walter Bodmer points out 'the widespread existence of co-operation and altruism between unrelated individuals in human societies', Andrew Whiten outlines his concept of 'the deep social mind' as the defining feature of humanity, while, in his account of the function of story-telling, Robin Dunbar (again the closest to my own concerns here) remarks that 'by stirring up the emotions, we create a sense of bonding between those involved'.[5] Moving from science into the more general area of cultural commentary, we can find the last point echoed by Francis Fukuyama:

> Human nature is very plastic, and we have an enormous range of choices conformable with that nature. But it is not infinitely malleable, and the elements that remain constant – particularly our species-typical gamut of emotional responses – constitute a safe harbor that allows us to connect, potentially, with all other human beings. (Fukuyama, 2002, p. 218)

This is pretty much a restatement of the eighteenth-century concept of human nature in which sympathy is communicated by the arousal of the passions.

2

The publication of Fukuyama's book coincided with a remarkable exhibition shown at the Getty Museum and at the National Gallery in London, Bill Viola's *The Passions*. While the present chapter has focused on the exemplary role of Shakespeare in the invention of a concept of human nature in the Scottish Enlightenment, I choose Viola's work by way of conclusion because it offers such a striking example of the continued relevance of those Enlightenment concerns to the modern world. Viola is a video artist, one of whose early works was actually called *The Science of the Heart*. In his more recent work, starting with *The Greeting* (1995), his aim has been, as he puts it, 'to get at the root cause of my emotions and the nature of emotional expression itself', adding that in the 1970s this was a 'forbidden zone' for artists, 'a place you didn't go' (Viola, 2003, p. 199). Kames writes in the *Elements* that painting has less power to arouse the passions than words because 'a picture is confined to a single instant of time ... our passions, those especially of the sympathetic kind, require a succession of impressions' (Kames, 2002, p. 37). But what if the still picture could somehow be animated? This is what Viola set out to do in *The Greeting*, which is a life-size video projection of an image based on Pontormo's *The Visitation*. Using actors in brightly coloured, loose modern dress, Viola captures the intensely emotional moment of greeting between Elizabeth and the pregnant Mary, witnessed by a single onlooker. The 45-second sequence was shot on high-speed film at 300 frames per second, transferred to video and projected in extreme slow motion. Over the ten minutes it takes to view, the spectator is able to witness what Viola has called 'the passage of an emotional wave through a human being' (Viola, 2003, p. 200) made visible in the evolving nuances of facial expression and gesture. The extreme slowness of the work, occupying a new territory between painting and film, makes it deeply absorbing in a way that is different from the experience of either of those media. On one level it is possible to observe the rhetoric of emotional expression in a way that would have pleased eighteenth-century critics, but at the same time the pace of the work produces a deeply sympathetic engagement as the impossibly extended moment of emotion unfolds. This is achieved partly by the presence of the third woman, who looks out towards the spectator, creating a bond of wonder.

The Greeting acts as an introduction to *The Passions* sequence itself, which explores the four 'primary' emotions of joy, sorrow, anger and fear, and treats them, as Viola explains, 'like primary colors, elements that could be melded and shaped to create varying gradations and shades' (p. 200). Some of these are modelled on Flemish portraits showing individuals in extreme emotional states, while others present communal expressions of emotion. The most remarkable of the latter is *Observance*, where a group of figures walks slowly in procession towards the spectator, gazing at an invisible object just outside the frame. Their shared experience is registered by occasional gestures of comfort, but their expressions of grief and shock are unique to each individual. After reaching the front of the line, they then move back again as others take their place. It is a work that draws upon the elements of human nature to recreate, in modern idiom, the experience of sympathy that so interested the thinkers of the Scottish Enlightenment. It is also a work that demonstrates a quality central to the aesthetic of the Scottish Enlightenment and its wider European forms – that of the sublime. Cynthia Freeland has written very interestingly on Viola and the sublime, citing Burke in particular, who provides her with the title of her essay in a phrase describing the effect of the sublime. She quotes the following passage to point out the difference between Burke's view of the sublime ('the strongest emotion which the mind is capable of feeling' [Burke, 1990, pp. 36, 41]) and Kant's:

For sympathy must be considered as a sort of substitution, by which we are put into the place of another man, and affected in many respects as he is affected; so that this passion may either partake of the nature of those which regard self-preservation, and turning upon pain may be a source of the sublime or it may turn upon ideas of pleasure ... It is by this principle chiefly that poetry, painting, and other affecting arts, transfuse their passions from one breast to another, and are often capable of grafting a delight on wretchedness, misery, and death itself. (Freeland, 2004, pp. 39–40)

Burke's account of the sublime, Freeland argues, defines the essential character of Viola's art by associating the sublime with the principle of sympathy. It is also, of course, very close to the concerns of the present chapter.

In the mid-eighteenth century criticism found in Shakespeare the deepest artistic resource from which to illustrate its thinking about human nature. By using modern technology to re-examine and reaffirm the most basic elements of human nature, the passions, Viola's exploration of the science of the heart is both contemporary and timeless. While his work is clearly indebted to many different sources, including Sufism and Italian and Flemish devotional painting, its focus on the passions and on the principle of sympathy is rooted in the concerns of the eighteenth-century science of man. But it also speaks to us now because it uses modern media unimaginable to earlier artists to reveal to us the basis of our shared humanity in new ways. As far as Shakespeare himself is concerned, his adaptability to new media has provided the impetus for an extraordinary wave of popularization over the last two decades. It is certainly true that in the future the boundaries between human being and machine will become increasingly unstable, but there is every possibility that Shakespeare will remain a humanist icon not just in elite and traditionalist academic circles but within the domain of popular culture. After all, even time lords acknowledge that Shakespeare was 'the most human of humans' (*Dr Who*, 2005).

Notes

1. This is not, however, to imply that literary theory has been unaware of science (see, e.g., Belsey, 2006, pp. 111–27).
2. By contrast, the editors of *Reading the Early Modern Passions* contend that their aim is to challenge 'the current privileging of emotions as inward rather than social phenomena' (Paster, Rowe & Wilson, 2004, p. 13).
3. Cf 'consciousness of self, carried through all the different stages of life, and all the variety of action, which is the foundation of *personal identity*' (Kames, 1762, p. 233).

4. Fraser Tytler's third member of the school of Kames, James Beattie, seems likely to have influenced the young Wordsworth (see Wu, 2003, pp. 16–17). There are, however, several aspects of the *Preface to Lyrical Ballads* (Wordsworth's remarks on sympathy, the natural language of the passions and the social function of the poet) that suggest a more direct acquaintance with *The Elements of Criticism.*
5. Pasternak, 2007: Walter Bodmer, 'Foreword', pp. ix–xix (xvi); Andrew Whiten, 'The Place of "Deep Social Mind" in the Evolution of Human Nature', pp. 146–63; Dunbar, 2007, p. 47.

Works cited

Bate, Jonathan (ed.) (1992) *The Romantics on Shakespeare*, Harmondsworth: Penguin.

Belsey, Catherine (2006) 'Biology and Imagination: The Role of Culture' in Robin Headlam Wells and Johnjoe McFadden (eds), *Human Nature: Fact and Fiction*, London and New York: Continuum, pp. 111–27.

Bloom, Harold (1999) *Shakespeare: The Invention of the Human*, London: Fourth Estate.

Burke, Edmund (1990) *A Philosophical Inquiry into the Origin of Our Ideas of the Sublime and the Beautiful*, Oxford: Oxford University Press.

Campbell, George (1776) *The Philosophy of Rhetoric*, 2 vols, London.

Cavendish, Margaret, Duchess of Newcastle (1974) 'Letter 113, from CCXI Sociable Letters', in Vickers (1974), I, pp. 39–41.

Crawford, Robert (ed.) (1998) *The Scottish Invention of English Literature*, Cambridge: Cambridge University Press.

Dixon, Thomas (2003) *From Passions to Emotions: The Creation of a Secular Category*, Cambridge: Cambridge University Press.

Dr Who (2005) 'The Shakespeare Code', BBC Television.

Dunbar, Robin (2007) 'Why Are Humans Not Just Great Apes?', in Pasternak, 2007, pp. 37–48.

Fisher, Philip (2002) *The Vehement Passions*, Princeton: Princeton University Press.

Freeland, Cynthia (2004) 'Piercing to Our Inaccessible, Inmost Parts: The Sublime in the Work of Bill Viola', in Chris Townsend (ed.), *The Art of Bill Viola*, London: Thames and Hudson, pp. 25–45.

Fukuyama, Francis (2002) *Our Posthuman Future: Consequences of the Biotechnology Revolution*, London: Profile Books.

Herder, Johann Gottfried (1985) 'Shakespeare', in H. B. Nisbet (ed.), *German Aesthetic and Literary Criticism*, Cambridge: Cambridge University Press, pp. 161–74.

Kames, Henry Home, Lord (1751) *Essays on the Principles of Morality and Natural Religion*, Edinburgh.

Kames, Henry Home, Lord (1762) *The Elements of Criticism*, 2 vols, Edinburgh.

Kames, Henry Home, Lord (1768) *Remarks on the Principles of Morality and Natural Religion*, 3rd edn, London.

Kames, Henry Home, Lord (2002) *Elements of Criticism* (1840), reptd Honolulu: University Press of the Pacific.

Paster, Gail Kern (2004a) *Humoring the Body: Emotions and the Shakespearean Stage*, Chicago and London: University of Chicago Press.

Paster, Gail Kern (2004b) 'Introduction: Reading the Early Modern Passions', in Paster, Rowe and Wilson (eds) (2004), pp. 1–20.

Paster, Gail Kern, Katherine Rowe and Mary Floyd Wilson (eds) (2004) *Reading the Early Modern Passions: Essays in the Cultural History of Emotion*, Philadelphia: University of Pennsylvania Press.

Pasternak, Charles (ed.) (2007) *What Makes Us Human?*, Oxford: Oneworld.

Paulin, Roger (2003) *The Critical Reception of Shakespeare in Germany 1682–1914*, Olms: Hildesheim.

Pope, Alexander (ed.) (1723–5) *The Works of Shakespeare*, 6 vols, London.

Richards, I. A. (1936) *The Philosophy of Rhetoric*, London and New York: Oxford University Press.

Richardson, William (1774) *A Philosophical Analysis and Illustration of Some of Shakespeare's Remarkable Characters*, Edinburgh.

Rogers, Pat (1997) 'Theories of Style', in H. B. Nisbet and Claude Rawson (eds), *The Cambridge History of Literary Criticism*, vol. 4, Cambridge: Cambridge University Press, pp. 365–80.

Shakespeare, William (1997) *The Norton Shakespeare: Based on the Oxford Edition*, ed. Stephen Greenblatt (New York: W. W. Norton and Company).

Tytler, Alexander Fraser (1807) *Memoirs of the Life and Writings of Lord Kames*, Edinburgh.

Vickers, Brian (ed.) (1974–81) *Shakespeare: The Critical Heritage*, 6 vols, London: Routledge & Kegan Paul.

Viola, Bill (2003) *The Passions*, ed. John Walsh, Los Angeles: Getty Publications.

Voltaire (1877) *Oeuvres complètes*, ed. Louis Moland, Paris.

Wu, Duncan (2003) *Wordsworth: An Inner Life*, Oxford: Blackwell.

2
'a passion so strange, outrageous, and so variable': The Invention of the Inhuman in *The Merchant of Venice*

Stefan Herbrechter

When did we become posthuman?

Historically speaking, there is uncertainty if and when posthumanism started or when we became posthuman.[1] Conceptually, however, it is quite inevitable that with the 'invention of the human' the posthuman as one of his or her 'others' also becomes thinkable, representable, possible, necessary etc. As soon as some form of *humanitas* begins to characterize the species as a whole, non-human (un-, in-, pre- or posthuman) others start proliferating and the process of inclusion, exclusion and differentiation is set in motion.[2]

Given his central position within early modern Western culture at the beginning of roughly five hundred years of humanism, Shakespeare can be used as an important illustration in this context. Harold Bloom's monumental study *Shakespeare: The Invention of the Human* (1999) insists on the centrality of Shakespeare's position in the universal 'humanist' canon, which transcends individual national literatures through the creation of essentially 'human' characters such as Rosalind, Shylock, Iago, Lear, Macbeth, Cleopatra and, in particular, Falstaff and Hamlet, who represent 'the invention of the human, the inauguration of personality as we have come to recognize it' (Bloom, 1999, p. 4).

> The idea of Western character, of the self as a moral agent, has many sources: Homer and Plato, Aristotle and Sophocles, the Bible and Augustine, Dante and Kant, and all you might care to add. Personality, in our sense, is a Shakespearean invention, and is not only Shakespeare's greatest originality but also the authentic cause of his perpetual pervasiveness. (p. 4)

For Bloom, Shakespeare's importance does not so much lie in his central cultural aesthetic or social historical meaning as in his 'ingenious' creation of universal truths and profound spiritual and sublime (in short, in his authentic) 'humanity': 'Our ideas as to what makes the self authentically human owe more to Shakespeare than ought to be possible' (p. 17).

Bloom's insistent and almost 'dogged' liberal humanism represents of course the main target of the kind of constructivist or anti-essentialist antihumanism that characterizes new historicism and cultural materialism (especially, in the work of Stephen Greenblatt, Jonathan Dollimore, Terence Hawkes or Catherine Belsey). As a result of the politicization of Shakespeare studies in the last few decades Shakespeare is usually afforded an 'ambivalent attitude' towards rising and consolidating early modern humanist ideologies and modern anthropocentrism (cf. the discussion about 'subversion' and 'containment', which, from a cultural political point of view, are always 'present' as two characteristic moments in Shakespeare's play; cf. Dollimore, 1985, pp. 10–17). This ambivalence is then 'resolved' by both camps – the defenders of liberal humanism like Bloom or Brian Vickers, on the one hand, and champions of antihumanist materialism, on the other – and used for their respective ideological purposes. On one side we have the Marxist-materialist critique of capitalist modernity, which targets alienation and individualism as the main evils of liberal humanism, whereas on the other side, from a formal aestheticist point of view, Shakespeare is reclaimed as a monument of essential humanity and humanist cultural achievement.

Jonathan Dollimore in his 1998 commentary places this caricature of an opposition into a longer historical and theoretical context. Neither Shakespeare's invoked universal humanity nor his, or early modernity's, subversive radicality, neither the liberal humanist, individual genius nor the proto-postmodern decentred subject of theory offer the entire truth, because:

> The crisis of subjectivity was there at the inception of individualism in early Christianity, and has been as enabling as it has been disturbing (enabling because disturbing). In other words, what we might now call the neurosis, anxiety and alienation of the subject-in-crisis are not so much the consequence of its recent breakdown, but the very stuff of its creation, and of the culture – Western European culture – from which it is inseparable, especially that culture in its most expansionist phases (of which the 'Renaissance' was undoubtedly one). The crisis of the self isn't so much the subjective

counterpart of the demise, disintegration or undermining of Western European culture, as what has always energised both the self and that culture… what we are living through now is not some (post-)modern collapse of Western subjectivity but another mutation in its enduring dynamic. (Dollimore, 1998, p. 271)

This latest mutation could therefore without doubt be referred to as 'posthuman' or at least 'posthumanist subjectivity' – a new form of humanist identity in posthumanist clothes that calls forth our vigilance and scepticism. In the third edition of Dollimore's *Radical Tragedy* (2004), he gives his preliminary verdict on the outcome of the so-called 'culture wars' of the 1980s and 1990s that his book in many ways helped to spark: '*Radical Tragedy*, first published in 1984, attacked just these ideas: essentialism in relation to subjectivity, universalism in relation to the human, and the belief that there was an ethical/aesthetic realm transcending the political' (2004, p. xv). While the decentring of the subject and of universalism in late-capitalist society have become the everyday experience of our posthuman(ist) selves, 'aesthetic humanism', as Dollimore calls it, continues to survive in its commodified form as a kind of spiritualizing force. The conviction that art, literature and culture function as a humanizing force is (still) the foundation of the cultural industries as well as all educational institutions. Dollimore criticizes this attitude as rather 'complacent':

Far from being liberating, the humanist aesthetic has become a way of standing still amidst the obsolete, complacent and self-serving clichés of the heritage culture industry, the Arts establishment, and a market-driven humanities education system. The aesthetic has become an anaesthetic. (2004, p. xxii)

This is not the place to discuss the potential transformation of the traditional 'humanities' into, for want of a better word, the 'posthumanities' of the future; however, what Dollimore's analysis makes clear is that in the age of the exposed crisis of humanist education there is no way back for theory and criticism nor any clear-cut trajectory forward into some consensual posthuman(ist) utopia – a condition that Neil Badmington, with reference to Elaine Graham's work, calls 'oblique': 'a "critical post/humanism" must actively oblique the order of things, Humanism must be obliqued, knocked sideways, pushed off course, declined' (Badmington, 2004, p. 63). The oblique between 'post' and 'human' (post/human) proposed by Graham mainly serves to gain time and to create a critical space for a more thorough deconstruction of humanism, without which an uncritical reinscription of humanist ideology into posthuman(ist) forms would be inescapable. The liberal humanist and the Marxist anti-humanist positions described above can in fact be seen to compete for the same moral authority over so-called human 'nature'. Approaches within literary criticism are certainly not immune from this anthropocentric blindspot, even or maybe because they pose as posthumanist engagements with the latest 'scientific' insights, for example, by promoting a so-called 'cognitive turn'. One could take Robin Headlam Wells's *Shakespeare's Humanism* (2005) as an example, which takes a biological-cum-cognitive starting point in its attempt to 'transcend' the opposition between pro- and anti-humanists:

> Where 'humanity' was once seen as a purely cultural construct, a consensus is now emerging among psychologists and neuroscientists that our minds are the product of a complex interaction between genetically determined predispositions and an environment that has itself been shaped by generations of human culture. (Wells, 2005, p. 2)

Wells uses the idea of the co-evolution of genes and culture to reposition the question about human nature as central within Shakespeare's work, in the hope that

> by listening to what other disciplines have to say about human nature, criticism can move on from an outdated anti-humanism that has its intellectual roots in the early decades of the last century to a more informed modern understanding of the human universals that literature has, in Ian McEwan's words, 'always, knowingly and helplessly, given voice to'. (p. 5)

The rhetoric of 'departure' and 'overcoming' makes clear that one cannot simply write off humanism that easily. On the contrary, humanism with all its essentialist values relating to some mystical form of human 'nature', is currently being reinvented with the help of cognitive and neuroscientific concepts – supposedly ever changing yet ever true to itself.

A critical posthumanism would thus need to overcome the ideological confrontation between liberal humanists and cultural materialists, mindful of both the historical context and the current climate of cultural change. In terms of Shakespeare studies this means situating

Shakespeare's work formally and historically at a certain turning point within the process of 'post/humanization' – a process that already contains its own mechanisms of repression and exclusion and thus already inscribes its own demise and end. So, just as Shakespeare might be the possible starting point of a certain humanism he could also already anticipate its decline and ultimate ruin. A critical perlaboration of Shakespearean humanism should thus open up the possibility of a fundamentally different, more 'radical' understanding of 'humanity'.

Recalling Donna Haraway's 'Cyborg Manifesto' (1991 [1985]) – in which Haraway hints at the permeability of the boundries between human and animal and between humans and machines at the end of the twentieth century – Fudge, Gilbert and Wiseman (2002) explain that the early modern period provides other and much earlier problematizing accounts of humanness and humanism. The spreading of humanist and anthopocentric ideologies during the Renaissance and early modern period of the sixteenth and seventeenth centuries does not happen without tensions, contradictions and resistance. There is no immediate consensus about what constitutes some imaginary 'human nature'. This alone should be reason enough to abandon the simplistic idea of a monolithic (presumably eurocentic) humanism which might today be challenged by *one* (global or globalized) form of posthumanism. Instead a critical posthumanism needs to link back to those critical discourses that run within and alongside the humanist tradition. The contributions in Fudge, Gilbert and Wiseman's *At the Borders of the Human* (2002) provide some clarification in this respect by pointing out moments of ambivalence in the early modern relationship to animals, machines, the rise of the natural sciences, cartography, sexuality, new concepts of the body and embodiment, and modern medicine. Jonathan Sawday, for example, in his essay 'Renaissance Cyborg', emphasizes that body modification is not the privilege of our own, contemporary, period:

> Enhancing or altering the body form artificially, whether through adornment – tattoos, cosmetics, padded shoulders, bustles, cod-pieces, wigs – or through more invasive procedures – silicone implants, surgical modification, scarification, the piercing of ears, lips, and other features – may be traced through a bewildering variety of cultural and historical moments. (Sawday, 2002, p. 172)

Sawday illustrates this ambiguity by referring to a literary example, Shakespeare's Coriolanus and his progressing 'mechanization' during the course of the play, which corresponds to the more general mechanization of nature especially after Descartes: 'When did we first begin to fear our machines?', Sawday asks. 'Certainly, by the end of the seventeenth century, the dominance of the mechanistic model within European modes of understanding had become unassailable. The world, human society, the human and animal body, all could be analysed in terms of the functioning of machinery' (p. 190).[3]

Haraway's 'cyborgization' of the human can thus be seen to start at the same time as the historical rise of humanism and actually becomes an integral part of it. Without its ideological and philosophical anticipation the idea of cyborgization, literally, would have been unthinkable. As much as the metaphor of mechanisation of nature and of the human and human behaviour allows for greater 'scientific' control over the environment by humans (and machines), it also provokes the 'unease' towards this new and self-produced and self-producing other which threatens to become an indispensible instrument of identification and delimitation and thus to erode the very core of this newly created humanity:

> The modern human relationship with machines, from its emergence in the earlier part of the sixteenth century down to the present, has always been tinged with a measure of unease. 'They' have always been nearer kin to 'us' than we have cared to admit; and in that lies their fascination, as well as their potential horror. It is an uncomfortable prospect that what it is to be human may be defined by 'forms such as never were in nature'. (Sawday, in Fudge, Gilbert & Wiseman, 2002, p. 191)

In a similar move, Rhodes and Sawday, in *The Renaissance Computer* (2000), argue for an anticipation of contemporary information and media society in the early modern period. Almost in analogy with the temporal mode we proposed for posthumanism and the 'invention of the inhuman', Rhodes and Sawday describe a form of 'remediation' when they claim that '[t]he experience of our own new technology has enabled us to re-imagine the impact of new technologies in the past' (Rhodes and Sawday, 2000, p. 2).

Shylock's humanism

Shakespeare's 'invention of the human' thus implies the invention of the inhuman. A case in point is Shylock, the Jew, in Shakespeare's *The Merchant of Venice* (1600). Bloom's classic interpretation of this profoundly ambivalent character of an all-too-human and at the same time constantly dehumanized villain can serve as emblematic of a humanist, as opposed to a critically posthumanist, understanding of the human. The central question in this context concerns the anti-Semitism of the play, as Bloom explains at the opening of his chapter on *The Merchant*: 'One would have to be blind, deaf, and dumb not to recognize that Shakespeare's grand, equivocal comedy *The Merchant of Venice* is nevertheless a profoundly anti-Semitic work' (Bloom, 1999, p. 171). Humanists nevertheless venture either to defend Shakespeare against the accusation of anti-Semitism (e.g. in arguing that the text is not anti-Semitic but simply an ironic and critical reflection of rampant and popular Elizabethan anti-Semitism, which not only saves but even ennobles Shakespeare as an author not of but in his time), or they attempt to 'humanize' Shylock by characterizing him as a largely sympathetic figure and thus wilfully misunderstand the text. Bloom is aware of this contradiction and blames the ambivalence in Shakespeare's text on the rivalry between Shakespeare's 'arch Jew' and Marlowe's Barabas, in *The Jew of Malta* (1590). How else explain Shylock's bizarre cruelty and his thirst for Antonio's pound of flesh? 'Shylock simply does not fit his role; he is the wrong Jew in the right play' (Bloom, 1999, p. 172). What Bloom seems to be missing in Shylock is the typical Shakespearean sceptical irony. Instead, Shylock impresses through his linguistic precision and expressivity, which constitutes another 'contradiciton' at the heart of this social outcast – a contradiction which many modern and contemporary stagings have tried to 'even out' by giving Shylock a heavy 'foreign' accent.[4]

Bloom tries to make a Shakespearean virtue out of Shylock's 'vividness' and his extraodinary (human) realism in the face of the barbaric and comic evil he represents by interpreting Shylock as an example of the fascinating multidimensional character of human nature. Shylock is thus seen to shake 'our' fundamental and universal belief in human goodness and confronts this belief with 'our' racist, sexist and religious prejudice. Shylock simply is both, a comic villain and the embodiment of tragic and embattled humanity. In this respect, his final conversion to Christianity must represent a sadistic act of revenge by Antonio.

The other main characters of the play also do not escape in this interpretation without at least some blame. Antonio is just as curious an outsider as is Shylock. In addition Antonio seems to entertain a homoerotically tinged relationship with his friend and 'impoverished playboy', Bassanio. He suffers from the latter's betrayal, namely his decision to woo the rich heiress Portia, to pay off his debtors; however, first

Bassanio needs another cash injection from Antonio which, in turn, leads to the whole credit and 'pound of flesh' episode in the first place. This part of the story is driven by Shylock's hatred of Antonio who has spat at him in public and dehumanized him by calling him 'dog'. Portia, in contrast, who is sometimes seen as the real main character of the play, displays some degree of frivolousness in her noble and rather romantic Belmont, while acting rather cunningly and implacably as a dressed-up judge in court. She tricks Shylock, who is rather obstinate in his literal interpretation of the bond, and has no hesitation in completely reversing the situation by exposing him to ridicule, destitution, capital punishment and, ultimately, to public humiliation and violence in the form of an imposed conversion to Christianity. Thus it is not only Shylock who is characterized by his human, all-too-human, contradiction but the play as a whole challenges 'our' trust in the 'Christian' understanding of 'humanity'. Shakespeare's ambivalence, Bloom believes, 'diverts self-hatred into hatred of the other, and associates the other with lost possibilities of the self' (Bloom, 1999, p. 190). And this is where ultimately Shakespeare's 'invention of the human' is located for Bloom, namely, in the moral injunction that, in the name of universal humanity, we should not 'dehumanize' ourselves by giving in to our self-hatred or hatred of the other based on a projection of difference and alterity. It is probably also in this sense that Bloom's rather speculative concluding statement needs to be understood: 'I close by wondering if Shylock did not cause Shakespeare more discomfort than we now apprehend' (p. 191), for 'the playright, capacious soul, would be aware that the gratuitous outrage of a forced conversion to Venetian Christianity surpasses all boundaries of decency' (p. 191). Mission accomplished, one could say: 'man', in standing up to his very own inhumanity, has been 'rehumanized' and, emblematically, in the figure of the Shakespearean genius, has been extracted at least temporarily from the evil mechanism of self-hatred and hatred of the other, and has thus been reinserted into the anthropophile sphere of humanistic self-elevation – court adjourned – until the next humanist or humanitarian crisis. As a last reassurance, Bloom's final verdict is: 'Shakespeare was [merely] up to mischief' (p. 191).

A completely different, namely, posthumanist, way of reading is possible, however. In order to demonstrate this alternative, let us first look at Catherine Belsey's essay 'Cultural Difference as Conundrum in *The Merchant of Venice*' in her *Why Shakespeare?* (2007), as an example of poststructuralist 'anti-humanism' with both its undeniable merits and its limitations. In a by now classic move, Belsey shifts the ambivalence of the play onto its linguistic plane and characterizes it as 'a play that depends so extensively on the instability of meaning and the duplicity of the signifier' (Belsey, 2007, p. 160), which to a large extent is expressed in Shylock's stubborn 'literalness' during the court scene, as far as the bond is concerned. It is this literalness that will be 'outdone' by Portia, in order to 'undo' Shylock. Unlike Bloom and other humanist interpreters, who see this ambivalence as a pedagogical 'task', or as a moral 'admonition' to the reader or spectator, namely, to acknowledge and understand their own human nature, Belsey reads it in a deconstructionist vein, as an impossible structural necessity of the play and its cultural context: 'A prejudice conventional in its own period goes into the composition of *Merchant of Venice*. At the same time, the play includes elements that radically unsettle the prejudice it produces. *It differs from itself*' (p. 161). A central role is played by the contradiction between the untouchable and general nature of the law, on the one hand, and its necessarily linguistic interpretation, on the other – a point that Derrida (2001) had already made in a similar form, in his reading of the play. Belsey formulates the dilemma as follows:

> How, in other words, can the law be just to both Antonio and Shylock? And the answer, of course, is a quibble: flesh is not blood; a pound is not a jot more or less than a pound. Nowhere is the duplicity of the signifier thrown into clearer relief than in this exposure of the moneylender's worthless bond. Shylock's ultimate antagonist is the language in which his contract with Antonio is necessarily formulated – and he loses. (Belsey, 2007, p. 162)

The law is necessarily expressed in language ('inscribed in the signifier'); language, however, has its own dynamic and is 'anarchic' (p. 164). At this point, however, something very interesting happens in Belsey's reading, which, despite all its best intentions and absolutely consistent antihumanist conclusions, finds itself drawn back into the dialectic of de- and rehumanization as described by Bloom above. Belsey uses Derrida's *Monolingualism of the Other* (Derrida, 1998), in which he speaks about his forced exile from his 'own' and his 'only' native language, French. The experience of being an Algerian Jew under the protectorate of the Vichy regime is described by Derrida in the form of the following 'aporia': 'I have only one language; it is not mine' (Derrida, 1998, p. 15). Belsey uses this to come to a general, almost existential, maybe even 'humanitarian' insight: 'we none of "us" own the language we speak, which was already there when we came into the world' (Belsey, 2007, p. 163). 'In this sense, we are all aliens, all in exile from a state of perfect correspondence between what we want to say, or would want to say if only we knew what it was, and the signifying practices available to us' (p. 163). However, what this disarming, almost humanist-*cum*-existentialist, 'universalism' necessarily downplays is that not all forms of lingustic exile are equivalent. Instead, and this is one of Derrida's main arguments in *Monolingualism*, every linguistic exile depends on a culturally specific power struggle between individuals and institutions, which attempt to control and establish a monopoly over the fixation of meaning by claiming 'ownership' of (a) language. Shylock becomes implicated in such a power struggle and as an outsider is duly stigmatized and excluded. He is stripped of 'his' language (which even more than in Derrida's sense is not his 'own') and is punished for his cultural difference to safeguard the imaginary homogeneity of Christian society and Venetian law.[5]

The strategy that Belsey uses to 'save' Shakespeare from his 'own' contemporary culture seems ultimately, despite or maybe because of its diametrical opposition to Bloom's liberal humanism, as humanistically and universalistically motivated as in Bloom: 'How surprising, then that the play invests its fantasy-Jew with humanity. It is for this reason, however, that *The Merchant of Venice* does not just reaffirm prejudice, but draws attention to it' (Belsey, 2002, p. 167). If Shakespeare's text itself undermines or even 'deconstructs' the idea of a culturally homogenous identity it can be used as an early modern testimony against any exclusivity in the process of identity construction at any time in history. Belsey's reading consequently does not fail to engage in a critique of contemporary multiculturalism, at the same time as it justifies the ongoing interest in Shakespeare as a thinker of great humanitarian and existential questions ('the reason why Shakespeare's play continues to haunt the imagination of the West'): 'can a society preserve cultural difference and at the same time do away with social antagonism?' (p. 168). In relation to the contemporary, and especially the Anglo-American, cultural context, the question arises in the following *historically and culturally specific* form, despite its tacit universal assumptions: 'While enforced integration generates a justified resentment, our own well-meaning multiculturalism may inadvertently foster precisely the segregation, and thus the hostility, it was designed to prevent' (p. 168). The similarity of the procedure with that of Bloom's 'liberal humanism' in this context is indeed striking. The play opens onto the 'abyss' of inhumanity, projected onto the outsider who, in turn, exposes the inhumanity of the entire society of humans. The same dialectic of self-hatred, hatred of the other and cultural improvement that constitutes Bloom's humanist ideology ironically appears to be at work in Belsey's reading as well. Our argument would be that, as long as this dialectic is not questioned a critical posthumanist angle remains invisible.

The Merchant of Venice: posthumanism and misanthropy

Let us therefore briefly return to the 'essence' of humanity and look again at Shylock's famous speech in III.1 – a speech provoked by his previous personal and no doubt traumatic loss of his only daughter, Jessica, and Salarino's mocking reminder of her elopement. Shylock concludes his 'humanity speech' with the words: 'The villany you teach me I will execute, and it shall go hard but I will better the instruction' (III.1.56–7). Nothing, in fact, is more effective in unhinging humanism than this phrase, because the dialectic of similarity and difference is here at its turning point. The projected inhumanity, the repressed self-hatred returns, following the basic psychoanalytical logic of the repressed's return, and it begins to haunt the provisionally stabilized self, threatens it and causes it to repress afresh – which could be used to explain the extent to which the escalation of inhumanity is an essential aspect of humanity itself, maybe even its very engine, drive or 'telos'. The 'humanization' of history hides its own dehumanizing logic. Posthumanism can therefore not simply break with this logic because that would merely constitute a continuation of the escalating dialectic of humanization and dehumanization. Instead it is a question of a deconstructive 'working through' of humanism's represseds, of the inhuman and unhuman, in a radically different sense.

Scott Brewster summarizes this point in his Introduction to *Inhuman Reflections: Thinking the Limits of the Human* (2000):

> the inhuman is unsatisfactorily configured as somehow 'post' or as a mere *limen* or threshold, much less a crossing of the boundary. Rather it retains a sense of excess (plural potentiality) which continues to disseminate as it always has done and fulfilled an unfulfillable within the continuing 'technical mediation' of the human. (Brewster, 2000, p. 9)

This techn(olog)ical mediation of the human, which has to be taken into account in any critical genealogy of the inhuman or the posthuman, testifies to the fact that any form of 'becoming-machine'

(i.e. cyborgization as the one, predominantly contemporary, form of posthumanization) is always already a constitutive factor of being human connected necessarily with an 'originary technicity'.

Let us stress again that the prefix 'post-' in posthumanism can have a variety of meanings and that it allows for a number of discursive and argumentative strategies. Thus neither in terms of content nor use do the terms 'posthuman', 'posthumanity' and 'posthumanization' presuppose any consensus about meaning. These terms are politically, radically open, which is the fact that gives rise to the demand for a critical posthumanism in the first place – a critical posthumanism that both takes the issue of the posthuman seriously and problematizes, contextualizes and historicizes it, at the same time.

In this respect this chapter is in partial agreement with Halliwell and Mousley's approach in *Critical Humanisms: Humanist/Anti-Humanist Dialogues* (2003), which proposes to do justice to the complexity of humanism in its many disguises. On the one hand, Halliwell and Mousley distinguish between a romantic, existentialist, dialogic, civic, spiritual, secular, pragmatic and a technological humanism and, on the other, they also subdivide antihumanism, as a reaction against each of these humanisms, into three phases. The first of these phases lasts from the mid-nineteenth to the beginning of the twentieth century and contains important antihumanist precursors such as Darwin, Freud, Marx, Nietzsche, Saussure and Weber, who all engage in a critique of anthropocentric metaphysics. The second phase of the 1960s and 1970s is that of the antihumanists proper (Barthes, Deleuze and Guattari, Derrida, Foucault, Baudrillard and Lacan), which leads, finally, within the postmodern context of the 1970s and 1980s, to the third generation of a 'popularized' antihumanism. Among the proponents of the third phase Halliwell and Mousley include figures like Catherine Belsey, Geoffrey Bennington, Terence Hawkes, Christopher Norris, Peggy Kamuf, J. Hillis Miller and Paul Rabinow, who expose the 'cardinal sins' of 'Western metaphysics': logocentrism, phallocentrism and anthropocentrism. As antidotes they propose the decentring of language, the subject and the liberal humanist world picture in general. Despite the curious anglocentrism of Halliwell and Mousley's genealogy, their approach successfully problematizes the monolithic view of humanism by locating a radical self-criticism already within the humanist tradition and, on this basis, by arguing for a non-normative, 'post-foundational' humanism 'that refuses to define the human' (Halliwell and Mousley, 2003, p. 9) and thus escapes the 'tyranny of naming and quantifying the human' (p. 10). Against the 'reduction' of the human in the age of hypermodern, late capitalism, so-called 'high theory' and the endless 'plasticity of the human', Halliwell and Mousley propose a 'grounded humanism' which opposes 'alienation, depersonalisation and degradation' (p. 10) of the human and humanity. Despite Halliwell and Mousley's humanitarian reflex, however, it seems unlikely that the contemporary techno-savvy phase of posthumanization will have a lot of patience for such an attempt at rehumanizing. This is why our standpoint probably implies a kind of 'alterhumanism', rather than a rehumanization, as antidote for some of the undeniably dehumanizing tendencies within the prospect of posthumanization. However, projecting inhumanity onto the 'system' in order to preserve the principle of human(ist) freedom seems an illusion since 'human' and 'system' are thoroughly interrelated – humans create systems, which then 'reproduce' or shape humans as subjects or actors to guarantee the continuity of that system.

There is no choice but to face the prospect of posthumanism if one is serious about a critique of humanism and anthropocentrism without giving in to the rehumanization reflex, a choice which does not really seem prepared to question the humanist foundations. This might, for example, be particularly relevant for postcolonial theory and the discussion about how best to deal with ethnic difference and modern racism. The particular concern is that the dissolution of a universalist notion of humanity would foster a rerturn of old racisms in new forms. As justified as this concern might be, it cannot lead to a renewal of a leftist radical humanism in the name of a Kantian cosmopolitan tradition as, for example, suggested by John Sanbonmatsu (2004), who argues for, what he calls, 'metahumanism':

> With the arrival of post-humanism we may fast be approaching the zero hour of the critical tradition. With the subject as such now placed *sous rature* (under erasure), but this time not merely by clever critics but by scientists who *literally* manipulate the stuff our dreams of ourselves are made of, even the poststructuralist project self-destructs, as deconstruction is rendered irrelevant by the *fragmentation* of the ontological unity *Dasein*. This may seem a trivial point, but critical theory is already dangerously in collusion with the final obliteration of all things 'human' by capital ... Post-humanism will have to be met forthrightly – with a return to ontology and the grounding of thought in a meaningful account of human being. (Sanbonmatsu, 2004, p. 207)

A lot could be said about the problematic reference to Prospero in defence of 'metahumanism'. Indeed, it would be quite wrong to idealize humanist universalism for the reasons outlined above. The universalist ideal of a common and irreducible humanity that underlies, for example, the legitimation of any legislation against crimes against humanity has not succeeded in addressing the radical dehumanization underlying the entire history of colonialism and its current legacy of global migration and multiculturalism (this is Belsey's motif above). Neither has an essentialist notion of humanity prevented the Holocaust or other genocides since. In my view, the 'perversion' of inhumanity is part of the logic of humanism itself. This is why a deconstruction of the humanist tradition has never been more important than today, that is, in the face of a continued transformation of the human and of the humanistic question as such: what exactly constitutes the humanity of the human? It is precisely the connection between continuity, break and remembering that powers the dialectical drive, within humanism, between dehumanization and rehumanization. Only a deconstruction of humanism in its current globalized and technocultural posthumanist form and phase can unhinge this dialectic play and may eventually expose and disrupt it, provoking an opening towards a radically different, non-humanist, post-anthropocentric view.

From its tender beginnings in Greek and Roman antiquity to the present, humanism has always displayed a remarkable resistance and adaptability. It has overcome its theological and religious beginnings in the face of modern developments and challenges (such as science, evolution, psychoanalysis, existentialism, globalization and technologization) and has been secularized (because of the French Revolution), politicized (as a result of liberalism) and has absorbed the effects of capitalism itself, and has established itself as 'common sense' on an international and arguably global level. In its name, wars have been and are being fought, at the same time as the world's poor are being helped. Its educational values underlie the modern institution of the university. Its aesthetic shores up globalized Western culture. Its moral values do not cease to inspire tales of human self-aggrandisement *and* humility, or of good and evil of which the human in all his or her splendour *and* misery is capable and between which he or she constantly has to choose in order to overcome the suffering and the mortality that the human shares with the rest of humanity (and indeed with all known other species). Who could be so unfeeling and not be touched by this: humanism's 'heroic' self-account? Nevertheless, it is precisely the humanistic self-indulgence and uncritical complacency that might drive a critical posthumanist towards 'strategic misanthropy' – out of care for the human and a future of and for the human, including his or her natural and cultural environment, for 'who can fail to realize that the trope of misanthropy is the hope of society?' (Cottom, 2006, p. 150). And this might ultimately be the justification for calling Shakespeare a posthumanist *avant-la-lettre* ...

Notes

1. N. Katherine Hayles's account of *How We Became Posthuman* (1999) centres on the history of cybernetics and its main metaphor, information, with its associated 'belief that information can circulate unchanged among different material substrates' (p. 1). Hayles traces this history throughout roughly the twentieth century by distinguishing three stages: 'how information lost its body ... how the cyborg was created as technological artefact and cultural icon ... and how the human is giving way to a different construction called the posthuman' (p. 2). It is the present chapter's and, indeed, the entire volume's claim that this twentieth-century transformation from human to poshuman via (information) technology needs to be historically challenged and recontextualized.

2. Like any other invention, the invention of the human would follow the logic analysed by Jacques Derrida in 'Psyche: Inventions of the Other' (1989). It would be impossible to give a short summary of what is a very complex and multilayered argument in Derrida's essay. The fundamental 'aporia' at the heart of the 'invention of the new' is that it happens within an essential or 'structural' double bind of impossibility and necessity. For an invention to be 'new' it needs to happen outside the horizon of subjectivity. In contrast, for an invention to be recognized and legitimated as such, it needs an inventing subject (an 'author'). This is why, strictly speaking a radically new invention would only be possible as an 'invention of the other'. However, a fundamental undecidability remains as a result: is the other 'invented' (e.g. the inhuman by the human)? Or does the invention in fact come from the unknowable other (is the human the 'effect' of a 'repressed' and 'older' form of alterity)? There is no way to decide. Derrida, in this essay and throughout his work, shows that this undecidability underlies *and* threatens the entire history of metaphysical humanism. The present chapter therefore uses the phrase 'invention of the inhuman' in a 'deconstructive' sense to refer to the possibility of an entirely different, i.e. 'posthumanist', understanding of the human even 'before' his/her (its?) 'invention'.

3. While Coriolanus' gradual 'mechanization' is an essential aspect of his tragic downfall, there is also a very strong link to comedy and laughter in 'becoming machinic'. The key reference here is Henri Bergson's *Le Rire* (1910 [1900]). Bergson's famous definition of the comical – 'du mécanique plaqué sur du vivant' (p. 39), a certain mechanicity and inflexibility ('raideur') that covers the life-force (which, for the vitalist Bergson, is elasticity itself). A prime example of the comic dimension of increasing mechanization of a character in Shakespeare – or a kind of early modern form of 'cyborgization' – is indeed Shylock, whose discourse throughout acts III and IV becomes increasingly repetitive, 'stubborn' and 'literal' (cf. below).

4. It would indeed be interesting to read Shylock's Venetian 'language memoir' and compare it to Derrida's 'Franco-Maghrebian' experience in France, in

Monolingualism of the Other (1998), particularly the remarks on the forceful loss of accent and the idea of 'hyperbolic purity' (pp. 45–8) Derrida associates with 'enter[ing] French literature'. While Derrida's 'monolingualism of the other' refers to a total surrender of 'one's own' language as to that of the other, Shylock seems to speak the language of the other 'as if it was his', which, arguably, leads to his defeat, by language itself.

5. For Derrida, in fact, *The Merchant of Venice* is 'the play of translation' as such. In 'What Is a "Relevant" Translation?' (2001, p. 183), Derrida says: 'everything in the play can be retranslated into the code of translation and as a problem of translation ... At every moment, translation is as necessary as it is impossible. It is the law; it even speaks the language of the law beyond the law, of the impossible law, represented by a woman who is disguised, transfigured, converted, travestied, read *translated*, into a man of the law. As if the subject of this play were, in short, the task of the translator, his impossible task, his duty, his debt, as inflexible as it is unpayable.' It could be said that it is Portia, disguised as Balthazar, who plays the role of the inventor of the inhuman as and within the law, and who 'sets into motion the *difference* of the other' (Derrida, 1989, p. 61). The law, coded in one specific language, has always already 'translated' justice – which constitutes a 'madness' or injustice at the very heart of the law (and language; cf. Derrida, 1998, p. 10) that affects both the Christians in Venice and Shylock, the Jew, however, in very different ways, of course.

Works cited

Badmington, Neil (2004) 'Post, Oblique, Human', *Theory and Society* 10.2, pp. 56–64.

Belsey, Catherine (2007) *Why Shakespeare?* Basingstoke: Palgrave, now Palgrave Macmillan.

Bergson, Henri (1910 [1900]) *Le Rire – essai sur la signification du comique*, Paris: Félix Alcan.

Bloom, Harold (1999) *Shakespeare: The Invention of the Human*, London: Fourth Estate.

Brewster, Scott (2000) 'Introduction', in Brewster et al. (2000), pp. 1–12.

Brewster, Scott, et al. (eds) (2000) *Inhuman Reflections: Thinking the Limits of the Human*, Manchester: Manchester University Press.

Cottom, Daniel (2006) *Unhuman Culture*, Philadelphia: University of Pennsylvania Press.

Derrida, Jacques (1989) 'Psyche: Inventions of the Other', trans. Catherine Porter, in Lyndsay Waters and Wlad Godzich (eds), *Reading de Man Reading*, Minneapolis: University of Minnesota Press, pp. 25–65.

Derrida, Jacques (1992) 'Force of Law: The "Mystical Foundation of Authority"', in Drucilla Cornell (ed.), *Deconstruction and the Possibility of Justice*, New York: Routledge, pp. 4–67.

Derrida, Jacques (1998) *Monolingualism of the Other; or, The Prosthesis of Origin*, trans. Patrick Mensah, Stanford: Stanford University Press.

Derrida, Jacques (2001) 'What Is a "Relevant" Translation?', trans. Lawrence Venuti, *Critical Inquiry* 27.2, pp. 174–200.

Derrida, Jacques (2005) 'Justices', trans. Peggy Kamuf, *Critical Inquiry* 31, pp. 689–721.

Dollimore, Jonathan (1985) 'Introduction: Shakespeare, Cultural Materialism and the New Historicism', in Jonathan Dollimore and Alan Sinfield (eds), *Political Shakespeare: New Essays in Cultural Materialism*, Manchester: Manchester University Press, pp. 2–17.

Dollimore, Jonathan (1998) 'Shakespeare and Theory', in Ania Loomba and Martin Orkin (eds), *Post-colonial Shakespeares*, London: Routledge, pp. 259–76.

Dollimore, Jonathan (2004) *Radical Tragedy: Religion, Ideology and Power in the Drama of Shakespeare and His Contemporaries*, 3rd edn, Basingstoke: Palgrave, now Palgrave Macmillan.

Fudge, Erica, Ruth Gilbert and Susan Wiseman (eds) (2002) *At the Borders of the Human: Beasts, Bodies and Natural Philosophy in the Early Modern Period*, Basingstoke: Palgrave, now Palgrave Macmillan.

Greenblatt, Stephen (1980) *Renaissance Self-Fashioning: From More to Shakespeare*, Chicago: University of Chicago Press.

Halliwell, Martin, and Andy Mousley (2003) *Critical Humanisms: Humanist? Anti-Humanist Dialogues*, Edinburgh: Edinburgh University Press.

Haraway, Donna (1991) 'A Cyborg Manifesto' (1985), *Simians, Cyborgs, and Women: The Reinvention of Nature*, New York: Routledge, pp. 149–81.

Hayles, N. Katherine (1999) *How We Became Posthuman: Virtual Bodies in Cybernetics, Literature, and Informatics*, Chicago: University of Chicago Press.

Rhodes, Neil, and Jonathan Sawday (eds) (2000) *The Renaissance Computer: Knowledge and Technology in the First Age of Print*, London: Routledge.

Sanbonmatsu, John (2004) *The Postmodern Prince: Critical Theory, Left Strategy, and the Making of a New Political Subject*, New York: Monthly Review Press.

Sawday, Jonathan (2002) 'Renaissance Cyborg', in Fudge, Gilbert and Wiseman (2004), pp. 171–95.

Shakespeare, William (1996) *The Merchant of Venice* (1600), The New Cambridge Shakespeare, ed. M. M. Mahood, Cambridge: Cambridge University Press.

Vickers, Brian (1996) *Appropriating Shakespeare: Contemporary Critical Quarrels*, New Haven: Yale University Press.

Wells, Robin Headlam (2005) *Shakespeare's Humanism*, Cambridge: Cambridge University Press.

3
Shakespeare and the Character of Sheep

Bruce Boehrer

Extracted from my recent work on nonhuman identity in early modern literature (Boehrer, 2010, *passim*) the two halves of this chapter stand in relation to each other as does theory to its applications. The first section considers, in broad terms, the role played by the species divide in the development of sixteenth- and seventeenth-century models of literary character. The second section offers commentary on a specific Shakespearean passage – *Titus Andronicus* IV.4.89–93 – whose meaning is grounded in cross-species relations. Taken together, these two scholarly exercises move from the general to the particular while approaching the topic of Shakespearean posthumanism from the perspective of animal studies.

In a sense, of course, any discussion of posthumanism in Shakespeare must be considered anachronistic. Shakespeare's works predate the term 'posthumanism' itself by a good three centuries,[1] nor do they directly subscribe to any of the main intellectual trends – deconstruction, for instance, or feminism, or postcolonialism – that dominate the posthumanist project. But at the same time, Shakespeare remains essential to posthumanist scholarship, and not just because of his cultural cachet. Given his historical moment, Shakespeare serves as a forerunner to the triumphant phase of European humanist thought as defined by figures like Bacon, Descartes, Locke, and Hume, yet for this very reason Shakespeare is especially well placed to illustrate the challenges faced by humanism in its rise to philosophical preeminence. In effect, Shakespeare enables us to get past the category of the human because he remains tied – despite the influence of Pico and his fellows – to the prehuman. This is nowhere better illustrated than in the poet's enduring concern with the boundaries separating human from nonhuman species, and in his equally enduring reputation for excellence as a delineator of literary character. I take these two issues to be interrelated.

1

On the broad level, my argument here is simple: that the problem of literary character may best be understood from the standpoint of animal studies, as an instance of general philosophical and scientific problems in theorizing the human/animal divide.

That the concept of literary character *is* a problem – or at least entails problems – I take as axiomatic. It was certainly so for L. C. Knights when, in 1933, he published his classic essay 'How Many Children Had Lady Macbeth?'[2] A brief for New-Critical formalism, Knights's article also mounts an attack upon the methods of character-analysis that dominated earlier critical practice as exemplified by the study of Shakespeare:

> The habit of regarding Shakespeare's persons as 'friends for life,' or, maybe, 'deceased acquaintances,' is responsible for most of the vagaries that serve as Shakespeare criticism ... It is responsible for all the irrelevant moral and realistic canons that have been applied to Shakespeare's plays, for the sentimentalizing of his heroes (Coleridge and Goethe on Hamlet) and his heroines. And the loss is incalculable. (Knights, 1947, p. 30)

Knights's critique has produced a kind of queasy ambivalence in more recent literary criticism, which remains attached to the notion of character without really wanting to be; as Elizabeth Fowler summarized matters, 'Literary scholarship ... speaks of characters as if they were real people and, just as frequently, warns us that they are not' (Fowler, 2003, p. 5). The resulting dilemma receives fine comic expression at the hands of David Lodge, an author with credentials both as a theorist and as a writer of fiction. In the 1988 academic novel *Nice Work*, Lodge's narrator is awkwardly obliged to introduce a character who 'doesn't herself believe in the concept of "character"' – one 'Robyn Penrose, Temporary Lecturer in English Literature at the University of Rummidge' (Lodge, 1988, p. 21). And Penrose's objections to the concept – that is, 'that "character" is a bourgeois myth, an illusion created to reinforce the ideology of capitalism,' obscuring the crucial insight that '[t]here are no selves, only production, and we produce our "selves" in language' (pp. 21–2) – attest to the role of Marxist and postmodernist theory in assailing the legitimacy of character as a literary construct.

But the Marxist/postmodernist critique of literary character did not develop in a vacuum; it runs parallel to a broader assault upon the category of the human itself. This broader line of argument is typified by the poststructuralist tradition in current animal studies theory, which objects to the Benthamite and Kantian schools of animal-rights philosophy, represented by Peter Singer and Tom Regan respectively, on the grounds that these seek to protect non-human animals by extending to them a notion of human rights (or, in Singer's case, human ethical subjectivity) that is itself intellectually untenable.[3] Thus Derrida refuses both 'to assign, interpret, or project' meaning onto the animal other (this being, I take it, the impulse of traditional animal-rights theory), while likewise resisting the Cartesian reflex to 'suspend ... one's compassion and ... depriv[e] the animal of every power of manifestation' (Derrida, 2002, p. 387). Deleuze and Guattari replace the notion of being with one of becoming, located in 'an objective zone of indetermination or uncertainty ... that makes it impossible to say where the boundary between the human and animal lies' (1988, p. 273). Giorgio Agamben, arguing that '[i]n our culture, the decisive political conflict ... is that between the animality and the humanity of *man*,' concludes that 'what is decisive here is only the "between," the interval ... between the two terms, their immediate constellation in a non-coincidence' (Agamben, 2004, pp. 80, 83; my italics). Each of these positions assumes that to ground political or ethical action upon notions of the human is to perpetuate the very inequities that politics and ethics are intended to remedy; hence the deconstruction of the human emerges as a philosophical imperative.

There can be no doubt that literary criticism's discomfort with the concept of character is related to this growing theoretical impulse to deconstruct the human/animal divide. After all, if a given philosophical category (the human) proves defective, it follows that the category's major literary manifestation (character) should share in its inadequacies. In effect, I would argue, the notion of character develops in English writing as an early effort to evade this very philosophical crisis: as a means of manufacturing and perpetuating the distinction between people and animals.

This is not how the turn to character and character-criticism has usually been understood. Knights explains it in classic New-Critical fashion, as a failure of linguistic engagement – in the case of Shakespeare scholars, 'an inability to appreciate the Elizabethan idiom and a consequent inability to discuss Shakespeare's plays as poetry' (Knights,

1947, p. 26). Lodge's Robyn Penrose, for her part, follows the Brechtian *aperçu* that literary illusionism aims to transform audiences into 'the passive consumer[s] of a finished, unchangeable art-object offered to them as "real"' (Eagleton, 1974, p. 64); thus, for her, 'the rise of the novel (the literary genre of "character" *par excellence*) in the eighteenth century coincided with the rise of capitalism' and its endless search for pliable markets (Lodge, 1988, p. 21). For scholars following Ian Watt, the rise of literary character derives from the eighteenth-century tendency to 'pa[y] greater attention to the particular individual than had been common before' (Watt, 1957, p. 18), a tendency deriving from the philosophical skepticism of figures like Descartes, Locke, and Hume. While these narratives trace the ascendancy of literary character to different historical events (the development of new language practices, the birth of capitalism, the rise of scientific empiricism), they agree by locating it in the eighteenth century and identifying the novel as its exemplary genre.

Still, if one takes at face value the eighteenth-century passion for Shakespeare as a creator of characters, it challenges both the chronological focus on the eighteenth century and the generic focus on prose fiction. And in any case, as Fowler's recent work with Chaucer has shown, it is patently silly to suppose that pre-Enlightenment authors had no literary characters, if one defines these simply – in Fowler's preferred way – as 'social persons' (Fowler, 2003, p. 27). Moreover, even the term 'character' itself, as applied to the 'description, delineation, or detailed report of a person's qualities' (*OED* 'Character' sb. 14), predates the eighteenth century. The *OED's* earliest recorded instance of this usage comes from Howell's *Letters* of 1645, but even this is unfairly belated; with the publication of Hall's Theophrastan *Characters* in 1608, the English already possessed a fully-formed literary exemplar of the definition. Indeed, Theophrastus' works play a central role in establishing the noun 'character' as an English literary term, and in the process they reveal the word's embeddedness in an ancient tradition of philosophical meditation on the nature of human identity.

Theophrastus is best remembered for treatises in the fields we would now call biology and psychology.[4] These works span the disciplinary divide – between 'the representation of nonhumans' and 'the representation of citizens' (Latour, 1993, p. 28) – that Bruno Latour identifies with modernity's 'separation of natural and political powers' (p. 13). In this regard, they preserve the cross-disciplinary focus of Theophrastus' master, Aristotle, whom he succeeded in 322 BCE as head of the Peripatetic school in Athens. Indeed, if readers of Theophrastus have detected a 'botanical' impulse in his *Characters* (cf. Boyce, 1947, p. 5), that is because

Theophrastus himself was working squarely within an Aristotelian tradition in which '[t]he methodical treatment of *poiesis* in the *Poetics* is similar to the orderly classification of the body in the *History of Animals*' (Craik, 2007, p. 158). In this tradition, the study of rhetoric and the study of natural history, the study of people and the study of animals, emerge as parallel expressions of the same taxonomic impulse.

It may be objected that this is merely a matter of form, that in substance the two undertakings differ considerably. Perhaps, but the most recent translators of Theophrastus' *Characters* have traced its antecedents back to the lengthiest surviving verse-fragment by Simonides of Amorgos, consisting of character-sketches of women whose 'various vices (e.g. filthiness, cunning, extravagance) are explained by their creation from animals (e.g. the pig, fox, horse)' (Theophrastus, 2002, p. 17). If, as these same editors aver, 'the notion that individual good or bad traits of character may be isolated and studied separately' is 'basic' to the philosopher's 'whole enterprise' (p. 13), then the *Characters* participates in an ethical project that encompasses the world of non-human animals as well. That, at least, is a major assumption of those other heirs to Aristotle, the bestiarists, when they identify the behavior of the halcyon hen as 'an unexpected celebration of kindness' (*Book of Beasts*, 1984, p. 124), or attribute to horses the capacity 'to weep for man and feel the emotion of sorrow' (p. 86), or expound upon '[t]he merciful nature of lions' (*Bestiary*, 1993, p. 25). As quaintly familiar as such language may be, it points to the historical investment of character-study in observation of the non-human world.

Thus, from the standpoint of animal studies, it becomes appropriate to view the bestiary entry as a particular variety of character-study, and to view the Theophrastan character as a particular variant of the bestiary entry. In terms of early modern English literary history, this linkage becomes especially visible in the 'birds of prey' – Voltore, Corbaccio, and Corvino – who populate Jonson's *Volpone* (I.2.89), as well as in Nano's claim, in the same play, to have passed former lives as an '*ox and asse, cammell, mule, goat, and brock*' (I.2.22). *Volpone's* characterological bestiary draws simultaneously on the traditional figures of beast-fable and epic, deriving from post-Aristotelian animal lore, and on the stock figures of New Comedy, based on post-Aristotelian psychology. In the latter respect, the linkage to Theophrastus again seems clear enough; Menander is said to have been one of the philosopher's students (Diogenes Laertius, 1959, pp. 485–6; V.36–7). And later English usage retains the affinity between human and animal traits in the sense of 'character' as denoting 'the distinguishing features of a species or genus' (*OED* 'Character' sb. 8b).

But Jonson's carrion-birds by no means exhaust the characterological possibilities of the animal in early modern literature. If we accept Fowler's working definition of literary characters as 'social persons,' compounded from overlapping 'legal,' 'civic,' 'corporate,' 'economic,' 'kinship,' and 'literary' identities (Fowler, 2003, pp. 16–17), the heavy integration of animals into all these aspects of early modern society makes it hard to see how one could reasonably deny them status as literary characters in their own right. Consider Montaigne's *Apology for Raymond Sebonde*, which, apart from its inscrutable cat, abounds with sentient beasts: a magpie who, after 'a profound study and withdrawal within herself,' learns to mimic the sound of trumpets (Montaigne, 1958, p. 341); elephants who help each other escape from traps (p. 342); cranes and swallows with 'the faculty of divination' (p. 345); and so on. Or consider Baiardo in Ariosto's *Orlando Furioso* (1974), so cunning and faithful a steed to Rinaldo that he refuses to let the latter mount him lest his master might call off the horse's steadfast pursuit of Rinaldo's beloved Angelica (Ariosto, 1974, XIII.2.20–3). Or consider the beginning of Sidney's *Defense of Poesy*, where John Pietro Pugliano praises the horse as 'a peerless beast ... the only serviceable courtier without flattery, the beast of most beauty, faithfulness, courage, and such more ... that I think he would have persuaded me to have wished myself a horse' (Sidney, 1970, p. 3).

One might protest that, for Sidney, Pugliano serves as an object of derision, an exponent of 'unbelieved' opinions, who defends these with 'strong affection and weak arguments' (p. 3). But this fact speaks precisely to my broader point: that in early modern culture, the literal and figurative proximity of non-human to human animals elicited anxiety, generating what René Girard has called a 'crisis of distinctions' (Girard, 1972, p. 49). Pugliano's character as a horseman (or horse/man) inspires Sidney's disapproval, yet Pugliano also provides Sidney with the model and motive – 'self-love' (Sidney, 1970, p. 3) – for the latter's defense of verse. In fact, Sidney's relation to Pugliano is far too close for comfort. It is the archetypal relation of 'scholar' to 'master' (p. 4), fraught with tension and ambivalence, which qualities receive figuration across the species barrier. Thus it stands as a further irony that in Sidney's case, 'self-love' is the love of Philip, *phil-hippos*, bearing within itself the trace of the anathematized other.

This 'crisis of distinctions' can be presented more broadly in Kuhnian terms, as an emerging dilemma in the early modern discourse of species – in effect, as a philosophical problem for which Descartes and his followers presented a paradigm-shifting solution.[5] Erica Fudge has traced this dilemma to inconsistencies within the early modern understanding of how and when a human being may be regarded as truly rational and therefore truly human: on the one hand, 'infants are not fully human, insofar as human status can only be designated truly by the actions that evidence the possession of a rational soul' (Fudge, 2006, p. 48); on the other hand, 'a human can literally become an animal when acting without reason' (p. 66); and various subaltern categories of humanity (e.g. women, slaves, ethnic others) present further challenges to a conventional understanding of humanity as grounded in reason. In sum,

> [T]here are natural born humans who can only be human because they possess the rational soul. Then there are humans in possession of the rational soul who require education to become truly human. Finally, there are humans who possess rational souls, can be educated, but are still less human than the human. Thus the category begins to collapse into absurdity. (Fudge, 2006, p. 58)

Descartes solved this problem with mathematical elegance by elevating human reason to the status of a first principle, requiring no proof outside the philosopher's own inference. The way was thus clear to discount the apparent sentience of other animals by dismissing it as an anthropomorphic projection, so that how beasts behaved no longer told us anything about what they thought or felt.

To this extent, the Cartesian *cogito* is itself a product of the inward turn, an application of skepticism to the philosopher's own beliefs and instincts until what remains – skepticism itself – becomes the ground of his identity as a rational being. And appropriately enough, this inward turn takes the confessional mode as its proper form of literary expression:

> I judged that I was as prone to error as anyone else, and I rejected as false all the reasoning I had hitherto accepted as valid proof. Finally ... I resolved to pretend that everything that had ever entered my head was no more true than the illusions of my dreams. But immediately afterwards I noted that, while I was trying to think of all things being false in this way, it was necessarily the case that I, who was thinking them, had to be something. (Descartes, 2006, p. 28; IV.32)

In effect, the Cartesian self arises from and entails the exploration of a new notion of character: not an Aristotelian taxonomy of shared attributes, but rather a sense of personal identity as singular and doubtful, consisting in particularity and observation, privileging mind over body and interior over exterior. This, of course, is the mode of character celebrated in the grand literary achievements of the late seventeenth, eighteenth, and nineteenth centuries: the novel, the illusionistic theater, the cult of sentiment, and the critical veneration of Shakespeare.

Hence we may recognize this notion of character, in its originary Cartesian moment, as an instrument for defining and maintaining the species barrier. It is no accident that the *Discourse on Method* remains almost equally famous for two distinct philosophical postulates: the *cogito* and the *bête-machine*. These principles emerge hand-in-hoof from Descartes's meditations, in symbiotic and mutually-reinforcing relation: the former crafts a notion of humanity composed of inwardness and speculation, while the latter denies such qualities to the non-human. Taken together, these philosophical constructs offer a response to earlier notions of human character that had come by the early modern period to appear increasingly untenable. In the process, Descartes's principles also paved the way for new literary techniques of representing the human, techniques which in turn proved essential in consolidating the species distinction upon which they themselves were based.

But what then of Shakespeare? How is this very pre-Cartesian playwright conscripted so durably into the Enlightenment project of literary character-construction? We might start to answer this question by noting how haunted Shakespeare is by the relationship between people and other animals. From Launce and Crab to the asinine Bottom, from the 'inexecrable dog' Shylock (*Merchant of Venice* IV.1.128) to Banquo's currish murderers (*Macbeth* III.1.91–104), from Lear's 'pelican daughters' (III.4.75) to the man/fish Caliban, the poet's work seems like nothing so much as a protracted, uneasy meditation on the ties that bind species together, and the traumas that tear them apart. From this standpoint, Shakespeare's particular claim to fame may lie not so much in the characters he created as in the discomfort he expressed through them: that is to say, in the resonance and clarity with which he lent voice to the problem of distinctions that preceded the Cartesian moment. Perhaps there is something a bit complacent, even self-infatuated, in recent efforts to celebrate him as the inventor of the human. Perhaps we should remember him instead as the poet of humanity in crisis.

2

If this is so – if, that is, Shakespeare distinguishes himself as a poet fascinated by the indefiniteness of the human – it is largely because of what common observation tells us we share with the nonhuman: bodies, senses, lineage, behavior, if not the full panoply then surely the fundamentals of embodied experience. In the space remaining here, I want to suggest how this range of experience informs Shakespeare's work by tracing networks of meaning across the species divide. To that end, I shall revisit the standard commentary on *Titus Andronicus* IV.4.89–93 by reading that passage in the context of early modern treatises on animal husbandry. These treatises have come under increasing recent study for the light they shed on contemporary belletristic texts. By the same token, the rising popularity of such manuals in early modern Europe bespeaks a rapid growth of interest in the interrelated topics we would now call agriculture, animal husbandry, and veterinary medicine, a growth scholars have also related to such concurrent developments as the realignment of agricultural economies, the emergence of nationalism, and the advent of the new science. Thus Anthony Low posits the occurrence of a 'georgic revolution' in seventeenth-century England, an event 'with social, ideological, economic, and technological ramifications as well as literary consequences' (Low, 1985, p. 12). Stefano Perfetti has argued that the new 'science of animals' in early modern Europe 'found its expression in new literary genres and epistemic practices' (2007, p. 1). Wendy Wall has implicated Gervase Markham's husbandry manuals in the production of 'a national myth of the land ... that called into being national subjects by renaming their activities in terms of the collective unit of Englishness' (1996, p. 770). In such narratives, the vocabularies of economics, natural history, and national sovereignty develop through a process of mutual implication that also manifests itself in more traditionally literary writing.

I am interested here in what early modern husbandry manuals have to say about the ailments of sheep. Risibly humble though they may be, these animals still participate in the grand discursive practices studied by scholars like Low, Perfetti, and Wall. After all, it was British sheep that produced the British wool that produced the British economy that produced the British Empire; to this extent, we should not be surprised to find the emergent animal sciences frequently engaged with questions of their care and rearing. In his *Historie of Foure-Footed Beastes* (1607), for instance, Edward Topsell calls for a discourse of agricultural management that specifically takes ovine husbandry into account:

> Horses, Dogs, and almost euery creature, haue gotten fauour in Gentlemens wits, to haue their natures described, but the silly sheepe better euery way then they, and more necessary for life, could neuer

attaine such kindnesse, as once to get one page written or indighted for the safegard of their natures, I do therefore by these presence from my soule and spirit, inuite all Gentlmen and men of learning ... to giue their mindes to know the defects of this beast. (Topsell, 1973, pp. 618–19)

Inviting gentlemen to publish books about sheep 'to the safeguard of their natures,' Topsell calls for a prophylactic and therapeutic medical discourse whose object is 'to know the defects of this beast, but also to inuent the best remedies that nature can afford' for its ailments (p. 619). With its growing emphasis on empirical observation, seventeenth-century natural history proves receptive to his appeal. The result is a husbandry literature that speaks not just to the character of barnyard animals, but also to the relation between the nonhuman and the human; this relation, in turn, can be demonstrated to inform the language and behavior of specific Shakespearean characters.

So to my text. In Act IV of *Titus Andronicus*, Tamora prepares to solicit Titus' aid in defending Rome, which is under assault by an army of Goths led by Titus' son Lucius. When the emperor Saturninus expresses doubt that Titus will 'entreat his son' on Rome's behalf, Tamora replies:

> I will enchant the old Andronicus
> With words more sweet, and yet more dangerous,
> Than baits to fish, or honey-stalks to sheep,
> When as the one is wounded with the bait,
> The other rotted with delicious feed. (IV.4.89–93)

On the whole, editors have made little of this passage, resting content to gloss 'honey-stalks' as clover (cf. for instance Shakespeare, 1995, p. 242, n. 90; Shakespeare, 2004, p. 997, n. 91; and Greenblatt, 1997, II., p. 129, n. 7). Alan Hughes's revised New Cambridge edition of the play provides more information here than most, noting that '"Rot" is a liver disease of sheep' (2006, p. 137, n. 92) and that, according to the *OED*, 'Shakespeare is the only writer' to use the phrase 'honey-stalks' as a name for clover-blossoms (p. 137, n. 90). But this commentary both raises and ignores an obvious question: if Shakespeare is the only writer to use the phrase, and if Shakespeare's own usage of it requires an explanatory gloss, where does the gloss come from? How, for that matter, does the *OED* know the meaning of Shakespeare's unique phrase?

As it happens, both the *OED* and Shakespeare's modern editors get the gloss from Samuel Johnson, who first provides it, without any specific attribution, in his 1765 edition of Shakespeare's works: 'Honey-stalks are clover flowers, which contain a sweet juice. It is common for cattle to overcharge themselves with clover, and so die' (Shakespeare, 1807, VII., p. 55, n. 9). From there it has migrated into standard editorial usage, but not without at least some dissent. For instance, John Monck Mason objects in 1785:

> Clover has the effect that Johnson mentions, on black cattle but not on sheep. Besides, these *honey-stalks*, whatever they may be, are described as rotting the sheep, not as bursting them, whereas clover is the wholesomest food you can give them. (Mason, 1973, p. 306)

So the standard explanation of Shakespeare's phrase is introduced without attribution, one hundred and fifty years after the poet's death, by a highly influential literary scholar whose attainments in the field of veterinary medicine remain, however, somewhat less well attested, and whose explanation in this case encountered disagreement fairly early on. If editors have held on to Johnson's gloss, one suspects, they have done so mostly for want of an alternative.

By the same token, if we were to seek confirmation for Johnson's gloss, the obvious place to do so would be in Elizabethan and Jacobean publications dealing with the care, feeding, and ailments of sheep. Yet if we turn to early English husbandry manuals for such help, we will at first be disappointed; despite a pervasive concern with rot and related ailments engendered by unhealthy diet, the husbandry manuals do not mention 'honey-stalks' at all. However, they are much exercised about other unwholesome feeds, especially those that impart excessive moisture to the animals. For instance, Leonard Mascall counsels that 'in Winter & Spring time, ye ought for to keepe [sheep] close, till the day haue taken all the gelly or netty rime from the earth, for in time the gelly is on the grasse, [it] doth ingender ... heauinesse of the head, and a looseness of the belley' (Mascall, 1620, pp. 208–9). Gervase Markham advises against feeding sheep on 'lowe and moyst grounds, which are infectious' (1614, p. 68). Gabriel Plat declares that 'Sheep that feed upon such grounds as yeeld silkish soft grasse, are sooner rotted, then those that feed upon a drier, and a hard grasse' (1974 [1639], p. 62). Conrad von Heresbach (as translated by Barnabe Googe) warns shepherds not to put their flocks out to graze 'tyll the sunne haue drawen up the deawe, and hurtfull vapours of the ground' (1971 [1577], p. 140), and in general these writers seem concerned about the noxious effects of dew upon tender ovine bellies.

Notable among the dews in question is one sort with loose biblical associations, which Topsell describes as follows:

> In India ... it raineth many times a dew like liquid honey falling vppon the hearbs and grasse of the earth: wherefore the shepheards lead their flocks vnto those places, wherewithal their cattle are much delighted ... Such a kind of dew the Haebrewes call *Manna*, the Grecians *Aeromelos*, and *Drosomelos*: the Germans *Himmelhung*: and in English Honny-Dew; but if this bee eaten vpon the herbs in the month of May, it is very hurtful vnto them. (1973 [1607], p. 603)

Elsewhere again, Topsell warns that 'If in the spring time Sheepe do eate of the dew called the Hony-dew, it is poyson vnto them and they dye thereof' (p. 611). Thirty years later, Gabriel Plat remarks, 'some are of the opinion, that Honey-dewes cause' sheep to become 'rotten' (1974, p. 70). As for clover, by contrast, Markham declares it 'most wholesome for sheep' (1614, p. 79).

My immediate point about Tamora's words should be clear by now. The husbandry manuals suggest that those words do not involve a reference to clover at all, but rather that 'honey-stalks' is a convenient nonce-formulation referring to any vegetation laden with honey-dew and therefore noxious to sheep. But if we stay with the husbandry manuals for a moment longer, we may discover something else worth noting: specifically, that the husbandry writers themselves don't seem very clear about what 'honey-dew' is supposed to be. Instead, their use of the term tends to conflate three different things: the Biblical manna of Exodus 16 (as in the passage from Topsell cited above), the aphid-secretions identified by the *OED* as the term's principal referent (and illustrated by a passage from Googe's Heresbach ['Honeydew,' sb. 1]); and the plant-nectar gathered by bees in the production of honey. This last substance, in turn, is conventionally identified with the honey-dews troublesome to sheep; thus Plat dismisses the argument that honey-dews cause rot in sheep by noting that 'there are more honey-dewes in sound yeares for Sheepe, then in rotten yeares,' and that 'when Sheepe are most subject to this disease [i.e., rot], the Bees are likewise most subject to die in the Winter time with famine' (1974 [1639], p. 70). This honey-dew is both etymologically and semantically identical to mildew – or 'Meldew,' as Markham calls it (1614, p. 79).[6] As Plat explains:

> Mildew ... is thus caused: When the flowers ... are in their pride ... the Sunne ... exhaleth some part of their sweetnesse, and converteth

the same into Common Aire; which in the night is condensed, and falleth into dew ... This dew being unctuous and clammie ... getteth power to suffocate, and strangle the vegetative vertue of the Corne ... and to the end that all things might be conducible to the generall profit; I will spend a few lines in commendation of this creature of God, the Bee; who getteth her riches totally, out of nothing but what else would be lost; for whatsoever she getteth, is that which the flowers by their attractive vertue draw to them in the night, out of the dew that falleth. (Plat, 1974 [1639], pp. 59–60)

This mildew, which strangles and rots vegetation, likewise engenders rot in sheep.

For his part, Shakespeare's fascination with rot is well attested. As Robert Appelbaum has recently pointed out (2006, pp. 18–27), it acquires a persistent culinary dimension that asserts itself memorably in Hamlet's vision of his father's 'funeral bak'd-meats' appearing at his mother's wedding-feast (I.2.180); likewise, Appelbaum has noted the anticipation of this image that occurs in *Titus Andronicus* when Titus bakes Tamora's sons into a pie (Appelbaum, 2006, pp. 27–8). We are now in a position to see Tamora's honey-stalks as another instance of this same preoccupation with decay and putrescence, elaborated this time through the vocabulary of animal husbandry. And once again, the image anticipates a complementary moment in *Hamlet*, where the prince draws Gertrude's attention to two portrait miniatures, one of his father, the other of his uncle: 'Look you now what follows:/ Here is your husband, like a mildewed ear,/ Blasting his wholesome brother' (III.4.63–5). Here Claudius is translated into a metaphorical version of Tamora's honey-stalks, communicating his corruption to Hamlet Sr. much as Tamora imagined conveying hers to Titus. Hamlet's participle 'blasting' clearly draws on its verb's sense 'To blow or breathe on balefully or perniciously' (*OED* 'Blast,' v. 7), which in turn derives from the corresponding noun, meaning 'A sudden infection destructive to vegetable or animal life' (*OED* 'Blast,' sb. 6). Given the density of Hamlet's image, he could be imagining his father either as a plant or as a grazing animal; in either case, he is employing the language of animal husbandry that Shakespeare explored earlier, in *Titus*, to similar effect.

Such imagery, though fairly unusual, is not confined to Shakespeare; other writers, too, draw on the vocabulary of ovine disease. Fresh from the stocks in *Bartholomew Fair*, Ben Jonson's Justice Overdo persists with his project of reforming the fair's manners, insisting that 'The shepherd ought not, for one scabbed sheep, to throw by his tar-box' (III.3.26–7).

Frustrated in her amorous designs, John Fletcher's Amaryllis in *The Faithful Shepherdess* seeks the assistance of a local shepherd 'whose nigh starved flocks / Are alwayes scabby' (B4v); later in the same play, the swain Perigot swears that he loves Amaryllis, 'and if I falsely swear, / Let [Pan] not guard my flocks, let Foxes tear / My earliest Lambs, and Wolves while I do sleep / Fall on the rest, a Rot among my sheep' (E4v). However, this imagery finds its most memorable poetic expression in Milton's 'Lycidas:' 'The hungry Sheep look up, and are not fed, / But swoln with wind, and the rank mist they draw, / Rot inwardly, and foul contagion spread' (125–7). Commenting upon this passage, Stella Revard has seen in it an allusion to the plague of 1637, which 'many thought ... was a judgment of God upon the people of England and their unworthy clergy' (Revard, 2003, p. 255). But any such reference has also been relayed through the intervening language of the early modern husbandry manuals, as has the poem's preceding complaint, 'As killing as the Canker to the Rose, / Or Taint-worm to the weanling Herds that graze, / ... / So, *Lycidas*, thy loss to Shepherds ear' (45–9). Googe's translation of Heresbach prescribes a remedy for 'the Taint, or Stingworme' (1971, p. 134b), and like most husbandry manuals, tends to present it primarily as a threat to cattle and horses. (Markham does observe, however, that 'Sheep are as subject to wormes in their guts and stomackes as any other cattell whatsoeuer' [1614, p. 78].) As for the 'rank mist' that spreads 'rot' and 'contagion' to Milton's 'hungry Sheep,' it is clearly conceived as a kind of devotional mildew.

If these passages prove notable because they employ concepts and language that circulate widely in contemporary agricultural treatises, they deserve further attention for their frequent translation of this material into the spiritual and ethical register. From Tamora's image of honeyed deceit, through Overdo's penal tar-box and Perigot's false oath, to Milton's wind-swollen flock, the idea of ailing ovine bodies seems to encounter its representational double in the diseased human conscience and the corrupted human soul. As a result, the sick sheep in question inhabit a space of representational duality. On the one hand, these ailing creatures derive their meaning from a specific set of agrarian conditions; they attest to a distinct way of experiencing the relation between human beings and domestic animals. Yet in the process they are abstracted from those same conditions, conscripted into a signifying order that in effect de-natures them. In a move that is the opposite of reification, real sheep lose their materiality and are re-constituted within the realm of the symbolic. The ovine body becomes a figurative placeholder for the human soul.

Johnson's gloss of the phrase 'honey-stalks' in *Titus Andronicus* does not pay much attention to this duality; on the contrary, it tends to downplay the notion of rot through which Tamora's simile connects animals to *animae*. Given the great critic's personal history, this neglect is easy enough to understand. After all, Doctor Johnson was preeminently a creature of the city: an urban intellectual whose limited encounters with the countryside are largely immortalized in tones of disdain. It is small enough wonder that the writer who famously viewed London as a synecdoche for life should also, in Boswell's words, 'at no time [have] had much taste for rural beauties' (1936, p. 81). More remarkable is the fact that Johnson seems to have seen no necessary overlap between the literary arts and the *artes rusticae*. Boswell records an exemplary exchange between Johnson and Lord Monboddo during the former's Hebridean tour: when Monboddo declared 'that Virgil seemed to be as enthusiastic a farmer as he, and was certainly a practical one,' Johnson retorted, 'It does not always follow, my lord, that a man who has written a good poem on an art has practised it ... [I]n Philips's *Cyder, a Poem* all the precepts were just, and indeed better than in books written for the purpose of instructing, yet Philips had never made cider' (Shakespeare, 1807, p. 54). This is more than the contentiousness of an urbanite unwilling to concede any preeminence to country life; Johnson's remark matter-of-factly presupposes a taxonomy of knowledge wherein literary attainments comprise an autonomous field of endeavor, owing none of their authority to practical experience of non-literary matters. Given this mindset, one can understand how Johnson's gloss on *Titus Andronicus* might appear innocent of the knowledge afforded by early modern husbandry manuals.

But Johnson's sense of disciplinarity should probably not be taken as the Elizabethan rule. On the contrary, Henry S. Turner has recently argued for 'a convergence of literary and scientific epistemologies' in sixteenth-century England, 'during a period when both fields were in a crucial moment of formation' (Turner, 2006, p. 12). Turner's model of disciplinary overlap encompasses not only the theory of mathematics and geometry but also 'contemporary developments in early modern technology' (p. 3) deriving from the 'mechanical sciences' (p. 25), and in doing so, it suggests the extent to which now-separate fields of intellectual inquiry could be mutually implicated in the production of early modern culture. If this is the case for geometry and mathematics, one might reasonably ask, why would it not also be so for those sciences and technologies now associated with biology and agriculture? England in the 1590s was still, after all, very much an agrarian nation, and like much of London's population at the turn of the seventeenth century, Shakespeare had come to the city as a sort of refugee from rural life. As for the interrelation between natural history and literature, one finds it on prominent display in such verse genres as pastoral, georgic, and the beast-fable, with all of which Shakespeare was well familiar.

In fact, the idea that science (whether theoretical or applied) and literature might comprise mutually exclusive fields of inquiry proves central to the development of what Bruno Latour has called 'the Modern Constitution', a redistribution of knowledge that insists upon 'the absolute dichotomy between the order of Nature and that of Society' (Latour, 1993, p. 40). For Latour, this new disciplinary constitution – despite its many strengths – has rendered 'analytic continuity ... impossible' by denying that a single phenomenon might be 'simultaneously real, social, and narrated' (p. 7), and Latour dates the establishment of the Modern Constitution to the half-century or so before Johnson publishes his edition of Shakespeare. By contrast, Shakespeare's 'honey-stalks' can only be rightly understood as a site of disciplinary convergence: a distinctive (indeed, a unique) poetic formulation that owes its status as such not to literary but rather to agricultural observation. Likewise, this same passage marks a convergence of species – an instant in which human beings become sheepish and sheep become human – that pulls against the compartmentalizing tendencies of the Modern Constitution. It may be a small moment in Shakespeare, but even small moments deserve to be glossed carefully, and the implications of this particular gloss may prove deeper than its occasion at first seems to warrant.

Notes

1. The *OED*'s earliest recorded usage of the noun 'post-humanism' and its variants is dated 1940 ('post-humanism,' sub.).
2. One could add concurring testimony from more recent theorists on the subject. Deidre Shauna Lynch quotes with approval John Frow's assertion that 'literary character remains the "most problematic and ... undertheorized of the basic categories of narrative theory"' (Lynch, 1998, p. 1; Frow, 1986, p. 227). James Phelan's *Reading People, Reading Plots* presents itself as an analysis and attempted solution of 'the main problem of character' (1989, pp. 20–1). The third chapter of Martin Price's *Forms of Life* is subtitled 'Problems of Character' (1983, p. 37). Elizabeth Fowler complains that '[o]ur tools for the study of literary character are surprisingly primitive compared to those we have developed for ... other formal aspects of fiction' (2003, p. 3).
3. For the utilitarian argument, see Singer (2002, pp. 1–23); for the Kantian argument and its variance with utilitarianism on the question of rights, see Regan (2004, pp. 218–8, 349–57).

4. Theophrastus' numerous lost works, as listed by Diogenes Laertius, also include nine different treatises on animals, as well as works on comedy, acting, poetry, meter, 'Introduction and Narrative,' and 'Mankind' (Diogenes Laertius, 1959, pp. 489–503; V., pp. 42–50).
5. For the notion of paradigm-shift and its relation to preceding crises of understanding, see Kuhn (1970, pp. 66–91).
6. The *OED* derives the first syllable of 'mildew' from the Old Teutonic *meliþ*, or honey, and lists 'honey-dew' as the word's first – and now obsolete – sense ('Mildew,' sb. 1).

Works cited

Agamben, Giorgio (2004) *The Open: Man and Animal*, trans. Kevin Attell, Stanford: Stanford University Press.

Appelbaum, Robert (2006) *Aguecheek's Beef, Belch's Hiccup, and Other Gastronomic Interjections*, Chicago: University of Chicago Press.

Ariosto, Lodovico (1974) *Orlando Furioso*, trans. Guido Waldman, Oxford: Oxford University Press.

Bestiary (1993) *Bestiary, Being an English Version of the Bodleian Library, Oxford M.S. 764*, ed. and trans. Richard Barber, Woodbridge: Boydell.

Boehrer, Bruce (2010) *Animal Characters: Nonhuman Beings and Early Modern Literature*, Philadelphia: University of Pennsylvania Press.

Book of Beasts (1984) *The Book of Beasts, Being a Translation from a Latin Bestiary of the Twelfth Century*, ed. and trans. T. H. White, rpt, New York: Dover.

Boswell, James (1936) *Boswell's Journal of a Tour to the Hebrides*, ed. Frederick A. Pottle and Charles H. Bennett, New York: Literary Guild.

Boyce, Benjamin (1947) *The Theophrastan Character in England to 1642*, Cambridge: Harvard University Press.

Craik, Katherine A. (2007) '"The Material Point of Poesy:" Reading, Writing, and Sensation in Puttenham's *The Arte of English Poesie*,' in Mary Floyd-Wilson and Garrett A. Sullivan, Jr. (eds), *Environment and Embodiment in Early Modern England*, New York: Palgrave, pp. 153–70.

Deleuze, Gilles, and Félix Guattari (1988) *A Thousand Plateaus: Capitalism and Schizophrenia*, trans. Brian Massumi, Minneapolis: University of Minnesota Press.

Derrida, Jacques (2002) 'The Animal That Therefore I Am (More to Follow),' trans. David Wills, *Critical Inquiry* 28.2 (Winter), pp. 369–418.

Descartes, René (2006) *A Discourse on the Method*, trans. Ian Maclean, Oxford: Oxford University Press.

Diogenes Laertius (1959) *Lives of Eminent Philosophers*, trans. R. D. Hicks, 2 vols, Cambridge: Harvard University Press.

Eagleton, Terry (1974) *Marxism and Literary Criticism*, Berkeley: University of California Press.

Fletcher, John (1634) *The Faithfvll Shepherdesse*, London.

Fowler, Elizabeth (2003) *Literary Character: The Human Figure in Early English Writing*, Ithaca: Cornell University Press.

Frow, John (1986) 'Spectacle Binding: On Character,' *Poetics Today* 7.2, pp. 227–50.

Fudge, Erica (2006) *Brutal Reasoning: Animals, Rationality, and Humanity in Early Modern England*, Ithaca: Cornell University Press.

Girard, René (1972) *Violence and the Sacred*, trans. Patrick Gregory, Baltimore: Johns Hopkins University Press.

Heresbach, Conrad von (1971) *Foure Bookes of Husbandry* (1577), trans. Barnabe Googe, facs. Amsterdam: Da Capo.

Jonson, Ben (1925–52) *Ben Jonson*, ed. C. H. Herford and Percy and Evelyn Simpson, 11 vols, Oxford: Clarendon Press.

Knights, L. C. (1947) *Explorations: Essays in Criticism Mainly on the Literature of the Seventeenth Century*, New York: George W. Stewart.

Kuhn, Thomas S. (1970) *The Structure of Scientific Revolutions*, 2nd edn, Chicago: University of Chicago Press.

Latour, Bruno (1993) *We Have Never Been Modern*, trans. Catherine Porter, Cambridge: Harvard University Press.

Lodge, David (1988) *Nice Work*, London: Secker and Warburg.

Low, Anthony (1985) *The Georgic Revolution*, Princeton: Princeton University Press.

Lynch, Deidre Shauna (1998) *The Economy of Character: Novels, Market Culture, and the Business of Inner Meaning*, Chicago: University of Chicago Press.

Markham, Gervase (1614) *Cheape and Goode Husbandry*, London.

Mascall, Leonard (1620) *The Gouernment of Cattell*, London.

Mason, John Monck (1973) *Comments on the Last Edition of Shakespeare's Plays* (1785), facs. New York: AMS.

Milton, John (1988) *The Riverside Milton*, ed. Roy Flannagan, Boston: Houghton Mifflin.

Montaigne, Michel de (1958) *The Complete Essays of Montaigne*, trans. Donald Frame, Stanford: Stanford University Press.

Perfetti, Stefano (2007) 'Philosophers and Animals in the Renaissance,' *A Cultural History of Animals*, ed. Bruce Boehrer, gen. eds Linda Kalof and Brigitte Resl, 6 vols, Oxford: Berg, pp. 1–32.

Phelan, James (1989) *Reading People, Reading Plots: Character, Progression, and the Interpretation of Narrative*, Chicago: University of Chicago Press.

Plat, Gabriel (1974) *A Discovery of Infinite Treasure, Hidden since the Worlds Beginning*, London, 1639; facs. Amsterdam: Theatrum Orbis Terrarum.

Price, Martin (1983) *Forms of Life: Character and Moral Imagination in the Novel*, New Haven: Yale University Press.

Regan, Tom (2004) *The Case for Animal Rights*, Berkeley: University of California Press.

Revard, Stella P. (2003) 'Lycidas,' *A Companion to Milton*, ed. Thomas N. Corns, Oxford: Blackwell, pp. 246–60.

Shakespeare, William (1807) *The Dramatick Works of William Shakespeare*, ed. Samuel Johnson, 9 vols, Boston.

Shakespeare, William (1995) *Titus Andronicus*, ed. Jonathan Bate, London: Routledge.

Shakespeare, William (1997a) *The Norton Shakespeare*, ed. Stephen Greenblatt, 4 vols, New York: W. W. Norton and Co.

Shakespeare, William (1997b) *The Riverside Shakespeare*, ed. G. Blakemore Evans et al., Boston: Houghton Mifflin.

Shakespeare, William (2004) *The Complete Works of Shakespeare*, ed. David Bevington, New York: Pearson Longman.

Shakespeare, William (2006) *Titus Andronicus*, ed. Alan Hughes, rev. edn, Cambridge: Cambridge University Press.

Sidney, Sir Philip (1970) *Sidney's Defense of Poesy*, ed. Lewis Soens, Lincoln: University of Nebraska Press.

Singer, Peter (2002) *Animal Liberation*, New York: Ecco.

Theophrastus (2002) *Theophrastus: Characters. Herodas: Mimes. Sophron and Other Mime Fragments*, ed. and trans. Jeffrey Rusten and I. C. Cunningham, Cambridge: Harvard University Press.

Topsell, Edward (1973) *The Historie of Foure-Footed Beastes*, London, 1607; facs. New York: Da Capo.

Turner, Henry S. (2006) *The English Renaissance Stage: Geometry, Poetics, and the Practical Spatial Arts 1580–1630*, Oxford: Oxford University Press.

Tusser, Thomas (1973) *A Hundreth Good Pointes of Husbandrie* (1557), facs. Amsterdam: Da Capo.

Wall, Wendy (1996) 'Renaissance National Husbandry: Gervase Markham and the Publication of England,' *Sixteenth Century Journal* 27.3 (Autumn), pp. 767–85.

Watt, Ian (1957) *The Rise of the Novel: Studies in Defoe, Richardson, and Fielding*, Berkeley: University of California Press.

4
Homeostasis in Shakespeare

Gabriel Egan

René Descartes was wrong, and Shakespeare could have told him so. Descartes's hard distinction between the inanimate and the merely living machine-matter, on the one hand, and the mind made of an immaterial essence, on the other, no longer convinces anyone. Since Charles Darwin we have accepted not a hard distinction but a continuous spectrum (indeed, a chain) of complexity and sensitivity connecting the low-order life forms and the higher, and recently it has become apparent that high-order rationality too is just a sophistication of simpler kinds of biological responsiveness. As Antonio Damasio has shown, the apparatus for thinking is built upon the simpler messaging systems common to animals and plants and that, essentially, we think and feel with our bodies and not with disembodied minds (Damasio, 1995). The realization of this embodiment is a key element in the recent 'affective turn' in cultural and literary theory, and it confirms Raymond Williams's strangely oxymoronic claim that in 'structures of feeling' our beliefs and practices – our mental and physical lives – interpenetrate one another (Clough and Halley, 2007; Williams, 1977, pp. 128–35). It is not surprising that with this closing of the gap between humans and all other life (lower forms around us now, and the lower forms from which we evolved), scientists are increasingly finding evidence that the behaviours we call culture, morality, and politics occur in communities of animals (De Waal, 1982; De Waal, 2001; Whiten, Horner and De Waal, 2005). As the editors of this collection note in their introduction, a 'strategic move away from anthropocentric premises' is necessitated by new knowledge of what we have in common with animals, but this does not entail a rejection of all of humanism. This chapter will identify ethical imperatives that, for Shakespeare, seem to be built into human nature by certain facts of life that science is only now fully bringing to light.

In the 1970s the chemist James Lovelock developed an extraordinary hypothesis in which our planet's atmosphere is not the precondition that allowed life to develop on Earth, but is itself the product of life-forms, which made the world comfortable for themselves. This seemed to require that the life-forms collaborated in adjusting their outputs, which idea appeared so far-fetched that early research papers by Lovelock were routinely rejected by academic journals. Lovelock continued working on his hypothesis, and introduced into it the further complexity of the chemical reactions between the atmosphere and rock surfaces as they weathered (a process that bacteria can accelerate) and also the oceans full of algae. The result was a chemical model of a complex interconnected chain of reactions whose ultimate effect was to regulate the conditions on Earth for the benefit of its life-forms. This model he called Gaia. With the entire Earth unified in this way, it seems artificial to distinguish between the parts that are obviously alive (the biota) and the inanimate oceans, rocks and clouds. These inanimate parts are tightly coupled in chemical processes with the biota, and the proper perspective is to treat the entire Earth as a super-organism composed of many kinds of subsidiary organisms. This idea Lovelock first presented in a sequence of papers (the most significant being Lovelock, 1972; Lovelock and Margulis, 1974a, 1974b) and then as a series of books (including Lovelock, 1979, 1988).

Darwin's hypothesis showed that a chain of being unites all of life on Earth in a single, subtly complex, process, and Lovelock's Gaia hypothesis extends this idea up to the planetary scale and down to the mere matter comprising the land, sea and air. In its strongest form, Gaia sees the whole Earth as a living organism, one that might even (in Daniel Dennett's deliberately provocative phrase) have finally grown a nervous system: us (Dennett, 2003b). In its weakest form, which shades off into Earth Systems Science, the Gaia hypothesis treats the Earth's chemical and thermodynamic processes not as life itself but as a collection of tightly coupled feedback loops producing planetary homeostasis, or self-regulation. We see homeostasis all around us, but it can be hard to recognize and explain. For instance, the moon takes exactly as long to turn once on its axis as it does to orbit once around the Earth, which is why it always presents the same face to us, the face it has presented to millions of our ancestors. In the geocentric model of the universe this had been explained by the moon being fixed to a crystal sphere encompassing the Earth and turning with it as the sphere rotated. But once Copernicus and Galileo had worked out the correct locations and motions of the heavenly bodies and Isaac Newton and Johannes

Kepler had derived the forces governing them, the moon turning at just the right rate to keep its face to us looked like a celestial miracle of coincidence. It was almost the twentieth century before George Howard Darwin, Charles Darwin's son, figured out how the laws of gravity make the Earth–moon system self-regulating (Darwin, 1898). If we managed to perturb the moon, giving it an extra spin in order to see around the other side, it would react by turning back to show its familiar face to us, and solely because of gravitational forces.

Earth Systems Science is finding self-regulation in places nobody suspected before, thereby reactivating pre-Enlightenment views on matter, the universe and life. Shakespeare's characters debate self-regulation and find it at work in things we consider to be alive and in things that, until recently, we did not. The Earth shook at Owen Glendŵr's birth, of that the protagonists agree. But why did it shake? Owen Glendŵr says it was out of fear:

> GLYNDŴR   The front of heaven was full of fiery shapes,
> Of burning cressets; and at my birth
> The frame and huge foundation of the earth
> Shaked like a coward.
>   (*1 Henry IV*, IV.1.13–16)[1]

Hotspur accepts the shaking but not the cause: 'I say the earth was not of my mind / If you suppose as fearing you it shook' (III.1.20–2). At best, the Earth but belched or farted at Glendŵr's birth:

> HOTSPUR   Diseased nature oftentimes breaks forth
> In strange eruptions; oft the teeming earth
> Is with a kind of colic pinched and vexed
> By the imprisoning of unruly wind
> Within her womb, which for enlargement striving
> Shakes the old beldam earth, and topples down
> Steeples and moss-grown towers. At your birth
> Our grandam earth, having this distemp'rature,
> In passion shook.
>   (*1 Henry IV*, III.1.25–33)

As Edmond Malone pointed out (Shakespeare, 1821, III.1.33, n. 3), the same image of winds trapped in the Earth occurs in Edmund Spenser's *The Faerie Queene* (III.9.15.2–9) and one of Shakespeare's narrative poems: 'As when the wind, imprisoned in the ground, / Struggling for passage, earth's foundation shakes' (*Venus and Adonis* 1046–7). But in Spenser's poem and *Venus and Adonis* the wind has agency – has a desire for release – and the Earth is merely its prison, a foundation to be shaken. Hotspur, in contrast, sees the Earth as the agent here: the Earth breaks wind to correct itself by relieving the build-up of internal pressure.

These ideas have been an embarrassment to criticism. Shakespeare seems to share his characters' belief in a vital and alive universe rather than a mechanical one. We can tell Shakespeare's view because Hotspur is pricking Glendŵr's pomposity, yet he does not challenge the idea that the Earth responded as a living creature. Hotspur merely substitutes flatulence for fear as the cause of this response. As late as 1765, Samuel Johnson was able to read Hotspur's explanation as 'a very rational and philosophical confutation of superstitious errour' (Shakespeare, 1765, III.1.28, n. 6), meaning that Glendŵr is superstitious and Hotspur's explanation is rational. In the notes to his 1768 edition Edward Capell wrote that as an explanation of earthquakes 'the Poet's physics are certainly right', albeit 'the dress he has put them in … is suited to the mouth they proceed from' (Capell and Collins, 1779–80, p. 159). I do not suppose Johnson and Capell meant that they accepted Hotspur's image as literally true. I imagine they saw it, much as we would until recently, as a metaphor that comes closer to the truth than Glendŵr's idea of a fully conscious world capable of fearing his nativity.

Until recently, most scientists would have said that, howsoever metaphorical, Hotspur's explanation is unhelpful since there is nothing remotely biological at work in earth tremors. Indeed, the Gaia hypothesis was at first resisted by Earth Systems scientists precisely because it seemed biological. The Gaia hypothesis now incorporates plate tectonics and earthquakes, and hence encompasses the phenomena Hotspur tries to explain (Worsley, Nance and Moody, 1991; Berner, 1991). Earthly exhalation is also where Gaia started, for the atmospheric disequilibrium it set out to explain is the rich concentrations of oxygen and methane that could not co-exist for long were not living creatures replenishing them by respiration and farting/belching. Hotspur was right: the living Earth belches and dead planets do not. It might be objected here that atmospheric methane comes from individual organisms' digestive processes not the whole Earth's. Gaia shows that this distinction between part and whole is false: the living Earth is its collection of parts, as is the organism. The average human has about ten times as many microorganisms – separate creatures with their own DNA and reproduction cycle – living in her digestive tract as she has cells in her body, and it is these that make her farts and her belches as they break down her food. If we think our effluxes are our own, then we must accept that the Earth's are its own.

Zoologists used to object that the Gaia hypothesis is anti-Darwinian, since planet-wide regulation of the atmosphere seems to imply cooperation that is at odds with natural selection's privileging of the local and the temporary advantage. Gaia, they objected, would require organisms planning ahead for their collective good, which cannot be right. Lovelock's answer invoked a principle that Darwinists only started to think carefully about since the 1960s: the environment to which an organism adapts is not a static background but includes the dynamic behaviour of other organisms, including others of its own species. Moreover, the environment can be altered by an organism. This last point is crucial, since an inheritable trait might be even more advantageous to a creature's descendants than it was to the creature that first developed it, simply because that trait changed the environment against which the adaptation's usefulness is to be measured. This means that determining whether a trait is doing an organism some good (in the evolutionary sense) may be harder than it might at first seem.

In his latest work to address how natural selection might have generated planet-wide homeostasis, Lovelock explicitly puts the case in transgenerational terms regarding mutual interchange between an organism and its environment:

> [T]he first organisms must have used the raw materials of the Earth's crust, oceans, and air to make their cells. They also returned to their environment their wastes and dead bodies. As they grew abundant, this action would have changed the composition of the air, oceans, and crust into an oxygen-free world dominated chemically by methane. This means that soon after its origin, life was adapting not to the geological world of its birth, but to an environment of its own making. There was no purpose in this, but those organisms which made their environment more comfortable for life left a better world for their progeny, and those which worsened their environment spoiled the survival chances of theirs. Natural selection then tended to favor the improvers. (Lovelock, 2004, pp. 3–4)

In other words, competition between, on the one hand, early organisms that left the area around themselves a bit easier for their progeny to live in and, on the other, those that left it a bit harder for their progeny to live in would have favoured the former. The progeny of the well-behaved had the advantage. This hypothesis does not fall foul of the fallacy of group selection, as Richard Dawkins claimed when he objected that Gaia requires the kind of selflessness that natural selection destroys because 'a mutant plant which saved itself the costs of oxygen manufacture ... would outreproduce its more public-spirited colleagues' (Dawkins, 1982, p. 236). Rather, Gaian natural selection is now taken seriously by mainstream Earth Systems Science (Lenton, 1998).

Of course, Elizabethans had no direct access to any such insights. But in the theologically centred morality of Shakespeare's time the ethic of reciprocity embodied in the Christian Golden Rule – 'do to others as you would have them do to you' (Matthew 7.12) – was obviously a component of interactions within the family, or within a community, or between natives and strangers. Shakespeare repeatedly dramatized how morality emerges from such interactions, both within a generation and, crucially for my argument, across generations of descendants. The Golden Rule seems to govern social interactions within a single generation – the 'others' are those around you now – while natural selection required for Gaia occurs trans-generationally and is concerned with behaviours whose impacts upon evolutionary fitness can only be discerned over time. Shakespeare on occasion addresses such Gaian interactions, by dramatizing selfish behaviour that seems advantageous to the individual considered synchronically but, when considered diachronically, trans-generationally, is revealed as disadvantageous. He was aware that if one's behaviour is inherited by one's children, one faces a kind of Golden Rule played out over time and hence, in crude but I think defensible terms, heredity encourages goodness.

The earliest example of this principle in Shakespeare's work is Lady Anne's curse on Richard Gloucester, in which she imagines him having a child as monstrous as himself:

LADY ANNE   If ever he have child, abortive be it,
Prodigious, and untimely brought to light,
Whose ugly and unnatural aspect
May fright the hopeful mother at the view,
And that be heir to his unhappiness.
(*Richard III*, I.2.21–5)

John Jowett thought that Anne's reference to deformity 'glances only indirectly at' Richard's own condition (Shakespeare, 2000, I.2.21, n.) whereas Antony Hammond was sure that Anne is 'describing Richard's own birth' and wondered whether she realizes that she is doing this

(Shakespeare, 1981, I.2.23, n.). Without speculating about the contents of Anne's mind, we can say for sure that 160 lines earlier (about 8 minutes of stage time) Richard called himself 'deformed, unfinished ... half made up' (I.1.20–1), so the audience hears Anne cursing Richard with having a child like himself. King Lear pronounces the same curse on his daughter Gonoril:

> LEAR   If she must teem,
> Create her child of spleen, that it may live
> And be a thwart disnatured torment to her.
> Let it stamp wrinkles in her brow of youth,
> With cadent tears fret channels in her cheeks,
> Turn all her mother's pains and benefits
> To laughter and contempt, that she may feel –
> That she may feel
> How sharper than a serpent's tooth it is
> To have a thankless child.
>   (*History of King Lear*, IV.268)

Viewed as a parenting strategy, Gonoril's selfishness defeats itself and the Golden Rule is upheld, not synchronically but diachronically over the generations.

Later Lear realizes a layer of further potential reciprocity: what if he is subject to the same curse he made upon Gonoril? That is to say, might not Gonoril herself be a deserved punishment to him just as he wishes her child to be a deserved punishment to her? The sight of Edgar prompts this thought:

> LEAR   What, has his daughters brought him to this pass?
> (*To Edgar*) Couldst thou save nothing? Didst thou give them all?
> FOOL   Nay, he reserved a blanket, else we had been all shamed.
> LEAR (*to Edgar*)
> Now all the plagues that in the pendulous air
> Hang fated o'er men's faults fall on thy daughters!
> KENT   He hath no daughters, sir.
> LEAR   Death, traitor! Nothing could have subdued nature
> To such a lowness but his unkind daughters.
> (*To Edgar*) Is it the fashion that discarded fathers
> Should have thus little mercy on their flesh?
> Judicious punishment: 'twas this flesh begot

> Those pelican daughters.
>
> > (*History of King Lear*,
> > 11.56–68)

Lear comes to realize the errors of his ways, and in this regard we may usefully contrast him with the childless king Richard III. Richard has hopes to start his own line of monarchs, but his imagery of generation runs precisely counter to the principle of transgenerational correction I have been outlining. Richard seems to think that by generation he will undo his crimes rather than be called to account for them:

QEEN ELIZABETH
> Yet thou didst kill my children.

KING RICHARD
> But in your daughter's womb I bury them,
> Where, in that nest of spicery, they will breed
> Selves of themselves, to your recomfiture.
>
> > (*Richard III*, IV.4.353–6)

The childless Macbeth is much like Richard in brutally hacking his way to the throne only to find that it gives little joy without a child to pass it on to. Indeed, we may suppose that these kings are able to be brutal because they are childless: had they to face the transgenerational consequences of passing on these traits they would learn that selfishness is self-defeating. In their introduction, the editors of this volume sketch Andy Mousley's defence of humanism's interrogations of 'how to live?', and here is a concrete example in Shakespeare's suggestion that the facts of life militate against anti-social behaviour. Perhaps goodness, like freedom, evolves (Dennett, 2003a).

The last plays of Shakespeare's career are especially concerned with relations between the generations. In *The Winter's Tale*, Paulina presents the new-born baby Perdita to Leontes and remarks on its likeness to him:

PAULINA
> It is yours,
> And might we lay th' old proverb to your charge,
> So like you 'tis the worse. Behold, my lords,
> Although the print be little, the whole matter
> And copy of the father ...
>
> ...
>
> And thou good goddess Nature, which hast made it
> So like to him that got it, if thou hast

> The ordering of the mind too, 'mongst all colours
> No yellow in't, lest she suspect, as he does,
> Her children not her husband's.
> *(The Winter's Tale*, II.3.96–108)

Paulina means to show Leontes that he was wrong to suspect that the baby is another's child. But, having asserted that the baby is like its father, Paulina must hope that Perdita is unlike her father in one quality at least: that she is not yellow (the colour of jealousy) lest she think that her children are not her own. This is of course absurd, since the uneven burden of sexual reproduction affords women one certainty: they can at least be sure that the children they give birth to are their own.

Even if heritable, Leontes's jealousy could not be transmitted down the female line, as Paulina appears to recognize as she says this. The Variorum edition of the play cites a number of critics who regard this absurdity as intentional illogic on Paulina's part, meant to show Leontes his own illogic (Shakespeare, 2005, Through Line Numbering (TLN), 1029–30, n.). On the other hand one might argue that this is unintentionally inflammatory and that, having his attention drawn to the certainty of motherhood, Leontes might feel the pain of paternal uncertainty all the more keenly. From the point of view of natural ethics – the kind of Gaian self-regulation that Shakespeare is thinking about – Paulina seems to have put her finger on a problem, since trans-generational relations cannot visit Leontes's disorder upon him in the way that they can revisit Gonoril's ingratitude upon her.

The neo-Darwinian approach to generation distinguishes our ideas from those of the high Enlightenment, and when allied to Lovelock's Gaia hypothesis the effect is that long-standing certainties about the place of humankind in the universe are transformed in ways that philosophers are only beginning to appreciate. According to N. Katherine Hayles, the break that marks the transition to a posthuman condition occurred with the mathematical demonstrations that information could be measured as a quantity distinct from the medium conveying it, and that a machine could exhibit complex homeostasis by using information about itself to regulate its own performance (Hayles, 1999). For Hayles, the humanist subject invented by the Enlightenment depended on an untenable Cartesian distinction between the body and the unembodied mind, and the posthumanist subject is in danger of abandoning the body altogether. The human characteristic we value most is consciousness, which impresses us much more than the (also complex) capacity to catch a fast-moving ball while running or to digest food, and consciousness she argues – following Antonio Damasio (1995) – is embodied. Thus 'Human mind without human body is not human mind' (Hayles, 1999, p. 246).

In this, however, Hayles's own anthropocentrism distorts the argument, for the humanist subject of the Enlightenment is just as effectively decentred in the new ecological approach that finds in the wider Earth systems (the movements of energy and chemicals in ocean currents, wind and weathering) the homeostatic processes that we once thought were characteristics peculiar to life. Hayles's posthuman condition in which a hard distinction between mechanical and living processes breaks down is also the early modern condition and was familiar to Shakespeare. Indeed, we might even say that Hayles is premature, for there are important ways in which the now-dominant neo-Darwinian approach to life might be an oversimplification regarding the distinction, first made by August Weismann, between the genetic information, akin to recipes, passed down the generations by sex, the so-called germ line, and the bodies built from these recipes, the so-called somatic line. According to Weismann the latter cannot affect the form: an individual's genes are in no way modified by its behaviour. In fact, it seems that the germ line is not quite so isolated from the somatic line as would be suggested by the analogy with information and media.

Work on epigenetics and imprinting, in which the expression of genes may be conditioned by the sex of the parent from which they are inherited (or, more controversially, conditioned by the experiences of the parent), suggests that genetic data are not entirely isolated inside their chromosomes. While this does not amount to a return to Jean-Baptiste de Lamarck's notion of inheritance in which each generation's particularities (the ironsmith's large biceps, the bicycle-courier's powerful calves) are passed on to descendents (the view that Weismann overturned), it suggests interactions that blur the germ/soma distinction. The idea that maternal experiences during gestation affect a foetus has a long tradition and of course emerges in Shylock's story of Laban's trick with his uncle's sheep (*The Merchant of Venice*, I.3.89) and in Edmund's conviction that his fierce personality was imprinted on him by the passionate sex enjoyed by his parents when they made him (*The History of King Lear* 2.10–15).

A particular kind of transgenerational relationship, parent–child incest, is the special focus of the last plays. In *Pericles*, Antiochus has corrupted the normal linear fanning out of family trees by fulfilling in himself the functions of father and husband. This turning in upon itself of the family is extended so that Antiochus also becomes, as Pericles puts it, 'both a father and a son' (1.170), which peculiar claim we will return to shortly. Marina performs a similar turning inward of family relations when she revives Pericles from his swoon: 'Thou … begett'st him that did thee beget' (21.183). The widespread taboo against sexual incest in almost all cultures has its biological origins in the genetic binarism of allele pairs in the human chromosome, one half of which came from the mother and one from the father. Many traits, including potential diseases, may be carried by an individual without being expressed because only one of the two alleles codes for that trait; the recessive allele has no effect because of the dominance of its partner that does not code for the trait. Such a recessive trait will be expressed only when both alleles at a given gene-locus code for it, which rarely happens when unrelated individuals mate. But because a brother and sister or a parent and child share 50 per cent of their genes they are quite likely to have the same recessive allele at a given point in their genomes. The children of their incestuous mating are quite likely to inherit the recessive allele from both parents, which is the condition required for the recessive trait to be expressed. Children born of incestuous mating are for this reason much more likely than others to have genetically inherited diseases, which is what the incest taboo exists to prevent.

Rather than being a cultural phenomenon, the incest taboo is a genetically determined behaviour that has been naturally selected: genes which make a parent and child, or a brother and sister, revolted by the thought of sex with one another are likely to do better in the centuries-long evolutionary competition than genes that do not. The latter genes are more likely to find themselves in unhealthy infants who die of genetically inherited disease before adulthood, and hence are less likely to get passed on to the next generation. Natural selection exhibits self-regulation, homeostasis, across the generations, and this offered Shaksespeare a model for his compulsive reworkings of self-healing family relationships – siblings forgiving parents and one another – in his last plays. Genes that do better by raising a taboo against incest need to give individuals a way of determining their consanguinity, and the most obvious way is to make individuals able to recognize their relations in order to avoid having sex with them. When a genealogy is drawn as a family tree, the incest taboo operates to promote the fanning out of lines of descent and to prevent the formation of genetically closed loops of relative-sex which are comparatively sterile because the resulting children have an increased propensity to die before adulthood. The family tree of a recurrent incestuous relationships would tend towards a denuded bough, its branches withering from disease.

Pericles's sexual desire for the daughter of Antioch is articulated in arboreal terms: 'To taste the fruit of yon celestial tree' (1.64). It is not clear if the daughter is the fruit and her father the celestrial tree, or perhaps she is the tree and the fruit is the sexual enjoyment of her. Her father, however, calls her 'this fair Hesperides, / With golden fruit' (1.70–1) which metaphor casts his daughter as a living contradiction, since she is the object of men's desire and simultaneously the guardian of that object. The riddle Pericles has to solve is written from the mute daughter's point of view ('I am ... ') and, as riddles often are, it is based on an apparent contradiction:

> PERICLES   I am no viper, yet I feed
> On mother's flesh which did me breed.
> I sought a husband, in which labour
> I found that kindness in a father.
> He's father, son, and husband mild;
> I mother, wife, and yet his child.
> How this may be and yet in two,
> As you will live resolve it you.
> Sharp physic is the last.
>
> (*Pericles* 1.107–15)

Even once this is solved as being about incest, the problem of the riddle is not entirely eliminated, since although we can see how her incestuous father would be her father and husband, it remains unclear why he would be her 'son'. Equally mysterious is why she thinks herself not only his wife and child but also his 'mother'. Parallel phrasing occurs in Pericles' soliloquy after Antiochus leaves:

> PERICLES   Where now you're both a father and a son
> By your uncomely claspings with your child –
> Which pleasures fits a husband, not a father –
> And she, an eater of her mother's flesh,
> By the defiling of her parents' bed,
> And both like serpents are, who though they feed
> On sweetest flowers, yet they poison breed.
>
> (*Pericles* 1.170–6)

Here Antiochus paradoxically becomes his own son and his daughter a consumer of her mother's flesh.

The point of the paradox emerges if we draw a family tree and consider how incest breaks its conventions by generating loops of inbreeding. In the drawing of pedigrees – the form of family trees Shakespeare would have been familiar with, having had to produce one to apply for a patent of gentility in 1597 – horizontal lines link mates and vertical lines are used to link parents and their offspring, as in Figure 4.1.

In such a schema there is no simple way to represent incest. One possibility is a loop (see Figure 4.2).

This requires an additional directionality that the orthogonal tree structure is not supposed to possess: a slanted line representing sex with an offspring. Alternatively, the individual occupying the position of mate and offspring can be repeated (see Figure 4.3).

A family tree that should fan out is made by incest to fold back on itself, or else it requires contradictory self-division, as in the daughter of Antiochus being both the fruit and the guardian of that fruit. Shakespeare's taste for likening family relations to pendant fruits such

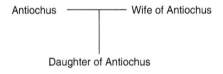

Figure 4.1

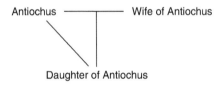

Figure 4.2

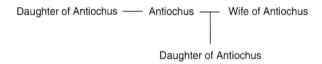

Figure 4.3

as 'dangling apricots' is fully expressed in the celebrated Gardening Scene (III.4) in *Richard II* and in Richard of Gloucester's 'I love the tree from whence thou sprang'st, / Witness the loving kiss I give the fruit' (*Richard Duke of York*, V.7.31–2). Sterility is a common consequence of inbreeding, and Pericles' impresa of a denuded bough green only at the top (the lower branches being dead) might stand for his avoidance of this evil. Antiochus calls Pericles a tree ('so fair a tree / As your fair self', 1.157–8) and Pericles fears that his life may be 'cropped' (1.184). Moreover, Pericles thinks of himself as one of that topmost class in a hierarchical social structure which protects the lower branches:

> PERICLES   Our men [will] be vanquished ere they do resist,
> And subjects punished that ne'er thought offence,
> Which care of them, not pity of myself,
> Who am no more but as the tops of trees
> Which fence the roots they grow by and defend them,
> Makes both my body pine and soul to languish,
> And punish that before that he would punish.
>
> (*Pericles* 2.27–33)

The play's arboreal imagery carries this double sense of diachronic generational fanning out over time and of synchronic social order. As a top branch, Pericles fears that Antiochus, 'To lop that doubt' (that Pericles will broadcast his sin), will cut him off; lopping means cutting off branches; and other uses (such as cutting off heads or limbs, here as in the Gardening Scene in *Richard II*) are figuratively derived from this primary sense.

The avoidance of incest is a purpose of many social practices which are, at root, driven by the genetic imperative to avoid harmful recessive genes meeting at the same locus in the genotype. The means by which organisms avoid incest is the ability to recognize their siblings, offspring and parents, and distinguish them from others with whom they may mate. *Pericles*, like *The Winter's Tale* and *Cymbeline*, is much concerned with this ability to distinguish, and it gives us reason to reconsider the rejection of the categorization that calls these plays the Romances or, still more neutrally yet also being resisted (McMullan, 2007, pp. 65–126), the Late Plays. Thaisa does not even know if she has a daughter, the shipboard delivery being somehow forgotten:

> THAISA   That I was shipped at sea
> I well remember, ev'n on my eaning time,

> But whether there delivered, by th' holy gods
> I cannot rightly say.
>
> (*Pericles* 14.4–7)

She does not know it, but the child was a girl so there is no danger of their later meeting and incestuously mating. But Pericles does indeed meet Marina without knowing who she is, and his language upon recognizing her invokes precisely the contradictory self-parenting language of Antiochus and his daughter: 'Thou that begett'st him that did thee beget' (21.183).

The genetic pressure not to commit incest unknowingly is at least part of the motivation unconsciously driving Pericles' and Marina's tense consideration of the means by which identity might be determined, as with her 'Is it no more / To be your daughter than to say my mother's name?' (21.196–7) which might carry the additional sense of 'is mentioning your wife enough to stop you thinking of me sexually?' In the source for Shakespeare's play *The Winter's Tale*, Robert Greene's *Pandosto*, the father Pandosto unwittingly and extensively woos his lost daughter Fawnia and even threatens to rape her if she will not yield to him (Greene, 1588, F4r–G3v). This part of the plot Shakespeare attenuated but did not excise in his version of the story:

FLORIZEL   At your request
My father will grant precious things as trifles.
LEONTES   Would he do so, I'd beg your precious mistress,
Which he counts but a trifle.

(*The Winter's Tale*, V.1.220–3)

Incest also lies just beneath the surface of *Cymbeline* in the strong affection of Guiderius and Arviragus for their sister Imogen which only her disguise suppresses: 'Were you a woman, youth, / I should woo hard' (III.6.66–7). Indeed, read as the product of a culture that seemingly understood (as we would not) Gertrude's marriage to her dead husband's brother Claudius to be a kind of incest in *Hamlet*, the avoidance of sibling incest is also the opening problem of *Cymbeline* since the king wished his daughter to marry his new queen's son (I.1.4–6). This unwanted marriage would have been a kind of grafting following the 'lopping' of Cymbeline's rightful male heirs, Guiderius and Arviragus, who at the end are again 'jointed to the old stock' as the prophecy handed down by Jupiter requires (V.3.236, V.4.441–2). It takes passionate complaints and overt threats from the ghosts of his parents and siblings to wring this rectification of Posthumus' wrongs from the negligent foster-father Jupiter ('Thou orphans' father art', V.3.134), as we should expect since Shakespeare's last plays are so insistently concerned with the correction of transgenerational wrong.

An eco-critic might be expected to stress the cyclical nature of time in these plays, and their use of myths of regeneration to suggest that nature gathers in all with its recurrent return to a starting point. However, it is at least as useful to attend to their dramatizations of self-regulation (homeostasis) achieved by transgenerational correction in which bad behavioural traits inherited by offspring plague the perpetrator. Shakespeare would seem, then, not only to have anticipated the Gaian model of a vitally alive Earth, but also the role of heredity in the evolution of morality as described by Frans de Waal, Daniel Dennett and Richard Joyce among others (Flack and De Waal, 2000; Dennett, 2003a; De Waal, 2004; Joyce, 2006). Of course he anticipated neither of those things; rather, unencumbered by the sharp distinction of matter and mind that dominated Enlightenment science he (rightly, we now know) assumed that the mechanical and the organic lie along a continuous spectrum, or chain of being. Like his contemporaries, Shakespeare had insights that we would call posthumanist.

Notes

1. All quotations of Shakespeare are from Shakespeare (1989).

Works cited

Berner, Robert A. (1991) 'Atmospheric Oxygen, Tectonics, and Life', in Stephen H. Schneider and Penelope J. Boston (eds), *Scientists on Gaia*, Cambridge: Massachusetts Institute of Technology Press, pp. 161–6.
Capell, Edward, and John Collins (1779–80) *Notes and Various Readings to Shakespeare. Vol. 1: All's Well That Ends Well; Antony and Cleopatra; As You Like It; The Comedy of Errors; Coriolanus; Cymbeline; Hamlet; 1 Henry IV; 2 Henry IV; Henry V; 1 Henry VI; 2 Henry VI; 3 Henry VI; Henry VIII; Julius Caesar; King John; King Lear; Love's Labour's Lost*, London: Henry Hughs.
Clough, Patricia Ticineto, and Jean Halley (eds) (2007) *The Affective Turn: Theorizing the Social*, Durham: Duke University Press.
Damasio, Antonio R. (1995) *Descartes' Error: Emotion, Reason, and the Human Brain*, London: Picador.
Darwin, George Howard (1898) *The Tides and Kindred Phenomena in the Solar System*, London: Murray.
Dawkins, Richard (1982) *The Extended Phenotype: The Gene as the Unit of Selection*, Oxford: Oxford University Press.

De Waal, Frans B. M. (1982) *Chimpanzee Politics: Power and Sex among Apes*, London: Cape.

De Waal, Frans B. M. (2001) *The Ape and the Sushi Master: Cultural Reflections by a Primatologist*, London: Allen Lane.

De Waal, Frans B. M. (2004) 'Evolutionary Ethics, Aggression, and Violence: Lessons from Primate Research', *Journal of Law, Medicine and Ethics* 32, pp. 18–23.

Dennett, Daniel C. (2003a) *Freedom Evolves*, London: Penguin.

Dennett, Daniel C. (2003b) 'How Has Darwin's Theory of Natural Selection Transformed Our View of Humanity's Place in the Universe?', in William K. Purves, David Sadava, Gordon H. Orians and H. Craig Heller (eds), *Life: The Science of Biology*, 7th edn, vol. 2: *Evolution, Diversity, and Ecology*, Sunderland: Sinauer, p. 523.

Flack, Jessica C., and Frans B. M. De Waal (2000) '"Any Animal Whatever": Darwinian Building Blocks of Morality in Monkeys and Apes', *Journal of Consciousness Studies* 7, pp. 1–29.

Greene, Robert (1588) *Pandosto: The Triumph of Time*, Short Title Catalogue (STC) 12285, London: Thomas Orwin for Thomas Cadman.

Hayles, N. Katherine (1999) *How We Became Posthuman: Virtual Bodies in Cybernetics, Literature, and Informatics*, Chicago: University of Chicago Press.

Joyce, Richard (2006) *The Evolution of Morality. Life and Mind: Philosophical Issues in Biology and Psychology*, Cambridge: Massachusetts Institute of Technology Press.

Lenton, Timothy M. (1998) 'Gaia and Natural Selection', doi:10.1038/28792, *Nature* 394, pp. 439–47.

Lovelock, James E. (1972) 'Gaia as Seen through the Atmosphere', *Atmospheric Environment* 6, pp. 579–80.

Lovelock, James E. (1979) *Gaia: A New Look at Life on Earth*, Oxford: Oxford University Press.

Lovelock, James E. (1988) *The Ages of Gaia*, The Commonwealth Fund Book Program, Oxford: Oxford University Press.

Lovelock, James E. (2004) 'Reflections on Gaia', in Stephen H. Schneider, James R. Miller, Eileen Crist and Penelope J. Boston (eds), *Scientists Debate Gaia: The Next Century*, Cambridge: Massachusetts Institute of Technology Press, pp. 1–5.

Lovelock, James E., and Lynn Margulis (1974a) 'Atmospheric Homeostasis by and for the Biosphere: The Gaia Hypothesis', *Tellus* 26, pp. 2–10.

Lovelock, James E., and Lynn Margulis (1974b) 'Biological Modulation of the Earth's Atmosphere', *Icarus* 21, pp. 471–89.

McMullan, Gordon (2007) *Shakespeare and the Idea of Late Writing: Authorship in the Proximity of Death*, Cambridge: Cambridge University Press.

Shakespeare, William (1765) *The Plays, Vol. 4: The Life and Death of Richard the Second; The First Part of King Henry the Fourth; The Second Part of King Henry the Fourth; The Life of King Henry the Fifth; The First Part of King Henry the Sixth*, 8 vols, ed. Samuel Johnson, London: J. and R. Tonson [etc.].

Shakespeare, William (1821) *The Plays and Poems, Vol. 16: Richard II; Henry IV Part I*, 21 vols, ed. Edmond Malone and James Boswell, London: F. C. and Rivington [etc.].

Shakespeare, William (1981) *King Richard III*, ed. Antony Hammond, The Arden Shakespeare, London: Methuen.

Shakespeare, William (1989) *The Complete Works*, ed. Stanley Wells, Gary Taylor, John Jowett and William Montgomery, electronic edition prepared by William Montgomery and Lou Burnard, Oxford: Oxford University Press.

Shakespeare, William (2000) *Richard III*, ed. John Jowett, The Oxford Shakespeare, Oxford: Oxford University Press.

Shakespeare, William (2005) *The Winter's Tale*, ed. Robert Kean Turner, Virginia Westling Haas, Robert A. Jones, Andrew J. Sabol and Patricia E. Tatspaugh, *The New Variorum Edition of Shakespeare*, New York: The Modern Language Association of America.

Whiten, Andrew, Victoria Horner and Frans B. M. De Waal (2005) 'Conformity to Cultural Norms of Tool Use in Chimpanzees', doi:10.1038/nature04047, *Nature* 437, pp. 737–40.

Williams, Raymond (1977) *Marxism and Literature*, Oxford: Oxford University Press.

Worsley, Thomas R., R. Damian Nance and Judith B. Moody (1991) 'Tectonics, Carbon, Life, and Climate for the Last Three Billion Years: A Unified System', in Stephen H. Schneider and Penelope J. Boston (eds), *Scientists on Gaia*, Cambridge: Massachusetts Institute of Technology Press, pp. 200–10.

Part II
'Posthumanist' Readings

5
Care, Scepticism and Speaking in the Plural: Posthumanisms and Humanisms in *King Lear*

Andy Mousley

I

What or who is humanist in *King Lear*? The question is symptomatic of a *post*humanist – or 'critical humanist' – perception that humanism is diverse and does not name a single, static set of ideas (for a discussion of critical humanism, see Halliwell and Mousley, 2003, pp. 1–17). Posthumanism, in this sense, means 'post' any humanism that took itself to be the definitive version of humanism and aspired to the universality of a grand narrative. It means seeing beyond the humanism which stole the limelight from other humanisms by privileging ideas about our sovereignty or specialness or rationality over, for example, humbler attempts to rescue the human from the dehumanizing effects of industrial modernity. Posthumanism, according to this conception of it, means opening up humanism to contestation and critique, or as Ivan Callus and Stefan Herbrechter argue in their introduction to this volume, embracing 'the new plurality' and 'the new questions that are put to humanism, anti-humanism, posthumanism, even transhumanism alike' (pp. 4–5).

But what is, or might be, the style and tone of posthumanist critique? Specifically, how might posthumanism operate as a 'caring' critique of the kind that Callus and Herbrechter are keen to advance in wanting their posthumanism to express '"care" for the human, humanness, humanity'? Critiques, as will be discussed more fully below, can be carried out at varying degrees of impersonal – 'dehumanizing' – distance from their objects of enquiry. Of course, the implication of such a mode of critique might be to persuade us that there are better ideas to invest in than the ones by which we might once have been seduced. Critique in this sense is not disinterestedly distant but *engages us* emotionally as well as rationally in questions about value, and in the case of posthumanist critique, with what meanings and values can or should be assigned to such terms as 'human', 'posthuman', 'humanist'. Critique can nevertheless be cold, and posthumanist critique so 'post'-human that it leaves us with nothing to attach to. My concern in this chapter is thus partly with posthumanism's 'mode of engagement', with *how* it appeals to, and cares for, the human, or fails to do these things, and with how Shakespeare in particular and literature in general might be central to the kind of caring which it practises.

II

A critical posthumanism, as Callus and Herbrechter imply, may be in tune with the long tradition of 'dissensus' that has existed within the humanities, but insofar as its sympathies are broadly in tune with the anti-essentialist intellectual trajectories associated with postmodernism, it is also a sign of the intellectual times, a sign, that is, of the need to speak in the plural about our objects of enquiry: modernism*s*, feminism*s*, renaissance*s*, humanism*s*. The reasons for pluralizing are often good, democratic ones, because disregarded or underrepresented aspects of a phenomenon get to represent that phenomenon where they did not previously. But speaking in the plural can also make it difficult, in the case of humanism, to see the humanist wood for the humanist trees. The danger of pluralizing humanism – and the human – to such an extent that they disappear entirely, and to the point where caring therefore becomes largely irrelevant, will be addressed later, but, first, posthumanist plurality needs to have its say, by outlining some of the humanisms and versions of the human in contention in *King Lear*. That they are in contention gives us a clue as to why we might decide to attribute value to this play in particular and to literature in general. If literature only took us to the same places, if it only confirmed who we already think we are, if it did not unsettle our preconceptions – in this case about what it is to be human – then its value would be limited. However, and to anticipate a later phase of my argument, if *King Lear* was not in the least bit anthropocentric, then it would be a thoroughly alienated 'object', entirely voided of human concerns (cf. Altieri, 2007, p. 72). It is because of the play's impact on the emotions that we are able to *feel* the force of aliena-tion or unsettledness or 'posthumanist' questions about what it is to be human. However unhinged the human becomes, the unhinging is represented in affective terms, with passion, through 'flesh and blood' entities we are encouraged to recognize as human, or a credible version of it, even as the term 'human' is put into question.

III

Edmond is probably the first 'humanist' to appear in the play. He qualifies as a humanist on account of his secular individualism. In Act I, he mocks his father's astronomical beliefs, renounces the determinism of higher or outside forces and, like many a Machiavellian stage villain, takes matters into his own hands. If there is a determinism at work in the world, then it comes from within rather than from without because, for Edmond, as we shall see later, character is destiny. Although Machiavellian stage villains need to be differentiated from Machiavelli himself, Machiavelli's *The Prince* (1532), in prioritizing human over divine causality, laid the foundations for a secular humanism that could and did move in an individualistic direction.

However, from a changed humanist perspective – an 'ethical humanist' perspective – Edmond is simultaneously an anti-humanist for, in retaliation to the dehumanizing label given to him of 'bastard', he adopts an instrumental attitude toward other people, treating them less as 'people' with intrinsic value just because they are people than as objects. Indicative of a general cultural anxiety about the instrumentalization of human relations strongly associated with, but not reducible to, the burgeoning of capitalism in the early modern period, Edmond moves people around like pawns. The ethical humanism that objects to the inhuman objectification of others translates the term 'human' as 'humane'. This humane-ness is not guaranteed. It can be – and is – 'lost and found'. It can be overwhelmed by other facets of the human, such as – paradoxically – the 'inhuman'. At the end of the play, however, Edmond, suddenly 'moved' by the speech of his brother, magically re-discovers his feelings for others and resolves to do 'some good' before he dies.[1]

Lear's progress through the play is also a hopeful 'ethical humanist' narrative, but unlike the generically expected transformation of Edmond (the villain with, eventually, a heart of gold), Lear's progress is granted a greater degree of psychological and emotional complexity. Lear's narrative, like Edmond's sea-change, nevertheless suggests that what was lost can be found again, that humanity's humane-ness can be retrieved. Having only ever but 'slenderly known himself' (I.2.292–3), Lear, according to this humanist narrative, acquires a degree of self-knowledge, which means, in this case, ethical self-knowledge. In a moment, on the heath, of Aristotelian recognition, he begins to see and feel his way out of his 'all-too-human' tragic flaw – diagnosed as status anxiety wedded to a narcissistic attempt to wrap others around his faltering ego – towards a sensitivity to the suffering of others. This moment is redemptive of his ethical consciousness. In this respect, as Jonathan Dollimore argues in his influential, materialist critique of what he calls 'essentialist', humanism is 'quasi-religious' (Dollimore, 2004, p. 193). It is as if, to press the religious connotation home, Lear is resurrected: out of the destruction of his old self come renewal and a rediscovery of humankind's 'spiritual essence' (p. 194).

The ethical humanist perspective outlined above need not be so spiritualized as to preclude an egalitarian social politics. Ethical humanism has moved in such an egalitarian direction in several Marxist-humanist readings of the play. What distinguishes humanist from anti-humanist Marxisms is that where the latter – as exemplified by Dollimore – tends to distrust any kind of essentialism and consequently drops the term 'human' from its vocabulary (except to attack it), the former measures the human cost of oppressive economic and social systems, looks optimistically towards a future in which human beings might flourish rather than perish, and is committed to the egalitarian notion that all human beings should be able to live their lives free from the evils and indignities of economic and social injustice. Kiernan Ryan's moving and powerful reading of *King Lear* exemplifies the hopeful social politics that lies at the heart of Marxist humanism. '*King Lear*', writes Ryan, 'edges us into an understanding which turns the class-divided view of society, then as now, on its head' (Ryan, 2002, p. 99). For Ryan, the play 'leaves us no choice but to identify' the causes of the tragedy 'as the indefensible subjection of men and women to the injustices of a stratified society, and to seek the implied solution in the egalitarian standpoint created and vindicated by the play as a whole' (p. 100). A major contributor to this egalitarianism is Lear's admission that he has taken 'too little care' of the 'houseless poverty' in his kingdom (III.4.33 and 26), and his plea to the rich and privileged that they should 'expose [themselves] to feel what wretches feel' in order to 'shake the superflux to them / And show the heavens more just' (III.4.34–6).

It is not only social and economic justice which is at stake in the optimistic deployment by humanist critics of the term 'human', but also a more capacious sense of how human beings, including those who have benefited from social and economic inequalities, might grow and become more fulfilled. Lear's case is again instructive, for Lear's emerging egalitarianism can be understood not only as an altruistic movement from narcissism to other-orientedness, but also to a fuller, richer subjectivity. Cocooned in a world of his own making, a world in which the role of others is instrumentalized and scripted – 'Which of you shall say doth love us most' (I.1.51) – Lear cannot grow. If he is only capable of hearing what he wants to hear, how can he develop? Insofar as the play invites identification with Lear as a person who is 'like us', this question is also our question. We can all be narcissistic, and, if Freud is to be believed, narcissism is a primary human experience that we more or less successfully unlearn as we become aware that the person – usually a mother – who initially met all our needs has needs of her own. That Lear does not succeed in getting his own way is painful for him, but it is the key to growth, the key to seeing beyond his narcissistic self to a richer repertoire of emotions and perspectives than was available to him previously.

Although the extent to which Lear changes is debatable (cf., for example, Dollimore, 2004, p. 192–3), this emphasis on growth – closely connected to the growth of his ethical consciousness but not synonymous with it – leads us into yet another way of thinking about humanism in the play. Like Kiernan Ryan's reading, Terry Eagleton's reflections on *King Lear* in *After Theory* (2003) come from the Marxist-humanist tradition, but they also intersect with a literary-critical humanist tradition in which works of art are revered for being oracular sources of enlightenment that bring about psychological, emotional and intellectual growth (in both their characters and readers) (Eagleton, 2003; for further discussion of this literary-critical tradition, see Mousley, 2007, pp. 1–30). For Eagleton, Lear's education is a 'sentimental' – as well as socialist – education, which repairs the damage done by his 'sensory deprivation':

> To perceive accurately, we must feel; and to feel we need to free the body from the anaesthesia which too much property imposes on it. The rich are insulated from fellow feeling by an excess of property, whereas what impoverishes the bodies of the poor is too little of it. For the rich to repair their own sensory deprivation would be for them to feel for the privations of others. And the result of this would be a radical social change, not just a change of heart. In Shakespeare's imagination, communism and corporeality are closely allied. (Eagleton, 2003, p. 184)

It is quite difficult to disentangle the voices of Eagleton and Shakespeare in this passage. Possibly this is for the reason given by Robert Watson. 'Few modern Shakespeareans', writes Watson, 'would dare to say explicitly that our courses will teach "what Shakespeare had to say about life"' (Watson, 1988, p. 123), but, he continues, further on in his argument:

> Though we are not in a position to claim that what we want is what God or nature dictates (as racists, sexists, and imperialists like to claim), we have something almost as good: we can recommend a philosophy, a theology, or a mode of conduct under the pretext that Shakespeare recommends it. (Watson, 1988, p. 126)

For Watson, teachers of literature are closet romantics whose belief in the 'enhanced enlightenment' that authors can bring complicates their *un*belief in the 'author-as-oracle' (pp. 124, 121). Once open and explicit, such humanist belief in the oracular power of literature has been overshadowed by the 'sceptical turn' that literary studies since the advent of modern critical theory has often taken.

Ethical humanism can therefore be placed alongside humanist faith in the educability of human beings and in the 'special' enlightenment that literature can bring. Both of these versions of humanism give us some cause to be optimistic about ourselves. Humanist optimism is itself not uniform, however, as it has varied in degree and has attached itself to different human attributes. Confidence in human capacities forms one strand of Renaissance humanism and is expressed in one half – the hopeful half – of Hamlet's disquisition on the nature of 'man': 'How noble in reason, how infinite in faculty, in form and moving how express and admirable, in action how like an angel, in apprehension how like a god – the beauty of the world, the paragon of animals' (II.2.305–9), and this celebratory outlook is continued, though with decisively important variations, in the enlightenment faith in human rationality and science, and in the romantic eulogizing of human imagination and creativity. A general commitment to the notion that humanity might give us cause for wonder and hope (as well as despair), reappears in nineteenth- and twentieth-century Anglo-American humanist literary criticism, which was often motivated by a concern with the preservation, via the literary canon, of human/e values in a world where such values were perceived to be under threat. The idea that literature might redeem us from ourselves and the nightmare of human history was sometimes expressed as a trite and simplistic optimism, as when James Gibson, for example, commenting on Thomas Hardy's poem 'In Time of "The Breaking of Nations"' writes that 'in this poem Hardy comments on the permanence of such simple things as work and love. Man must cultivate the earth so that he can eat, and we will continue to fall in love. Not even the madness of war can change these basic certainties' (Hardy, 1975, p. 81). However, in the hands of its subtler practitioners, such as A. C. Bradley, idealization of humanity's redeeming features was far from trite. Suggesting that central to the experience of Shakespearean tragedy is the 'impression of waste' (Bradley, 1992, p. 16), Bradley argues provocatively about the way that what is worshipful about humanity ends up tragically devouring itself:

> Everywhere, from the crushed rocks beneath our feet to the soul of man, we see power, intelligence, life and glory, which astound us and seem to call for our worship. And everywhere we see them perishing, devouring one another and destroying themselves, often with dreadful pain, as though they came into being for no other end. (Bradley, 1992, p. 17)

Bradley, however, avoids the pessimistic and nihilistic conclusion that 'all is vanity' (p. 17). What survives in *Lear* – just – is the 'only real thing' in the world which is 'the soul, with its courage, patience, devotion' (p. 286). The qualification of 'just' is necessary because Bradley does not shy away from the prospect of a humanity that tears itself apart. If we take 'humanism' to mean any kind of essentialist discourse about the human, then this is an equally humanist perspective, though empty of the easy optimism that fills some of the other versions.

IV

Humanism in *Lear* and in general, then, does not add up. There are different humanisms and humanist narratives in contention in the play, from the secular individualism of Edmond, to the egalitarian sense of a common humanity – meaning humane-ness – discovered by Lear, to the reawakening of the senses that Lear also experiences in his 'unaccommodated' (III.4.100–1) state, to the pessimistic conclusion that we are, at best, a mixture of good and bad and, at worst, bad. Humanism is in contention in the play because what is 'in' human nature is contentious: fantasies of omnipotence (Lear, Edmond, Goneril, Regan); cruelty (Lear, Edmond, Goneril, Regan); nothing, because 'men', says Edmond, 'are as the time is' (V.3.30–1); love and compassion (Cordelia and, belatedly, Lear); loyalty (Kent, Edgar, Cordelia); the capacity for forgiveness (Cordelia; for further discussion of the use of the term nature in *King Lear*, see Danby, 1949). Where a traditionalist such as Kent uses the vocabulary of restraint – 'Reserve thy state,' he advises Lear, and 'in thy best consideration check / This hideous rashness' (I.1.149–50) – and observes those 'natural' loyalties and allegiances which make of ambition an aberration, the play's individualists tend not to observe boundaries and allegiances, or, if they do, they observe them only temporarily and with an eye to their own advantage. Edmond, for example, swears allegiance to 'nature', whom he calls his 'goddess', but the loyalty he pledges is actually a loyalty to himself and to a positive version of his own bastardly 'nature': 'Why brand they us/With "base", with "baseness", bastardy – base, "base" –/Who in the lusty stealth of nature take/More composition and fierce quality/Than doth within a dull, stale, tired bed' (I.2.9–13). 'Nature', here, is not what Gloucester has in mind when he mourns the violation of what he sees as natural human affiliations. For Gloucester, nature, referring to the natural world which human beings are part of, and influenced by, is behaving 'unnaturally': 'These late eclipses in the sun and moon portend no good to us. Though the wisdom of nature can reason it thus and thus, yet nature finds itself scourged by the sequent effects' (I.2.36–7). The 'sequent effects' are those already referred to violations of natural bonds: 'Love cools, friendship falls off, brothers divide; in cities, mutinies; in countries, discord; in palaces, treason; and the bond cracked 'twixt son and father ... Machinations, hollowness, treachery, and all ruinous disorders follow us disquietly to the grave' (I.2.104–12). For this communal and ecological conception of nature, Edmond substitutes a notion of 'nature', based on a version of humours theory, which lines up with his individualistic credo and enables him to celebrate the unrestrained vigour and vitality granted to him by virtue of his lust-induced birth. He also severs the connection between nature and (social) custom – 'Wherefore should I/ Stand in the plague of custom' (1.2.2–3) – and turns nature instead into an individuating principle.

What is 'natural' to one character in *King Lear*, then, may not be natural to another. Perhaps most conspicuously, because most painful to the play's central character, the 'bond of childhood', which for Lear is one of the sacred 'offices of nature' (II.2.351) is not recognized by the play's wayward, aggressively individualistic children. This makes them, in Lear's eyes, 'unnatural hags' (II.2.452), but such is the play's constant equivocation with the word nature that we might wonder whether enmity within the family is just as 'natural' as love.

We can therefore credibly invoke the term 'posthumanist' to describe the equivocation of a term – 'nature' – which thereby becomes impossible to speak of except in the plural and with a considerable degree of scepticism. Where one or another humanist discourse might attempt to stabilize words like 'nature' and 'natural', so that they can operate as the basis for ethical and/or political imperatives, posthumanism destabilizes them, for, as Callus and Herbrechter argue, posthumanism constitutes 'a strategic move away from anthropocentric premises: the human can no longer be taken for granted, humanity as a universal value is no longer self-legitimating, humanism as a reflex or self-reflex cannot be trusted' (p. 5). But what is the nature – and extent – of posthumanism's distrust? What kind of scepticism is posthumanism? It is to these questions that I now want to turn, with the eventual aim of arguing that humanism and posthumanism need not and should not be seen as out-and-out antagonists or in terms of the teleological supersession of the one (humanism) by the other (posthumanism).

V

If a defining characteristic of posthumanism is its scepticism about such foundational principles as 'the human', then it is clearly not the originator of scepticism. Scepticism has a long history, to which Shakespeare himself – as a 'modern' – may be seen as contributing. Locating 'the general historical beginning' of modernity in 'disenchantment with … older meaning-giving myths and structures' (Engle, 2000, p. 85), Lars Engle suggests that the 'most obvious early modern discourse which might model anti-foundationalism for Shakespeare is scepticism, which enjoyed a vigorous revival in the sixteenth century' (p. 86). Scepticism in Shakespeare takes different forms, from the critical consciousness of a Hamlet, who questions principles, such as the principle of revenge, purportedly based on 'natural' human instinct (the natural instinct to avenge the murder of one's father, for example), to the cynicism of an Iago or Edmond, who routinely trash the assumed naturalness of shared systems of belief, sometimes in the name of their own individualistic notions of nature, but sometimes in the name of a 'nature-less' and anti-essentialist constructionism: 'men', to recall Edmond, 'are as the time is' (for detailed discussion of the varieties of scepticism in Shakespeare, see Mousley, 2007, chs 1–4).

The variety of sceptical attitudes in Shakespeare is mirrored by the variety of the sceptical tradition in general, for since what Engle refers to as 'the general historical beginning' of modernity in the Renaissance, scepticism has taken different forms and has had a number of 'close relatives'. Some of its past and present pseudonyms or near-neighbours have been disenchantment, disbelief, cynicism, secularism, critical consciousness, disengaged rationality, de-familiarization (for example, in Brecht's 'estrangement' or 'alienation' effects as well as in Russian formalism), the 'hermeneutics of suspicion' embraced by some versions of modern critical theory, anti-essentialism, anti-foundationalism, constructionism, postmodernism – and, now, posthumanism. Scepticism and its analogues are the product of what Max Weber took to be modernity's disenchantment of the world, its replacement of 'magic', religious belief and immanent meaning with rationality and 'models' of meaning. The connection between modernity, disenchantment and scepticism has been elaborated by a number of thinkers since Max Weber (1927; esp. ch. 30: 'Evolution of the Capitalistic Spirit', pp. 352–69), including Theodor Adorno and Max Horkheimer (1979, pp. 3–42; for a recent discussion of Adorno and Horkheimer's concept of disenchantment, see Haynes, 2005, pp. 65–7), Jürgen Habermas and more recently Charles Taylor. In *Sources of the Self* (1989), Taylor suggests that the disengagement entailed by various forms of rationality from Descartes to the present day 'demands that we stop simply living in the body or within our traditions or habits and, by making them objects for us, subject them to radical scrutiny and remaking' (Taylor, 1989, p. 175). Rather than functioning as an obvious and immediate site of identification, the human itself becomes one such alienated or de-naturalized 'object', an object, that is, from which a sceptical, questioning, disengaged subject is partly or wholly removed. As sceptics, we become suspicious of all received wisdom, including received wisdom about 'the human', and tend to rename such 'wisdom' as 'ideology'.

My reasons for locating posthumanism in a longer history of scepticism are twofold: first, to show how Shakespeare, as a contributor to modernity's sceptical disenchantment of the world, might have been 'posthumanist'; and second – as already suggested – to ask what *kind* of scepticism posthumanism is and, related to this, to ask what *kind* of sceptical posthumanist we might take Shakespeare to be. If scepticism has come in different shapes and sizes, and if posthumanism is the shiny new scepticism, then it is important to try to establish the nature and extent of its scepticism. An iconoclastic sceptic will tend to empty terms entirely of the claim they have on us: he or she might say that human nature does not exist, that it belongs to the realm of myth, that it is always and everywhere an ideological construct. *Anti*-humanism was one such form of scepticism in that it tended to render its designated objects – liberal humanism, transcendent subjectivity, universalism, essentialist conceptions of 'man' – obsolete. But *post*-humanist scepticism seems less iconoclastic, at least as represented by this volume's editors. '*Posthumanist Shakespeares*', write Callus and

Herbrechter, 'does not want to be dogmatic about the resurfacing of the human and humanism in their fragilized forms. It wants to show "care" for the human, humanness, humanity' (p. 4). This appeal – to having a care of the human – seems to me to be an important intervention (or re-intervention) in posthumanist discourse. It would be difficult to care for something believed not to exist, or thought to be *only* the stuff of ideological misrecognition. And it would be equally difficult to see who or what might be left to do any caring, if 'the subject' and all philosophies of the subject were entirely abandoned, in favour of a subject-less theory of language, discourse, cybernetics or digital codes.

If a bloodless techno-speak or social constructionism retooled as technological determinism sometimes threatens to engulf posthumanist discourse, thereby eradicating any kind of subjectivity effect, in other, more 'emotional' variants of posthumanism, the human reappears. In his proto-posthumanist book, *The Ecstasy of Communication* (1987), for example, Jean Baudrillard argues that 'the religious, metaphysical or philosophical definition of being [has] given way to an operational definition in terms of the genetic code (DNA) and cerebral organization ... We are in a system where there is no more soul, no more metaphor of the body' (p. 19). If, in Baudrillard's terms, the metaphors of 'body' and 'soul' have lost their potency to describe the parameters of selfhood, then there can be 'no more individuals, but only potential mutants' (p. 51). Instead of using modernist tropes of exile and alienation, Baudrillard writes in terms of 'metastasis' as 'a deprivation of meaning and territory' and as an expression of the interminable spreading of disease, a malignant cancer that rends the core of the humanist self and for which there is no treatment (p. 50). *Nevertheless*, Baudrillard's writing evokes the recognizable human emotions of euphoria and mourning, celebration and loss: the death of the humanist 'self' or 'soul' is at once cause for celebration because it transcends the limits that might otherwise circumscribe the human, and the occasion for mourning because of the loss of foundational principles.

Like Baudrillard, N. Katherine Hayles's seminal book, *How We Became Posthuman* (1999) also invites us to feel the agony and ecstasy of becoming posthuman, and to share her hopes and fears in a way that again paradoxically recalls us to an albeit threatened sense of our human-ness and makes us 'care' about what we might be in danger of losing (or liberated from):

> If my nightmare is a culture inhabited by posthumans who regard their bodies as fashion accessories rather than the ground of being, my

dream is a version of the posthuman that embraces the possibilities of information technologies without being seduced by fantasies of unlimited power and disembodied mortality, that recognizes finitude as a condition of human being. (Hayles, 1999, p. 5)

However questioning and pluralizing posthumanism might be, however much it might want, as Callus and Herbrechter argue, to 'confront humanism with its "specters" – the inhuman, the superhuman, the nonhuman in all its invented, constructed or actual forms' (p. 5), the maintenance of some degree of belief in, and care for, 'the human, humanness, humanity', means that, in these posthumanist discourses at least, we are 'not yet' completely and irreversibly 'post'-human.

Insofar as a caring posthumanism is an emotionally charged posthumanism, it can be aligned with the turn or return to 'affect', not only in literary studies but also across a number of other disciplines, including cognitive poetics, neuroscience, bio-culturalism and evolutionary psychology. While these emerging fields of enquiry do not form a unity, those which emphasize the universality or at least the longevity of human emotions indicate that the human, rather than being on its last legs, is making a comeback. This revival is or should not be immune to the challenges of a posthumanism which simultaneously registers *its* recognition of the human by caring about it. Moreover, it is no accident that a number of different theorists of the emotions should be turning to literature for their inspiration, since the kind of knowledge that literature offers us is knowledge 'with feeling' (cf., for example, Zeki, 2009). Thus a *caring* posthumanist scepticism, a scepticism which not only questions our investments in the human but also generates concern, to the point of angst, about the human condition might also find a natural ally in the literary in general and in Shakespeare, as the epitome of the literary, in particular. What is 'inside' us – inalienably part of us – is not clear in *King Lear*. In another context, this might be cause for celebration, even 'humanist' celebration: the absence of a fixed human nature might be called 'freedom', and the choice about what we are or might be that accompanies this freedom might be called 'agency'. But in tragedy – especially a tragedy such as *King Lear* – equivocation breeds anxiety in the same way that it does for Hamlet when he wonders where human beings belong in the scheme of things: whether they are the 'paragon of animals' or the 'quintessence of dust' (*Hamlet*, II.2.309–10).

We care – to the point of becoming anxious – about the absence of foundational principles in *King Lear* because the play never entirely relinquishes a commitment to representing 'the dynamic of ideas passing into and out of people', as John Danby once put it (Danby, 1949, p. 18). *King Lear* is in this fundamental sense anthropocentric. It is committed to representing human as opposed to supra-human realties. While it is true that characters sometimes look 'upwards' – often in vain – to the benevolent operation of a supra-human deity or deities, the focus of the play is upon the psychological, emotional and physical impact of such recognizable human experiences as those of pain, suffering, love, lovelessness, joy, dread, fear, anxiety and exile. Stephen Greenblatt (1990) has an altogether different, more historicist focus than the perspective I am offering here, but there is a passage in which he almost perfectly encapsulates my point about the play's anthropocentric commitments. Lear's anxieties, which reflect those of the makers of 'maintenance agreements' between fathers and children, are listed by Greenblatt as follows:

> [T]he terror of being turned out of doors or of becoming a stranger even in one's own house; the fear of losing the food, clothing, and shelter necessary for survival, let alone dignity; the humiliating loss of parental authority; the dread, particularly powerful in a society that adhered to the principle of gerontological hierarchy, of being supplanted by the young. (Greenblatt, 1990, p. 95)

Are Lear's anxieties not 'all too human' anxieties, anxieties which have a levelling effect upon him and shock him out of his inflated, 'more than human' self-conception where the terms 'man' and 'king' were conflated? Does Greenblatt's ultimately historicist, or new historicist, imperative in his *Lear* essay still nevertheless rely upon a trans-historical recognition of what makes people scared, like 'being turned out of doors' or 'becoming a stranger even in one's own house'?

As suggested, Greenblatt's essay on *Lear* is not principally about the play's mimesis of universal human realities but social ones, and especially those realities that have a bearing upon issues, which were central to new historicism, of power. According to Greenblatt, Lear tries to compensate for his own anxiety by 'arousing it in others', so as to maintain his position and authority. 'He wants his children', writes Greenblatt, 'to experience the anxiety of a competition for his bounty without having to endure the consequences of such a competition.' But then he adds, suggestively: 'he wants, that is, to produce in them *something like the effect of a work of art, where emotions run high* [my italics] and practical effects seem negligible' (p. 93). Not only do emotions run high in a work of art but, in a work of art whose primary commitment is to the representation and understanding of human experience in and for itself, rather than as a means to the end of, say, an understanding of God, then human emotions are not only likely to run high but also to be complexly overdetermined. So Greenblatt's Lear is a Lear broadly amenable to such Freudian categories as projection: anxious himself, he projects anxiety onto his children in order to alleviate his own.

We would probably not – or not so readily – apply affective-psychological terminology to a medieval morality play like *Everyman*, for the world of *Everyman* is theocentric, not anthropocentric. It therefore poses a challenge to readers brought up on psychologically 'realistic' characters, because the play is less interested in human than in supra-human realities and accordingly uses characters allegorically, as vehicles rather than tenors. The play is in this sense prehumanist, meaning 'pre' that form of humanism which takes human life to be an object of interest and enquiry in its own right. If the Renaissance was not solely responsible for the evolution of anthropocentric perspectives, then it was an important agent in its development. Renaissance art, with its interest in the realistic depiction of the human form, bears this out. Renaissance painters did not suddenly stop depicting religious themes but, where they do, it is often the fleshliness and physical human suffering – of Christ, for example – that strikes the eye and arouses the senses, to the extent, sometimes, of overwhelming his divinity. In her discussion of the painting *The Body of the Dead Christ in the Tomb*, by the sixteenth-century artist Hans Holbein, Julia Kristeva emphasizes the way that the laws of nature seem to have consumed Christ's divinity, for the picture, according to Kristeva, 'seems to give expression to the idea of a dark, insolent, and senseless eternal power, to which everything is subordinated' (Kristeva, 1989, p. 109). Here, the physical body and its decay are realities which give the lie to divinity. This particular expression of human reality – comparable to Hamlet's depressing image of 'man' as no more than the 'quintessence of dust' – is a far cry from the uplifting versions of humanism outlined earlier. It nevertheless testifies to an anthropocentric commitment.

VI

As in Holbein's *The Body of the Dead Christ in the Tomb*, the suffering human body is at the centre of the action of *King Lear*. Having lived in a state, to recall Eagleton, of 'sensory deprivation', Lear on the wild and stormy heath experiences the opposite: sensory overload. As much as he attempts to deny the physical impact of the 'thought-executing fires' and 'oak-cleaving thunderbolts' (III.2.4–5), by focusing on the mental storm caused by 'filial ingratitude' (III.4.14), Lear is not able to resist the storm. It is too much to bear, or, as Kent puts it, in yet another of the play's uses of the word 'nature': 'Man's nature cannot carry / Th' affliction nor the fear' (III.2.48–9). This anthropocentrism is emphatically not celebratory of human capacities and achievements, but rather an acknowledgment of the limits of the human. These limits are not only defined by the frailty of the flesh to which Lear increasingly admits: 'Here I stand your slave, / A poor, infirm, weak and despised old man' (III.2.19–20), 'They told me I was everything; 'tis a lie, I am not ague-proof' (IV.5.104–5). They are also defined in affective terms, in terms, that is, of fears, anxieties and insecurities: the fear of abandonment; the chronic sense of insecurity arising from a world that has become utterly inhospitable; the fear that the human, natural and supernatural worlds have become entirely unpredictable; the fear that the human condition is a condition of metaphysical homelessness or, as Lear suggests, absurdity – 'When we are born, we cry that we are come / To this this great stage of fools' (IV.5.178–9).

The physical and emotional onslaught is unbearable for those characters who experience or witness it. But these 'raw' experiences save the human from the 'nothing' that it sometimes seems in danger of becoming as a result of the play's 'posthumanist' scepticism. They tell us what our limits are and when these limits have been traversed. The remedy, such as it is, for the breach of human equilibrium is 'repose', the 'foster-nurse of *nature* [my italics]' (IV.3.12). Perhaps we can readily assent to this piece of folk wisdom? After all the uncertainty surrounding the terms 'nature' and 'natural', perhaps we cling to a use of the word that seems uncontentious. Yes, Lear with his 'bereavèd sense' (IV.3.9) needs rest and so, perhaps, do we, for our senses have also been assaulted. But through this assault, we rediscover what we are always, the play implies, in danger of forgetting, that we are 'all too human'.

King Lear is thus an antidote to amnesia. Like all tragedies, it stirs primary emotions, such as fear, or at least it attempts to, for there is no absolute guarantee that we will be moved in the way I have been describing. Despite the several emotional 'hits' that *King Lear* attempts to score, when Gloucester has his eyes gouged, for example, or when Lear near the close of the play enters with the dying Cordelia 'in his arms' (V.3.231), we might be such 'men of stones' (V.3.232) that we fail to react. But we should at least know how we are supposed to react.

Only a society in which affect has died – only a decisively 'post'-human society, a society in which we have forgotten ourselves – would not know this.

VII

The degree to which the object of posthumanist sceptical enquiry is distantiated matters. Too much distance would turn us into coldly detached observers, would turn 'the human' precisely into an *object*. Too little distance would mean that we are not sufficiently removed from our *subjective* identifications to critically question them. Broadly speaking, critical theory is good at the former, whereas literature is good at both, because, as I have been arguing, it translates concepts into impassioned concepts. If the human is lost, then we feel it as a loss or as a freedom or both. Lear's question – 'Who is that can tell me who I am?' (I.4.212) – is not a disembodied and disinterested philosophical enquiry, but an agonizing question, felt upon the pulse, about (the lack of) his and our identity.

Notes

1. William Shakespeare (2005) *The Tragedy of King Lear: The Folio Text*, V.3.192; 218. Subsequent references to this edition are given within the text. I have used the folio text exclusively. My reading would not be substantially affected by the differences between the folio and quarto versions, although arguably there is at times more 'human' response in the quarto.

Works cited

Adorno, Theodor, and Max Horkheimer (1979) *Dialectic of Enlightenment* (1944), trans. John Cumming, London: Verso.
Altieri, Charles (2007) 'The Sensuous Dimension of Literary Experience: An Alternative to Materialist Theory', *New Literary History*, 'What Is Literature Now?' 38.1, pp. 71–98.
Baudrillard, Jean (1987) *The Ecstasy of Communication*, trans. Bernard and Caroline Schutze, New York: Semiotext(e).
Bradley, A. C. (1992) *Shakespearean Tragedy*, 3rd edn, first published 1904, Basingstoke: Macmillan Education.
Danby, John F. (1949) *Shakespeare's Doctrine of Nature: A Study of King Lear*, London: Faber and Faber.
Dollimore, Jonathan (2004) *Radical Tragedy*, 3rd edn, first published 1984, Basingstoke: Palgrave Macmillan.
Eagleton, Terry (2003) *After Theory*, London: Allen Lane.

Engle, Lars (2000) '*Measure for Measure* and Modernity', in Hugh Grady (ed.), *Shakespeare and Modernity*, London: Routledge, pp. 85–104.

Greenblatt, Stephen (1990) *Learning to Curse*, New York: Routledge.

Halliwell, Martin, and Andy Mousley (2003) *Critical Humanisms: Humanist/ Anti-Humanist Dialogues*, Edinburgh: Edinburgh University Press.

Hardy, Thomas (1975) *Chosen Poems*, ed. James Gibson, London: Macmillan Education.

Hayles, N. Katherine (1999) *How We Became Posthuman*, Chicago: University of Chicago Press.

Haynes, Patrice (2005) '"To Rescue Means to Love Things": Adorno and the Re-enchantment of Bodies', *Critical Quarterly* 47, pp. 64–78.

Kristeva, Julia (1989) *Black Sun: Depression and Melancholia*, trans. Leon Roudiez, first published 1987, New York: Columbia University Press.

Mousley, Andy (2007) *Re-Humanising Shakespeare: Literary Humanism, Wisdom and Modernity*, Edinburgh: Edinburgh University Press.

Ryan, Kiernan (2002) *Shakespeare*, 3rd edn, first published 1989, Basingstoke: Palgrave, now Palgrave Macmillan.

Shakespeare, William (2005) *The Tragedy of King Lear: The Folio Text*, in *The Oxford Shakespeare*, 2nd edn, ed. Stanley Wells et al., Oxford: Clarendon Press.

Taylor, Charles (1989) *Sources of the Self*, Cambridge: Cambridge University Press.

Watson, Robert N. (1988) 'Teaching "Shakespeare": Theory versus Practice', in James Engell and David Perkins (eds), *Teaching Literature: What Is Needed Now*, Cambridge: Harvard University Press, pp. 121–50.

Weber, Max (1927) *General Economic History*, trans. Frank H. Knight, London: George Allen and Unwin.

Zeki, Semir (2009) *Splendours and Miseries of the Brain*, London: Wiley-Blackwell.

6
Cyborg *Coriolanus* / Monster Body Politic

Mareile Pfannebecker

Is Coriolanus too stubborn, childish, stupid? Or is he too honest, noble, even 'too noble for the world' (III.1.257)?[1] These are hardly original questions for Shakespeare criticism, and, as Stanley Cavell notes, they have been bound up with taking sides for either patricians or plebeians (Cavell, 2003, p. 145). Does Coriolanus fail to negotiate with the people in a respectful manner to win their rightful votes; or is he too honest to ingratiate himself by false flattery with those who do not know their place? Characters in the play, however divided in their political allegiances, agree on one thing. Whether they regard him as noble, stupid or arrogant, all find him, as his mother Volumnia puts it, 'too absolute' (III.2.40). It is, indeed, in terms of this absolutism, this obstinacy and determination that both claims for his nobility and stupidity are put forward – and both assessments of Coriolanus come with imagery that positions him as obstinate beyond the limits of the human.

Attention has since shifted away from what Cavell critiques as predictable attempts to unearth unambiguous political messages in the play (2003, p. 145); yet the question of the political in *Coriolanus* remains.[2] It is in the multiple figures of stubbornness, in and beyond Coriolanus himself, that this chapter sets out to trace a figuring of politics in the play. The early modern commonplace of the body politic which appears in a variety of transmutations takes a central role here; together with stubbornly excessive Coriolanus, it points towards questions about the shape and limits of the political and how they are linked to those about the shape and limits of the human and of human life. Throughout Shakespeare's play, I will argue, notions of stupidity and nobility awkwardly coincide, both in renegade Coriolanus and the state body. In this context, Jacques Derrida's treatment of *bêtise* as stubborn stupidity in *The Beast and the Sovereign* opens up ways to explore how the theme of obstinacy in *Coriolanus* is relevant to human politics and a politics of the human.

Where Coriolanus' obstinacy is presented as virtuous, it is first of all as the determination of a soldier. 'I am constant', he declares when commander-in-chief Cominius asks him to honour his promise to join him at war (I.1.223). Where others praise this constancy as noble – and nobility to the patricians in this play is explicitly bound up with the *nobilis* of high birth (cf., for example, Menenius Agrippa's exclamation 'O true bred!' following Lartius' promise to fight in spite of injury [I.1.218]) – it is, more often than not, in terms that are exaltedly god-like, yet thing-like at the same time. When Coriolanus is assumed dead after fighting an army on his own, his general Titus Lartius has the following to say about him:

O noble fellow!
Who sensibly outdares his senseless sword
And, when it bows, stand'st up. Thou art lost, Martius.
A Carbuncle entire, as big as thou art,
Were not so rich a jewel. Thou wast a soldier
Even to Cato's wish, not fierce and terrible
Only in strokes, but with thy grim looks and
The thunder-like percussion of thy sounds
Thou mad'st thine enemies shake, as if the world
Were feverous and did tremble. (I.4.56–65)

Thus, Coriolanus: a sentient being more resilient than the dead metal of his sword; more valuable than, somewhat grotesquely, a red-glowing, man-sized precious stone; with effects on earth and sky normally reserved for the gods. Later on in the play, Menenius imagines Coriolanus to 'move like an engine', 'pierce a corslet with his eye' and 'talk like a knell' (V.4.15–17). Throughout, Coriolanus seems to know no fear, hunger, tiredness or greed (cf. esp. Cominius' formal speech of praise [II.2.76–116, and 118–23]).

God and thing meet in the living machine. It is no far stretch of the imagination from Lartius' description to classic sci-fi cyborgs: Jonathan Sawday sees 'the fantasy, or the nightmare of the cyborg' foreshadowed in Coriolanus as machine that turns against its makers, prominently his mother Volumnia, who raised him for war (Sawday, 2007, p. 163). There is much in the development of the tragedy that invites this link; but Coriolanus can be read as cyborg even before he becomes a threat to Rome, in images of what Lee

Bliss in her commentary calls 'a dehumanised, godlike yet strangely mechanical warrior' (II.1.131–2, n.). Coriolanus is larger-than-life, yet embodied mechanicity. Many a stage production has put great emphasis on Coriolanus' martial gear, but what makes Coriolanus an out-of-this-world war machine that strikes 'Corioles like a planet' (II.2.108) is no technical add-on. Instead, it is the mechanical tenacity of his actions. Coriolanus decides the outcome of whole wars, not so much as a leader,[3] but in his own unstoppable and precisely repeated movements of destruction, 'a thing of blood, whose every motion / Was timed with dying cries' (2.2.108 and 103–4). That an encounter with Coriolanus on the battlefield means certain death is an assertion repeated with persistent regularity, as earlier in the same act, 'Death, that dark spirit, in 's nervy arm doth lie / Which, being advanced, declines, and then men die' (II.1.133–4). The final four heavy stresses of this line, R. B. Parker suggests, lend inevitability (Shakespeare, 1994), they also help to make this grim reaper appear as ridiculous as chilling. The thing of blood, the absurd disembodied arm of death, in their invariable timing, make of Coriolanus not a thinking fighter but an automaton.

Noble, valued, superhuman; but also, a dead thing, a machine, and consequently, a thing put to work by others for something other than himself. 'Framed' a warrior by Volumnia (V.2.62–3), 'bred in the wars' by the Roman military system (III.1.325), more than once he appears programmed, beyond human fallibility but also beyond the capacity for decision making. In the repetitive action of his work he is not unlike the plebeians he so despises and dismisses as 'the mechanics of Rome' towards the end of the play (V.3.83). Volumnia makes this clear when, in spite of her class snobbery elsewhere, she shifts emphasis in her grim reaper reference towards employment and dependency. Coriolanus' existence is justified by his task with the same urgent necessity as that of an agricultural labourer, a hired hand:

> His bloody brow
> With his mailed hand then wiping, forth he goes,
> Like to a harvestman that's tasked to mow
> Or all or loose his hire. (I.3.29–32)

Coriolanus' tenacity as a warrior machine is marked as extraordinary, even as superhuman mechanicity; meanwhile, ordinary bodies and machines increasingly go together in early modern England. Sawday traces discursive interdependencies between seventeenth-century machine and anatomy books as part of an increasingly commonplace way of thinking human bodies as machine and vice versa (Sawday, 1999, pp. 178, 183–4). Significantly, about forty years after Shakespeare's *Coriolanus*, bodies and machines are thought in terms of each other in a different sort of cyborg:[4] Thomas Hobbes's *Leviathan*. When Hobbes asks: 'For what is the heart, but a spring; and the nerves, but so many strings; and the joints, but so many wheels, giving motion to the whole body, such as was intended by the Artificer?' he links bodies to machines as 'artificial animals' in order to set up an analogy between the divine and human artificers. Then, the text moves on swiftly to declare the greatest achievement of human art – where it imitates God's greatest work, man himself:

> For by Art is created that great LEVIATHAN called a COMMON-WEALTH or STATE (in latine CIVITAS) which is but an Artificiall Man; though of greater stature and strength than the Naturall, for whose protection and defence it was intended; and in which the *Soveraignty* is an Artificiall *Soul* as giving life and motion to the whole body. (Hobbes, 1997, p. 9)

Hobbes goes on to list, among other functions, penal law as the nerves of the state via 'reward and punishment' and the founding 'pacts and covenants' as the God-like, yet human, force at the origin which assembles the state body (p. 9). In his treatment of this passage in *The Beast and the Sovereign*, Jacques Derrida writes of Hobbes's state as a 'robot', 'like a gigantic prosthesis designed to amplify, by objectifying it outside natural man ... the power of the living, the living man that it protects, that it serves, but like a dead machine, or even a machine of death' (Derrida, 2009, p. 28). A sort of virtual cyborg state then, which doubles and expands the figure of 'natural' man by the artificial addition of laws and institutions that protect human life, if ultimately only by the threat of death that they exert both inside and outside the state body; but also a cyborg body made up by the mass of people held together in their rigidly regulated interactions. There is much here of the traditional image of the state as body politic, as an extension of the king's two bodies, but with the crucial difference that in Hobbes's version of a quasi-secular state monster, 'the matter thereof, and the artificer; both ... is man' (Hobbes, 1997, p. 10).

Hobbes's *Leviathan* asserts mechanical functions for human body and human community, and thus admits a certain continuity of humans and other animals with mechanical objects. Yet, the state machine also marks the limit of the human, the break with the rest of god's creation: made of men by men, it is manifestation and proof of men's reason, for it is based on their ability to make 'pacts and covenants' (p. 9), the laws and contracts that form the state skeleton; an ability, as Hobbes indicates later on in the *Leviathan*, which excludes animals as much as it excludes God (cf. chapter 16, 'Of the first and second Naturall Laws, and of Contracts' [p. 77]; cf. also Derrida's discussion [Derrida, 2009, pp. 54–5]). Thus the man-made, prosthetic state machine becomes what proves the human human.[5] In this sense, Hobbes's Leviathan is in line with Bernard Stiegler's assertion in *Technics and Time* that 'prosthesis is not a mere extension of the human body; it is the constitution of this body qua "human"' (Stiegler, 1998, pp. 152–3). In Hobbes, this emphasis on the artificial as what is politically and discursively human is deployed to stabilize: thinking of the state as a machine in the image of man helps Hobbes to assert political man as self-made, and thus as removed from direct divine intervention. By preserving the old figure of the body politic,[6] Hobbes also lends his Leviathan a certain organic immutability. As Derrida notes, Hobbes's Leviathan is 'vitalist, organicist, finalist *and* mechanicist'; it both claims for political man the independence of being 'producer and product of his own art' and at the same time proclaims the shape of the state that it lays out as unquestionably natural (Derrida, 2009, pp. 28, 27).

The figure of the body holds this machine together; it allows Hobbes's *Leviathan*, like it has allowed writing for the political status quo for centuries before him, to demand of the 'members' of the body politic that they perform their designated function, and accept sovereign power and the state as a whole as indivisible.[7] For if civil war, according to Hobbes, is the death of the body politic by division (Hobbes, 1997, p. 9), then the only way to keep it alive, and to preserve peace, is to preserve the powers that be. But, as Derrida points out:

[I]f sovereignty, as artificial animal, as prosthetic monstrosity, as Leviathan, is an artifact, if it is not natural, it is deconstructible, it is historical; and as historical, subject to infinite transformation, it is at once precarious, mortal, and perfectible. (Derrida, 2009, p. 27)

In other words, the cyborg state can never be as sure of its shape as Hobbes makes out; political representation, once it divests itself even partially of divine infallibility, will find it increasingly difficult to claim a unified and static form. If what makes this cyborg is a self-proclaimed artificiality of human life, it cannot help inviting mutation; if man makes himself human, then the human is never fixed – which is precisely what would make it monstrous.

What, then, about cyborg Coriolanus and the body politic? The Roman state in the play shares much of Hobbes's Leviathan's anthropomorphic physiognomy; it is also contractual, not god-given, with its functions under debate from the very start. As will be discussed below, one distinctive difference is that, unlike Hobbes's Leviathan, Shakespeare's portrayal of the Roman state draws attention to its continued malleability. But whatever shape the state, Coriolanus himself – Rome's prime war horse, the steed to which, Lartius declares, the rest of the army is mere decorative cover (I.9.13) – fails to take his specified place as a member of the body politic once off the battlefield. Practically invincible enemy, obedient tool of Rome at war and potential holder of high office and power, he is unable to integrate into the politics of the state body at peace. This is the Coriolanus of Act III who, returning the successful war hero, he fails to ask the people of Rome for their votes in a sufficiently humble fashion, and refuses the customary ritual of displaying his war wounds. He is unwilling to accept that there should be any interdependency between him and the populus, given that he fashioned his victory against the enemy, as is stressed throughout the play, 'alone'. He is even less willing to feign humility where he sees no cause for it. Coriolanus complains to his mother: 'Would you have me / False to my nature? Rather say I play / The man I am' (III.2.15–17).

However politically disastrous this particular 'dangerous stoutness' (III.3.128), as opposed to his tenacity at war, turns out to be for Coriolanus, critics have made much of it. Cynthia Marshall suggests that it is only Coriolanus' refusal, which, by putting difference on stage, 'creates the need for a multi-dimensional hero and constructs the place for such a character to occupy'; thus, Shakespeare's stubborn hero participates in the historical development of subjectivity as a concept of interior selfhood (Marshall, 1996, p. 104). Coriolanus' denial of the people's claims on his body as spectacle becomes self-assertion. Similarly, Arthur Riss, in the historical context of controversial land enclosures, reads Coriolanus' refusal to parade his wounds as a (nascent capitalist) privatization and individualization of a body that 'the dominant ideology demands be available for public use' (Riss, 1992, p. 55). Readings of this kind make Coriolanus the prototype for a modern character, and for modern man, in a liberal humanist sense: self-aware and self-determined.

Accordingly, Coriolanus claims personal sovereignty against the demands of tradition and a political system that he identifies as distinct from and disagreeable to him:

> Why in this wolvish togue should I stand here
> To beg of Hob and Dick that does appear
> Their needless vouches? Custom calls me to't.
> What custom wills, in all things should we do't,
> The dust on antique time would lie unswept
> And mountainous error be too highly heaped
> For truth to o'erpeer. Rather than fool it so,
> Let the high office and the honour go
> To one that would do thus. (II.3.103–9)

Subjects of the Roman state automatically follow 'what custom wills'; the staging of power must proceed according to 'ceremony' as Sicinius demands in the previous scene (II.2.136). Here, the machine is tradition and the state, not Coriolanus. As fickle as he is stubborn, where Coriolanus does agree, for the time being, to play the customary part, he perceives the violation against his personhood in the strongest possible terms: 'I will not do't, / Lest I surcease to honour mine own truth / And by my body's action teach my mind / A most inherent baseness' (III.2.121–4). His stubbornness here would not be that of the unthinking and relentless war machine but that of a rational mind that sees its integrity threatened by the mechanical action of an alien protocol forced upon his body. Coriolanus, accordingly, steps outside the body politic and its laws to be, and to protect, his own self: not an absolute, divine force of war, but absolutely self-determined, if only for the moment, and thus the little god that passes as liberal humanist man in the making.

Strangely, of all the characters in the play the representatives of the people get closest to supporting this image of Coriolanus. To them, it is precisely his excessive demand for self-determination that makes him 'a very dog to the communality' and a 'viper' who, given the chance, would 'depopulate the city and / be every man himself' (I.1.21, and III.1.265–7). According to Sicinius' portrayal, Coriolanus' narcissist misjudgement of his own position would threaten to destroy, even consume, the body politic altogether. If the tribunes picture Coriolanus as less than human, the logic of their rejection depends on his claim to be more than human: in this Rome, humanity means to function as part of the political whole.

Meanwhile, Menenius and Cominius tend to interpret Coriolanus' behaviour not as an excessive demand for self-determination, but as lack of it. Menenius sees his obstinacy not as pride but as unstoppable honesty:

> His nature is too noble for the world.
> He would not flatter Neptune for his trident
> Or Jove for's power of thunder. His heart's his mouth.
> What his breast forges, that his tongue must vent,
> And, being angry, does forget that ever
> He heard the name of death. (III.1.257–62)

This is double-edged praise, and in line with earlier descriptions of Coriolanus' robotic service at war: noble and honest with an otherworldly relentlessness, Coriolanus appears to have little choice. He must speak his mind regardless of all other considerations, here including his own safety as well as that of his family and friends. Being too noble for the world makes him, yet again, god and thing at the same time: it places him beyond the ability to reason, to calculate, to make decisions. Not only is he 'ill-schooled / in bolted language' (III.1.340); the rage-crazed Coriolanus of the marketplace seems lost to the bolts of culture, to the technology of communication. There has been much comment on the logical and grammatical incoherence of Coriolanus' angry speeches;[8] elsewhere, Coriolanus is not only unable to speak properly, but also stubbornly refuses to be the object of discourse, to 'hear his nothings monstered' (II.2.71). In Menenius' image of Coriolanus above, he does not refuse, he lacks articulation altogether. While Menenius credits what he describes as a missing distance between heart and mouth, between self and self-expression as noble in a way that would not seem out of place in eighteenth-century romanticism, his 'too noble' also hints at the catastrophic implications for Coriolanus' place in the body politic. Lacking articulation means lacking human art: the assumed rational ability to distinguish between interior thought and exterior display, the participation in language as construct and, perhaps most importantly here, the jointed art of politics. Which, at least in Hobbes's Leviathan, as the making of and abiding by contracts and laws, is the artificial extension of the human body that not only makes and secures the state but also proves reason and thus makes the human in the first place.[9]

That Coriolanus should be too stubborn to remember his own mortality is particularly significant here as, according to Hobbes, the political community is based on the shared fear of death (cf. *Leviathan*, ch. 27 'Of Crimes, Excuses and Extenuations' [Hobbes, 1997, pp. 146–55]). As is evident throughout the play, Coriolanus lacks the fear concomitant to hearing 'the name of death'; beyond the practical effects of this fearlessness, this forgetting of the name as the idea of death gives Coriolanus' lack of human rationality a dimension in time. Coriolanus forgets names throughout the play, but in Cominius' speech before the senate no traces of imagined pasts or futures seem to impact on Coriolanus' actions at all, as he 'rewards / His deeds with doing them, and is content /to spend the time to end it' (II.2.121–3). Coriolanus seems to have no human time-keeping, no understanding of death as a limiting factor, no being-towards-death in Martin Heidegger's sense as that which defines human existence. He just, stubbornly, lives. And thus he would also be absolutely, obstinately closed off against the human community, having neither Hobbesian fear to drive him into becoming an obedient part of the body politic, nor memory as the prerequisite to participation in law and language as the prosthetics of the state: Coriolanus as god, or thing, or both – but not as a human subject.

In the end, the two opposed camps implicitly agree on the impossibility of stubborn Coriolanus. Whether his obstinacy is portrayed as lack or excess of self, nobility or pride, it is always shown as excessive to the state. According to either interpretation of Coriolanus' behaviour, it comes as no surprise that he is expelled from the city and from the community. He cannot be a political leader because he cannot be political. He cannot be part of the body politic because he resists its mechanics, and is thus, according to Sicinius, 'a disease that must be cut away' or else cause the death of all (III.1.300). He ends up outside the city walls, in a sense that is perhaps not too far away from the famous passage close to the beginning of Aristotle's *Politics*:

> Hence it is evident that the state [*polis*] is a creation of nature, and that man is by nature a political animal. And he who by nature and not by mere accident is without a state, is either above humanity, or below it; he is the 'tribeless, lawless, hearthless one', whom Homer denounces – the outcast who is a lover of war; he may be compared to an unprotected piece in a game of draughts. (Aristotle, 1926, p. 28)

Thus it would not be the people of Rome, as 'the beast with many heads' that 'butts' Coriolanus away but his own lacking humanity (IV.1.1–2). Bertolt Brecht suggests that '[Coriolanus'] switch from being the most Roman of the Romans to becoming their deadliest enemy is due precisely to the fact that he stays the same' (Brecht, 1992, p. 264). Accordingly, his obstinate self-identity, regardless of whether it is conscious or automatic, stands in the way of the body politic as the place of articulation, engagement, translation and circulation. In a way, the opposed assessments of Coriolanus' political failure offered in the play conflate both of Aristotle's categories for apolitical man, the sub- and the superhuman, in his ferocious stubbornness; Menenius puts an image to this when he sees exiled Coriolanus as 'grown from man to dragon. / He has wings; he's more than a creeping thing' (V.4.10–11). There is much more in the play to make Coriolanus look fundamentally apolitical once he has left the city. Denying his family, 'wife, mother, child, I know not' (V.2.76), apparently leaving behind all markers of his former life, Coriolanus would be, in Cominius' words, 'a kind of nothing, titleless, / Till he had forged himself a name o'th'fire / Of burning Rome' (V.1.12–14) – 'a lover of war', indeed. Outside Rome, it would seem that there is nothing that still links him to law, tribe and hearth, to the *polis* and thus to humanity: Coriolanus as pure obstinacy, unaffected, unguided force. And once he is driven out of the city, he goes to work towards the only thing one might expect pure force to do: flatten everything.

But of course the play will not allow this. Whatever fantasies of pure force and complete isolation are offered, they are always offset by their failure. Aristotle's version of the city, while it seems to promise a clear boundary between those within and those without, already points towards the impossibility of the division; if Aristotle's lover of war, sub- or superhuman, is like an 'unprotected piece in a game of draughts', he is yet defined by his game. While there are real city walls, there is no being human, inside or outside, that is unmarked by their demarcations in some way. There is no such thing as pure force – and Coriolanus certainly is not one. Critics have noted this in a variety of ways. James Calderwood sees Coriolanus seek, and fail, to create 'a private verbal standard' outside Rome's corrupted sign system in which 'words are cemented to their meanings' (Calderwood, 1966, pp. 217, 214). Carol Sicherman suggests that Coriolanus' silences mark a belief in, and a failure of, communication without words, as in his meeting with Aufidius, where he expects, and fails, to be identified 'instantly, without words, rather as if two angels – enjoying intuitive rather than discursive knowledge – were encountering' (Sicherman, 1972, p. 192). More recently, Clark Lunberry sees Coriolanus try to express a sovereign self outside Rome's dirty politics by the pure language of his sword and sees him fail as neither the wounds on his body nor those he leaves on others' speak for themselves, but are subject to discourse – and thus subject to politics (Lunberry, 2002, p. 236).

There is no absolute escape from the city – not even by wiping it out. As Volumnia points out to her son, burning down Rome will only give him a bad name in future chronicles of the city – not a new one forged by himself, as Cominius imagines earlier on (V.3.141–8). There is no getting away from being named by others, and thus no getting away from engagement with their laws. And therefore, there is no getting out of being human, if that means to be *zoon politikon* – not even by death; when Coriolanus is murdered by the conspirators, his body yet signifies in Volscian politics. Coriolanus' stubbornness can neither make him 'author of himself' nor unthinking and unaffected force. Instead, he is torn between the various different and contradictory demands of the city as much as he is constituted by them in the first place.

It would be possible to end a reading of *Coriolanus* here, with the conclusion that its hero's tragedy rests in his wrong-headed, stubborn impulse, conscious or not, rational or not, of mistaking his position for that of an angel or a beast. Coriolanus fails to escape the human community and its physical, symbolic, linguistic, legal and economical machineries and his inevitable implication in them. Instead, I suggest that the uncanny and persistent manifestations of the more and less than human in *Coriolanus*, the strange images of a cyborg god-thing as embodied stubbornness, lend some life yet to a figuring of the political in the tragedy. One possible headline for this is tribune Brutus' view of Coriolanus as 'past all thinking / Self-loving' (IV.6.34). Here, Coriolanus' excessiveness makes for a very un-Cartesian self-manifestation; his placing of himself above his station, his, as tribune Sicinius puts it in the following line, 'affecting one sole throne / Without assistance', is marked as a narcissism beyond all thought. Coriolanus puts himself first but without thinking – 'bolder' than the devil, as his rival Aufidius has it, 'though not so subtle' (I.10.17–18).

I propose that there is a useful link to be made between this kind of purely stubborn, unthinking self-love and the kind of stubbornness that Derrida traces in a variety of contexts in *The Beast and the Sovereign* under the French term *bêtise*. Derrida links *bêtise* to 'stubborn obstinacy, the *conatus* of a perseverance in being'. Before any pre-existent concept, without identifiable determining cause, *bêtise* is 'headstrong stubbornness in being', that which wants 'to continue to be, to be what that is, self-identically, without thinking of anything else' and that manifests itself insofar as it '*posits*, posits itself and reposits itself in stubborn obstinacy, in pigheadedness [*entêtement*] without concept' (Derrida, 2009, p. 192). Thus, any kind of thing that is stubborn enough to be a living thing, a self-identical living thing – and not just a human self – would require, in order to be, a self-repetition, an 'autopositing' as Derrida calls it (p. 139). It is worth stressing Derrida's insistent use of this verb *poser*, here translated as 'posit', as it links, among other things, the perseverance of unthinking, pre-conceptual self-repetition of a living thing as described above to a 'conscious self-positing self' (p. 183) as well as to the positing of state and state power, as in Hobbes's prosthetic Leviathan (pp. 42, 98). These very different instances of *bête* stubbornness, whether they place their boundaries as those of human and other animal bodies, of humanist subjects or of social 'bodies', are always held in place by a repeated, forceful or even violent positioning that can no longer be fixed absolutely on either side of a nature/ culture, nature/law or nature/artefact division (pp. 42, 15). Concepts or mammals, laws or acephalic life forms, it makes any self-unity not a given but an assertion, an institution, a neither artificial nor natural (or both artificial and natural) claim of place that always depends on stubborn persistence.

So, the problem with Coriolanus' stubbornness, first of all, is that while it is variously presented as mechanical, automatic, bestial and divine, none of these categories can succeed in containing it outside the boundaries of the human as rational and thus as political. Coriolanus, even as he fails to 'play the man [he is]', displays the mechanics of staging self-unity as stubborn positing. Perhaps this is what is so outrageous about *Coriolanus*: it shows up the stupid stubbornness, the violent and ungraceful assertion of any sovereignty, of any self-identical entity at all – that all self-loving is past thinking, a stubborn repetition of a claim of place. The broader political implications for the play begin where this stubborn positing goes beyond the dramaturgy of sovereign selves. Derrida insists that *bêtise* is a non-conceptual stubbornness (2009, p. 192); but significantly, it is at work in all conceptuality and all rationality, in all its delineations and unifications. This means that if all self-loving is past thinking, all thinking is yet based on self-loving. It is one aspect of this irrational force of the rational that Derrida's essay 'The Force of Law', following Walter Benjamin's *Critique of Violence*, explores in the inevitable violence that keeps any law alive:

> [T]here is no law without enforcability, and no applicability or enforceabilty of the law without force, whether this force be direct or indirect, physical or symbolic, exterior or interior, brutal or subtly

discursive and hermeneutic, coercive or regulative, and so forth. (Derrida, 1990, pp. 927–8)

Just as there is no thought, there is no law, and no politics, without its own violent self-justification.

James Kuzner's reading of *Coriolanus* picks up on the ways in which the play shows the exile as judged by a law that does not do him justice, how the tribunes manipulate state structures and people in order to create, in Giorgio Agamben's terms, 'a state of exception' that makes Coriolanus 'bare life' and thus places him beyond eligibility for a formal trial, literally as much as juridically outside the city walls and the body politic (Kuzner, 2007, pp. 185–6). This is no doubt the manoeuvre played out, at least on one level of the action.[10] The tribunes' interpretation of the state, as it insists on taking Coriolanus literally and uses the letter of the law against him without remit or mercy, shows stubborn *bêtise* to match that of Coriolanus. But this, I suggest, does not mean that the play points towards a straightforward way out of the 'state of exception', and the state of Rome, in Coriolanus himself. Instead, it exposes that there is no claim of place that is not based in protective and violent boundaries, and thus in the inevitably bellicose prosthetics of stubborn life. Posited as rational or not, *bêtise*, stupid stubbornness, 'is always ... on the side of the victor' (Derrida, 2009, p. 183) – whether the victor is a renegade one-man war machine, a thick city wall, a well-defended idea of the state body, family institutions, some successful conspirators, or a concept of the human, the political, of reason or law.

This does not mean that *Coriolanus* comes down to a tableau of the 'war of all against all' that in Hobbes marks the absence of civil society and thus humanity (Hobbes, 1998, pp. 49–50). Or purely that, as in La Fontaine's fable, 'the reason of the strongest is always best' (1997, p. 10; translation modified). As suggested above, Coriolanus' tragedy can be read as his failure to be pure force. While his character is figured as noble, divine, invincible, unified, he is also mechanical thing – and therefore jointed, connected, dependent, provisional. He, and all 'sovereign' selves, share the problem Derrida identifies in state sovereignty in Hobbes's *Leviathan*: 'it is posited as immortal and indivisible precisely because it is mortal and divisible, contract or convention being destined to ensure for it what it does not have naturally' (Derrida, 2009, p. 42). Because there is no guaranteed, natural unity for self or state, *bêtise* is at work in its putting-into-place, in figuring and staging;[11] thus the hardening up, the increasingly armour-plated stubbornness of any (self-)institution involuntarily shows the continued vulnerability and openness that necessitates its closing-off in the first place. Where there is no force, and thus no life, without law, and yet no law is immortal, everything depends on the prostheses of unity – and they are always subject to change.

Shakespeare's *Coriolanus*, I suggest, draws attention to this. While the official body politic in the play much resembles Hobbes's Leviathan in its mechanicist yet organicist shape, its less official reconfigurations leave it quite distorted. If there is no pure force in Coriolanus, there certainly is none in the state. When Menenius confronts the rioting people, his fable of the belly is to remind the citizens of their place in the body politic, but he does not even manage to get them to agree on its shape. Before he can even assert the belly's rightful sovereignty over the rest of the body's members, Second Citizen butts in with a different version until he, too, is interrupted:

> Your belly's answer – What?
> The kingly crownèd head, the vigilant eye,
> The counsellor heart, the arm our soldier,
> Our steed the leg, the tongue our trumpeter,
> With our muniments and petty helps
> In this our fabric, if that they – (I.1.97–102)

The 'kingly crownèd head' sits awkwardly with the Roman republic and alludes to a more contemporary Jacobean body politic; but the citizen's version also confuses the orientation of Menenius' version as it names a different principal organ – the head rather than the belly. It then goes on in an impatient, even lazy enumeration of the body's members, farcically including horses for legs, rather than allocating the lower extremities to the working classes, as was commonly the case.[12] The substitution is an uneasy one as it blurs the distinction between the political metaphor and its referent. Horses are neither human body parts nor part of the constituency – and thus pull the whole state body into the ridiculous. Perhaps the horses also subtly raise the question whether the Roman Republic makes as much of a difference between human and animal labourers as its constitution suggests. Even as the citizen's version apparently accepts the notion of a body politic as such, and of the citizens' position within it, it draws attention to its artificiality as 'this our fabric'. When Menenius eventually finishes his version, the citizen refuses to take the interpretation of the fable as read: 'It was an answer. How apply you this?' (I.1.130). Fables, and political systems, are fabrications, and, much to Menenius' annoyance, how they are applied is always in question. He goes on to label Second Citizen a rascal and the people rats. As Riss points out, one reason for the failure of Menenius' tale is that he does not see that the people's literal, starving bellies stand in the way of his figurative use of the belly: 'They are too hungry to think abstractly' (Riss, 1992, p. 62). Here real stomachs, for the time being, assert sovereignty over rhetorical ones – and the people get their representatives and their grain.

If state sovereignty has to posit itself successfully as indivisible in order to be forceful, nothing will appear less so than when fictions of the state begin to divide and multiply and consensus disintegrates. Where the play is about the political and, via Aristotle, about the political as a definition of the human, the human is left fairly ill defined; this political human seems closer to the pamphlet depictions of multi-headed state monsters that would circulate in 1640s civil war England than to Hobbes's orderly Leviathan (cf., for example, 'The Kingdomes Monster' [1643]). Beyond the body politic, animate bodies are on the move in *Coriolanus*. Who is a dog of war, an ungrateful viper, a bear, a wolf or a lamb to whom is never finally determined, as multiplying animal figures swarm through the play, machine-like in their stubborn repetition: fable creatures, but never fixed in the place of an identifiable moral.[13] The provisional quality of allegiances, popularity, power; of ideas and ideals of political community; of who is family, friend or enemy show Coriolanus the cyborg not as a unified self but as part of multiple, unstable and unchangeable relations of force; even as he and various other agents try to assert themselves as definite and distinct.

Cyborgs in the play, whether the political cyborg Coriolanus or the cyborg body politic, show life to be prosthetic; to always depend on protective gear, on armour and on fictions which are not only liable to fail but also difficult to fix in place. This way, *Coriolanus* does not provide a way out of the city; instead, the play refuses to settle with the illusion that its shape is ever fixed or beyond question. I do not believe, as Kuzner proposes, that 'in seeking to exist outside Rome's fictions ... Coriolanus ... stands for other, more habitable forms of unprotected existence', that by embracing his 'bare life' he escapes citizenship and its 'boundedness' (Kuzner, 2007, pp. 175, 192). Rather, I suggest that the play shows existence, within and beyond professions of 'the human', as necessarily communal and political, always bounded by multiple and often contradictory relations of force. This is not to say that resistance is futile, only that there is no getting out of relationality, no escaping power relations. Politics, *Coriolanus* also suggests, are determined by boundaries which, like all boundaries, require violence. There are no politics without treading on someone, somebody, something. 'Tread not upon him!' (V.6.136), a Volscian lord exclaims as Aufidius stands on Coriolanus' body after he has been murdered in full view of the City's representatives. The assembled proceed 'to make the best of it' (V.6.148) and turn the bloody scene into a state funeral for political spin. In the final scene, the mechanics of treading on Coriolanus' body, in their untidy brutality, turn into eloquent representation of the powers that be, into rationalizing the force of law. *Coriolanus* demands a confrontation with political violence otherwise covered up. It shows interrelated cyborg mechanisms as fictions that are as real and bodily as they are posited and provisional, and thus it shows them open to challenge. It blocks the conceptual purity of 'the human' and 'the political' as much as the 'inhuman' and the 'apolitical'. This does not mean that it effaces differences. Instead, it posits an invitation to counter the rigor mortis of all kinds of absolute city walls with differently stubborn responses – however provisional.

Notes

1. All references to *Coriolanus*, unless indicated otherwise, are to the 2010 updated Cambridge edition.
2. Much of this recent interest in the politics of the play draws on Giorgio Agamben's *Homo Sacer*, particularly his development of 'bare life' and Carl Schmitt's 'state of exception' as the basis of modern government in the West (Agamben, 1998, pp. 8–9). Critics plot various ways in which a 'state of exception' can be read to destabilise notions of lawful power in *Coriolanus* (see Lemon, 2007, p. 246; Miller, 2009, pp. 286–94; Murakami, 2006, pp. 130–1; Kuzner, 2007, p. 179; for the last, also see discussion below).
3. There is some suggestion of Coriolanus as a motivating force (see, for example, I.6.66–75), but there is no evidence of Coriolanus' strategic prowess beyond Volumnia's tactical mention of 'honour and policy' in war (III.2.43). Instead, as the play stresses throughout, Coriolanus does his best fighting alone (I.4.55–6, I.8.7–8, II.1.135, II.2.104, V.6.119).
4. In 'The Cyborg Body Politic', Chris Hables Gray and Steven Mentor distinguish between Hobbes's early modern 'soulful automaton' and a late twentieth-century cyborg body politic, while admitting Hobbes's role in a 'process that [he] saw and helped institute, the proliferation of selves, the joining of machine to natural image to make a hybrid' (Gray and Mentor, 2001, pp. 455). Despite all the significant differences between early modern and postmodern states, an absolute distinction between the two based on the apparent absence of 'soul' in postmodern states runs the risk of overlooking not only the openness to 'cyborg' human/machine ambiguities in early modern text but also the hidden assertions of 'soul' as a sort of divine

sovereignty which, 'onto-theologico-politically', claims an indivisible and unquestionable core of state power in contemporary political systems (see Derrida, 2009, pp. 45–8, for his discussion of indivisible sovereignty in Hobbes, and discussion below).

5. This is the case even though Hobbes insists that political fitness is not innate. While, according to Hobbes, not all men achieve the artificial, learnt superior state of civil society (*On the Citizen*, chapter 1, 'On the state of man without civil society' [Hobbes, 1998, pp. 24–5]), he nonetheless confirms it as an exclusively human possibility.

6. For an influential early example see John of Salisbury's twelfth-century anatomy of the anthropomorphic state, *Policraticus* (1990). Menenius' fable of the belly derives from Plutarch's account of Coriolanus' life in an even earlier version of the long-lived political metaphor (Plutarch, 1965).

7. See Hobbes, 1998, p. 108: '*Dominion*, i.e. sovereign power, is indivisible, so that no one can serve two masters'.

8. Sicherman comments on Coriolanus' 'logorrhea' as his downfall and lists much of the other critical work focused on his 'excessiveness in words' (Sicherman, 1972, pp. 198 and 198n.16).

9. Cathy Shrank draws attention to the 'connection between civil and civic in early modern England' in Ciceronian discourse that allocates to reasonable speech the power to transform 'wild savages into kind and gentle folk' – a humanist standard of civic civility that Coriolanus spectacularly fails to meet (Shrank, 2003, pp. 423, 410).

10. That the tribunes' actions are not unambiguous is evidenced in the body of criticism, including Annabel Patterson's *Shakespeare and the Popular Voice*, which interprets the play as pro-republican (1989).

11. The proliferation of theatrical vocabulary in the play has been widely noted (see, for example, Lee Bliss's commentary on 'this unnatural scene' [V.3.185]).

12. One contemporary example is Edward Forset's *Comparative Discourse of the Bodies Natural and Politique* (1606), who aligns 'the meaner sort of mechanicall tradesmen' with the feet of the body politic (p. 48).

13. Dogs are one instance of this: Coriolanus is 'a very dog' to the people in I.1.21; the people are 'curs' to him in III.3.128; tribune Sicinius plans to manipulate Coriolanus into convenient anger like one sets 'dog on sheep' (II.1.231); Second Servingman claims that given the chance he would have beaten the disguised Coriolanus 'like a dog' (IV.5.48) and, finally, Volumnia warns Coriolanus that destroying Rome would give him a 'name / Whose repetition would be dogg'd with curses' (V.3.143–4). Murakami draws attention to the rhetorical competition between Menenius and the tribunes to associate predators with the opposing side and prey animals with their own (II.1.5–12) and how the competing versions leave 'a conflict between Martius and the people, including any claims to moral superiority' undecided (Murakami, 2006, p. 125).

Works cited

Agamben, Giorgio (1998) *Homo Sacer: Sovereign Power and Bare Life*, trans. Daniel Heller-Roazen, Stanford: Stanford University Press.

Aristotle (1926) *Politics*, trans. Benjamin Jowett, ed. H. W. C. Davies, Oxford: Clarendon Press.

Brecht, Bertolt (1992) *Brecht on Theatre: The Development of an Aesthetic*, ed. and trans. John Willett, New York: Hill and Wang.

Calderwood, James L. (1966) 'Coriolanus: Wordless Meanings and Meaningless Words', *Studies in English Literature 1500–1900* 6, pp. 211–24.

Cavell, Stanley (2003) 'Coriolanus and the Interpretations of Politics: "Who does the wolf love?"', *Disowning Knowledge in Seven Plays of Shakespeare*, 2nd edn, Cambridge: Cambridge University Press.

Derrida, Jacques (1990) 'The Force of Law: The Mystical Foundation of Authority', *The Cardozo Law Review* 11.5–6, pp. 919–1046.

Derrida, Jacques (2009) *The Beast and the Sovereign*, Vol. 1, trans. Geoffrey Bennington, Chicago: University of Chicago Press.

Forset, Edward (1606) *Comparative Discourse of the Bodies Natural and Politique*, London: John Bill.

Gray, Chris Hables, and Steven Mentor (2001) 'The Cyborg Body Politic', in Chris Hables Gray (ed.), *The Cyborg Handbook*, London and New York: Routledge, pp. 453–66.

Hobbes, Thomas (1997) *Leviathan* (1651), ed. Richard E. Flathman and David Johnston, New York: Norton.

Hobbes, Thomas (1998) *On the Citizen*, ed. Richard Tuck and Michael Silverthorne, Cambridge: Cambridge University Press.

John of Salisbury (1990) *Policraticus*, ed. and trans. Cary J. Nederman, Cambridge: Cambridge University Press.

Kuzner, James (2007) 'Unbuilding the City: Coriolanus and the Birth of Republican Rome', *Shakespeare Quarterly* 58.2, pp. 174–99.

La Fontaine, Jean de (1997) *Selected Fables: Fables Choisies*, ed. and trans. Stanley Appelbaum, Mineola: Dover.

Lemon, Rebecca (2007) 'Arms and Laws in Shakespeare's *Coriolanus*', in Constance Jordan and Karen Cunningham (eds), *The Law in Shakespeare*, Basingstoke: Palgrave, now Palgrave Macmillan, pp. 233–48.

Lunberry, Clark (2002) 'In the Name of Coriolanus: The Prompter (Prompted)', *Comparative Literature* 54.3, pp. 229–41.

Marshall, Cynthia (1996) '*Wound-man*: Coriolanus, Gender and the Theatrical Construction of Interiority', in Valerie Traub, M. Lindsay Kaplan and Dympna Callaghan (eds), *Feminist Readings of Early Modern Culture: Emerging Subjects*, Cambridge: Cambridge University Press, pp. 93–118.

Miller, Nicole E. (2009) 'Sacred Life and Sacrificial Economy: *Coriolanus* in No-Man's Land', *Criticism* 51.2, pp. 263–310.

Murakami, Ineke (2006) '"The Bond and Privilege of Nature" in *Coriolanus*', *Religion and Literature* 38.3, pp. 121–36.

Patterson, Annabel (1989) *Shakespeare and the Popular Voice*, Oxford: Blackwell.

Plutarch (1965) 'Coriolanus', *Makers of Rome: Nine Lives*, trans. Ian Scott-Klivert, London: Penguin, pp. 15–32.

Riss, Arthur (1992) 'The Belly Politic: Coriolanus and the Revolt of Language', *English Literary History* 59.1, pp. 53–75.

Sawday, Jonathan (1999) '"Forms such as Never Were in Nature: The Renaissance Cyborg', in Erica Fudge, Ruth Gilbert and Susan Wiseman (eds), *At the Borders of the Human: Beasts, Bodies and Natural Philosophy in the Early Modern Period*, Basingstoke: Macmillan, pp. 171–95.

Sawday, Jonathan (2007) *Engines of the Imagination: Renaissance Culture and the Rise of the Machine*, London: Routledge.

Shakespeare, William (1994) *The Oxford Shakespeare, The Tragedy of Coriolanus*, ed. R. B. Parker, Oxford: Clarendon Press.

Shakespeare, William (2010) *Coriolanus*, ed. Lee Bliss, Cambridge: Cambridge University Press.

Shrank, Cathy (2003) 'Civility and the City in *Coriolanus*', *Shakespeare Quarterly* 54.4, pp. 406–23.

Sicherman, Carol M. (1972) 'Coriolanus: The Failure of Words', *English Literary History* 39.2, pp. 189–207.

Stiegler, Bernard (1998) *Technics and Time*, Vol. I, *The Fault of Epimetheus*, trans. Richard Beardsworth and George Collins, Stanford: Stanford University Press.

7
Renaissance Self-Unfashioning: Shakespeare's Late Plays as Exercises in Unravelling the Human

Rainer Emig

Introduction

Shakespearean scholarship is generally rather embarrassed when it comes to the late plays *Timon of Athens* (*c*.1605–8) and *Pericles* (*c*.1607–8). Critics generally emphasize that their authorship is mixed, that they are either unfinished (as in *Timon of Athens*) or rather reported snippets from rehearsals (as in *Pericles*) than properly authored and authorized texts.[1] As such, however, they merely expose the workings of early modern authorship. They also show us very clearly that Shakespearean character and plot creation are a far cry from the romantic nineteenth-century myth of a single genius plucking original material out of nowhere. Their intertextual nature and complex assembly of fragments (which in *Pericles* requires the author of one of its sources, the late medieval chronicler John Gower, to appear as a clumsy narrator) hardly lead to satisfactory plots with meaningful resolutions – at least not for a modern reader and viewer.

The present chapter wishes to take up exactly this 'self-unravelling' of plots and characters into loose ends and contradictions (features which apparently did not irritate Shakespeare's contemporaries unduly) to show that there lurks something within early modern patterns and strictures of supposedly creating a newly autonomous self that pulls its representations back into the structures and material out of which they emerge. Language and texts as much as power, status, wealth and gender will be shown to be the building yet also stumbling-blocks of a figuration that, in its contradictory pull towards a textual (and ideological) openness and the closure of a newly achieved autonomy, exposes the contradictions within early modern self-fashioning. Obsessed with learning, it yearns to incorporate all human achievements, while a simultaneous thriving for individual empowerment forces it to strategically rough ride over the authorities and hierarchies implied in the material it has to employ for its miraculous self-creation. Issues such as over-expenditure and waste (as in *Timon of Athens*), incest and uneasy escapes from tyranny while simultaneously playing tyrant to those closest to oneself (as in *Pericles*) will be exposed as symbolic manifestations of this structural contradiction.

Humanism's alterities

In many ways it is as futile to investigate Shakespeare's humanism as it is to inquire into his potential posthumanism, since the term 'humanism' was a nineteenth-century invention rather than an established cultural concept or label in Shakespeare's time. Indeed, some Italian scholars referred to themselves as *humanisti*, and some of their British colleagues were aware of this. But neither the term nor the ideas behind it were common currency in British Renaissance culture (Davies, 1997, pp. 72–6).

Yet the German-speaking scholars who devised the label and were happy to apply it to Renaissance Europe did have something in mind that touches on early modern English culture, too. Since the days of romanticism, Shakespeare had been adopted as an honorary German writer. His character Hamlet was even seen to embody Germany itself,[2] an unfree and torn country, divided into numerous little states. The inclusion or exclusion of German-speaking regions elsewhere, such as in the Austro-Hungarian Empire, Switzerland, or German enclaves in North-Eastern and Eastern Europe, posed further problems.[3] Taking Hamlet as one's figure of identification – and by extension as the triumph of an assumed humanism over the odds of internal strife – was therefore as much a cultural as a political gesture. Yet Hamlet pays for his supposed integrity with his death – and only maintains it at the price of playing the madman and sacrificing those nearest and dearest to him.

Moreover, Hamlet is neither the culmination of Shakespeare's attempts at character-creation nor is he even particularly representative of Shakespeare's oeuvre. Much more common are flat characters or those that act against their own interests, and again more often than not the price for this has to be paid by others. When Stephen Greenblatt aims at celebrating the subject-creating power of Shakespeare among other early modern English figures, he also has to admit grudgingly that 'self-fashioning always involves some experience of threat, some effacement or undermining, some loss of self' (Greenblatt, 1980, p. 9). In the very opening of his seminal study *Renaissance Self-Fashioning*

Greenblatt had described the potential inherent in self-fashioning in a way that could also act as an abstract shorthand of the later idea of humanism: 'Self-fashioning is in effect the renaissance version of these control mechanisms [of culture], the cultural system of meanings that creates specific individuals by governing the passage from abstract potential to concrete historical embodiment' (pp. 3–4). As a new historicist Greenblatt refuses to locate the power of embodiment completely within the individual (this is what traditional liberal humanism had been – and is – wont to do). Yet he is curiously silent on how these control mechanisms and meanings come about. What he makes explicit, though, is that the processes of control and signification as well as the heroic feat of self-embodiment take place in relation to, indeed even require, an alterity that is perceived as negative: 'Self-fashioning is achieved in relation to something perceived as alien, as strange, or hostile' (p. 9).

Alterity in Shakespeare can sometimes be found outside accepted and acceptable human characters, as in the figure of Caliban in *The Tempest* or the witches in *Macbeth*. There, modern posthumanism's aliens would find early modern ancestors. Yet more frequently it is part of the set-up of protagonists and antagonists or even (as in *Hamlet*) to be found *inside* protagonists as part of their divided characterization that refuses to be reified into what traditional humanism likes to call their 'human nature'. Othello or Lear would be such protagonists whose tragedies are in exact correlation to the contradictions of their embodiment. Yet while Shakespeare's tragedies manage to contain this contradiction inside their genre conventions, things become less comfortable in plays where this neither works nor is even attempted. The so-called late plays offer examples where neither self-fashioning works nor an anachronistic attribution of humanism is easily possible. Two of these will be used in what is to follow to check whether concepts of posthumanism might instead be applicable to them in the sense proposed by the introduction to this volume as an attempt to work its way back to Shakespeare and construct genealogies between his work and a perceived or real shift away from a humanist knowledge paradigm, the possible advent of a new 'episteme', in which 'the human' again becomes a radically open category.

Timon of Athens – unravelling humanism's premature success story

A respected citizen, after being disappointed by his supposed friends, flees a society that he has learned to detest and becomes an antisocial hermit. Yet the miraculous discovery of a treasure leads him back into society in which he is now welcomed as a benefactor. This would make a neat humanist parable of the civilizing power of the essentially human that might be discovered in individual contemplation, but that is much better tested in communities – which it then refines into civil societies proper. Unfortunately, it is the reverse of what happens in *Timon of Athens*. The play[4] starts with an established and functioning civil society in which the character Timon plays a fully integrated part. Indeed the opening of the play presents a model of a humanist court where educated men engage in civilized exchanges:

> [*Enter Poet, Painter, Jeweller and Merchant at several doors*]
>
> POET   Good day, sir.
> PAINTER   I am glad you're well.
> POET   I have not seen you long – how goes the world?
> PAINTER   It wears, sir, as it grows.
> POET   Ay, that's well known.
>   But what particular rarity? What strange,
>   Which manifold record not matches? See,
>   Magic of bounty, all these spirits thy power
>   Hath conjured to attend. I know the merchant.
> PAINTER   I know them both – th'other's a jeweller.
> MERCHANT O, 'tis a worthy lord!
> JEWELLER   Nay, that's most fix'd.
> MERCHANT A most incomparable man, breathed as it were
>   To an untireable and continuate goodness –
>   He passes. (I.1.1–12)

Despite the elevated language and refined attitudes, the characters are not engaged in an exchange for the sake of individual and societal improvement. Their motives are mercenary, and Timon is the focus of their attention because he also represents the source of the wealth that maintains this society. Even the poet and the painter are there because they expect patronage. The poet's derogatory remark concerning the merchant and the jeweller is thus misguided. In fact, merchant and jeweller, with their more pragmatic attitude towards greatness in which 'worthy' stands for abstract value as much as for financial status, are turned into ironic oracles when they both make an ambivalent pronouncement of Timon's steadfastness ('most fix'd') and an uncanny prediction of what will happen to him ('He passes'). Shakespeare, one might argue, sees through the seemingly disinterested veneer of educated humanist society and spots, as a Marxist *avant la lettre*, the underlying economic and power structures that generate this society of privilege and the homosocial bonding of ambitious and upwardly mobile men.[5]

This, however, would not make him a posthumanist as much as a traditional antihumanist already at the stage when humanism was in the process of shaping itself into the formation to which German-speaking scholars would attach this label three hundred years later. Already the translation in geographic as in linguistic terms of writings such as the formative ones by Pico della Mirandola into an English context charged their original utopian playfulness with pragmatism. Thus, the original title of his *Oratio in coetu Romanorum* (Oration in the Roman Assembly), one that he was never allowed to deliver, in the first printed edition of 1496 became the now famous *De hominis dignitate* (On the Dignity of Man), in pirated editions from 1504 onwards and especially with the successful Basel edition of 1557, a title much more suitable for later attributions of 'humanism' (cf. Buck, 1990, p. xvii).

Scholars as diverse as Erasmus of Rotterdam (1466–1536), Sir Thomas More (1478–1535), Roger Ascham (*c.*1515–68) and Sir Thomas Hoby (1530–66) outlined diverse and critical forms in which the thought that would later be called humanism expressed itself. At the same time, all these characters knew where their bread was buttered, having in most cases risen from relative obscurity to the status of teacher and secretary of kings and queens (in the case of Ascham), diplomat (Hoby), Lord Chancellor (More), or internationally respected scholar (Erasmus). Only More and Hoby were men of some privilege from the start, although even More was seen as a social climber when he became the first layman Lord Chancellor. Erasmus was in fact illegitimate. Erasmus's *Praise of Folly* (1509), for instance, already contains a comment that fits the much later *Timon of Athens*:

> But the most foolish and sordid of all are your merchants, in that they carry on the most sordid business of all and this by the most sordid methods; for on occasion they lie, they perjure themselves, they steal, they cheat, they impose on the public. Yet they make themselves men of importance, because they have gold rings on their fingers. (Erasmus, 1970, p. 69)

There is, in fact, no reason why Timon of Athens's generosity towards the many men who surround him must inevitably lead to catastrophe. Generosity, traditionally known as 'largesse' or 'munificence', had been a virtue since antiquity (a preferred reference point of the Renaissance). It is Timon's own view that his generosity is excessive that eventually brings about a break with his environment and anti-social removal of his character from that which grants it a status as civilized. The play shows this decision as arbitrary and wilful. Its consequences for Timon are catastrophic. They turn him into an anti-social outsider. They also remove his status not only as a respected but also as a wise man. Clearly, if we talk about humanist principles in the play, these are assigned to the community and not the individual. But the question remains how such a refined specimen of a humanist character can turn into such an ardent antihumanist.

Here some posthumanist perspectives on the concept of the 'alien' come in handy. While it is facile to define posthumanism without a proper historical reference to humanism and to reify the complex idea of the alien in the commodified images provided by science fiction novels and films, the idea that the concept of the alien emerges from and remains entangled with the establishment of the self also has some bearing on Shakespeare's radically self-contradictory characters.[6] Timon, originally the essence of Athenian civilization (the title *Timon of Athens* does not so much refer to his elevated social status as to his belonging to one of the hotbeds of Classical civilization),[7] becomes its most vociferous enemy. Worse than that, since enmity would still imply interaction, he severs his connection from society and civilization completely and moves into a space that is not only geographically outside the bounds of civilization but incomprehensible to it. In short: he turns himself into an alien.

This is, of course, a paradoxical move. Or it should be – if being human was as essential as traditional humanism, despite its internal differences, insisted on. Yet already Pico della Mirandola lists among the attributes that he grants to man the miraculous, that of departing radically from his innate greatness:

> Ecquis hominem non admiretur? Qui non immerito in sacris litteris mosaicis et christianis, nunc omnis carnis, nunc omnis creaturae appellatione designator, quando se ipsum ipse in omnis carnis faciem, in omnis creaturae ingenium effingit, fabricat et transformat? Idcirco scribit Evantes Persa, ubi chaldaicam theologiam enarrat, non esse homini suam ullam et navigam imaginem, extrarias multas et adventitias.

> Who would not admire man, who is called by the sacred Jewish and Christian writings 'all flesh' and 'every creature', because he

fashions and transforms himself into any fleshly form and assumes the character of any creature whatsoever? This is why Evantes the Persian, in his description of Chaldaean theology, writes that man has no proper inborn form, but that many things that humans resemble are external and alien to them. (Pico della Mirandola, 1990, pp. 8, 10; trans. Rainer Emig)

In Shakespeare's *Timon of Athens*, we find praise of idealized humanity in lines such as the following uttered by the poet: 'Admirable! How this grace / Speaks his own standing! What a mental power / This eye shoots forth! How big imagination / Moves in this lip!' (I.1.32–4). What they praise, however, is a painting that the painter hopes to sell to the highest bidder. When the poet a little later praises Timon, he tellingly does so in a way that shows wealth and privilege as the media that communicate greatness, but also as burdens: 'His large fortune, / Upon his good and gracious nature hanging, / Subdues and properties to his love and tendance / All sorts of hearts' (I.1.57–60).

Timon's assumed 'good and gracious nature', however, turns out to be a misconception, for his generosity eventually loses him his fortune. Both poet and painter had repeatedly punned on fortune as wealth and Fortune as the fickle goddess in this scene. It is the misanthropic philosopher Apemantus who sees through Timon's generosity and calls it foolish. Interestingly enough, he is punished for this by being called the opposite of the civilized ideal at the time: 'He's opposite to humanity' (I.1.280). Already his name contains a pun on ape and man and implies that he is less than what a human being should be.

Soon, as has been indicated, the model citizen Titus also becomes the opposite to humanity. His dramatic change can, at least at first glance, still be explained by reference to humanist principles. Idealist that he is, he even views his self-inflicted bankruptcy as a chance to find friends who will support him in his trouble:

And in some sort these wants of mine are crowned,
That I account them blessings. For by these
Shall I try friends. You shall perceive how you
Mistake my fortunes: I am wealthy in my friends. (II.2.181–4)

A traditional Christian or a Stoic attitude would have seen value in enduring the humiliation of poverty. Yet a Renaissance attitude banks on human bonds and bonding, the homosocial bonds of privileged men. Yet all too soon this trust is disappointed, and it is revealing that with its frustration Titus' belief in a sociable and amicable nature of humankind also dwindles:

> These old fellows
> Have their ingratitude in them hereditary.
> Their blood is caked, 'tis cold, it seldom flows,
> 'Tis lack of kindly warmth they are not kind;
> And nature as it grows again toward earth
> Is fashioned for the journey, dull and heavy. (II.2.214–19)

Timon eventually snubs his former friends and allies with a banquet at which the offered dishes turn out to be mere lukewarm water. Even before this revelation, Timon prepares his aristocratic guests with a speech that clearly shows his disappointment with Renaissance ideas of the virtue of man lying in his deeds:

> For your own gifts, make yourselves praised, but reserve still to give, lest your deities be despised. Lend to each man enough, that one need not lend to another, for were your godheads to borrow of men, men would forsake the gods. (III.7.70–4)

This is strong stuff indeed, since it equates religion with investment, but also denies the idea of altruism by declaring good deeds a careful strategy to increase one's social standing. By offending his guests, Timon ruins his. After a tirade of invectives, he pronounces a telling verdict: 'henceforth hated be / Of Timon man and all humanity!' (III.7.103–4). Yet what does it imply? Is Timon not a man and part of humanity? Does his hatred include himself – in which case it would be the result of a frustrated idealism, a disappointed humanism? Or does he believe that he can stand outside humanity, in which case the question would be: as what? For his guests, the answer is clear: 'Lord Timon's mad' (III.7.113). Madness is a form of alterity that confirms the norms, as Michel Foucault has famously pointed out (Foucault, 1988). Yet is Timon's behaviour that of a simple madman?

Timon removes himself from the Athens that he has learned to revile. His parting curse, however, shows him as a careful analyst of Athenian society still:

> ... Matrons, turn incontinent;
> Obedience, fail in children; slaves and fools,
> Pluck the grave wrinkled senate from the bench

And minister in their steads. To general filths
Convert o'th' instant, green virginity,
Do't in your parents' eyes. Bankrupts, hold fast;
Rather than render back, out with your knives
And cut your trusters' throats! Bound servants, steal:
Large-handed robbers your grave masters are,
And pill by law. Maid, to thy master's bed,
Thy mistress is o'th' brothel. Son of sixteen,
Pluck the lined crutch from thy old limping sire,
With it beat out his brains. Piety, and fear,
Religion to the gods, peace, justice, truth,
Domestic awe, night-rest and neighbourhood,
Instruction, manners, mysteries and trades,
Degrees, observances, customs, and laws,
Decline to your confounding contraries –
And let confusion live! (IV.1.3–21)

He knows the structures of his society very well, and his wish to see them perverted through reversion is not a sign of an alien status, much less of a newly discovered alien 'nature' (whatever this might be).[8] Yet a divorce from mankind is what he aims to achieve. His method is a paradoxical one, since it resembles a traditional form of withdrawal from human society: becoming a hermit in a cave. His final statement even smacks (doubly paradoxically, since Timon must needs be a pagan) of Christian orthodoxy:

Timon will to the woods; where he shall find
Th' unkindest beast more kinder than mankind.
The gods confound – hear me, you good gods all! –
Th' Athenians both within and out that wall,
And grant as Timon grows his hate may grow
To the whole race of mankind, high and low!
Amen. (IV.1.35–40)

Timon curses all creation, but his bitterest scorn is reserved for mankind – and this includes himself:

... All's obliquy,
There's nothing level in our cursed natures
But direct villany. Therefore be abhorred
All feasts, societies and throngs of men!

> His semblable, yea himself, Timon disdains:
> Destruction fang mankind! ... (IV.3.18–23)

Yet does this make him a posthumanist or merely an antihumanist? The reference to the accursed nature of mankind is again Christian orthodoxy. That the character Timon continues to be defined as a man, a human being, and that he remains painfully aware of it, becomes evident when the place of his retirement is approached by the Athenian captain Alcibiades, who has in the meantime also turned against his own city:

> ALCIBIADES   What art thou there? Speak.
> TIMON   A beast, as thou art. The canker gnaw thy heart
>   For showing me again the eyes of man!
> ALCIBIADES   What is thy name? Is man so hateful to thee
>   That art thyself a man?
> TIMON   I am Misanthropos and hate mankind.
>   For thy part, I do wish thou wert a dog
>   That I might love thee something. (IV.3.49–56)

Alcibiades outlines Timon's crux neatly by countering the latter's sophist beast riddle with a hint both at names and at self-referentiality. Man is the signifying animal, and among his powers is self-naming, self-definition. By naming himself 'Misanthropos', hater of man, Timon also calls himself a man, while simultaneously trying to turn himself into a cliché, a character defined intertextually rather than as an individual essence. When he declares that he would prefer if Alcibiades were a dog, he also puns on the old identification of cynics with canines and implies that, as a fellow detester of norms he would find his questioner more sympathetic.

Timon continues by offending the two women who accompany Alcibiades with misogynist references to whores and venereal disease (indeed he repeatedly insinuates that society is a whore – a belated reference to his own weakness of buying his popularity). One of them, Timandra, tellingly responds by calling him 'monster' (IV.3.87). Then he poses Alcibiades a challenge that he cannot win:

> Promise me friendship, but perform none.
> If thou wilt not promise, the gods plague thee,
> For thou art a man; if thou dost perform,
> Confound thee, for thou art a man! (IV.3.73–6)

While at first glance a paradox, the challenge contains once again the basic ingredient of early modern humanism: the notion of sociability, the friendship of free and educated, that is, privileged, men. Yet Timon unsettles these foundations by not only implying that sociability is a performative act, since it rests on promises. He also points out that even the positive performance of friendship merely indicates that one is human, part of humanity, and therefore tied to its rituals and norms. Since Timon has recently become a victim of these symbolic agreements (whose possible violation is part and parcel of their force), he cannot see the merit in them. They both rely on one being a man and demand that one shows oneself a man – and thereby simultaneously and contradictorily use a model of humanity as essence and as role.[9]

Athens is to Timon like mankind: he cannot live with (or in) it, but neither can he exist without it. 'Without' here represents both deprivation and separation. He cannot be defined as a human being, a 'man' in the terminology of his time, outside civilized society. Yet, as a self-defined civilized man with ideals, he also cannot live in society either. As anthropocentric beings, humans can only think from the vantage point of human beings. Even positing the alien (be it as monster, subhuman, or animal) requires an anthropocentric starting point. As human beings born and raised in a particular civilization (and the merger of imagined Classical Greece and Renaissance England here does not double the perspective), their views will be those of this civilization, no matter how much they try to negate them.

Yet being tied to a human perspective does not automatically signal the unproblematic victory of a residual humanism. It is precisely society's symbolic measure of identity and value that undermines its definition of successfully achieved humanity in the very act of creating it. This symbolic measure also forms the connection of early modern humanism with orthodox antihumanism in the shape of Marxist thinking, for it is nothing but gold. Gold, and by implication the status that wealth guarantees, had been the measure of Timon's success at the start of the play as much as it proved the measure of his downfall afterwards. Yet the allure of gold cannot simply be overcome. Timon's servant, whom the play characterizes as devoted to his master throughout, formulates this naively when he declares: 'Whilst I have gold, I'll be his steward still' (IV.2.51).

Gold provides the means of identity, but as a universal exchange mechanism, it lacks any intrinsic value of its own. Marx formulates this in connection with what has replaced gold: money.[10] Yet an identity is what humanism's essentialism requires for the functioning of its miraculously self-creating human being. It is therefore telling that, when Timon discovers a treasure while digging for roots (a coincidence that introduces both an element of romance into the play and echoes of medieval *exempla* – along the lines of Chaucer's *Pardoner's Tale*), he abhors using his new-found wealth to buy himself back into society. Indeed he merely uses it to taunt Alcibiades as well as a couple of sailors, the poet, the painter and the senators who follow in his footsteps once news of Timon's treasure reaches them. The mere rumour of recovered wealth suffices to turn Timon from an outsider into a figure in demand.

The play's final twist, however, is that he uses the treasure neither for a restoration of his privileged status nor for revenge (along the lines of many texts, the most famous of which is Alexandre Dumas's *Count of Monte Cristo*). Criticism has been puzzled by this. Yet it makes sense when one sees Timon as an unwilling humanist, a more than willing antihumanist, yet a failed posthumanist. Realizing that he cannot escape being a representative of the human even by shunning human society, his figure remains tied to society's norms and mechanisms of exchange – in which gold stands for the ultimately empty self-production of worth in direct correlation to humanism's empty celibate machine of self-fashioning. The most radical thing that he can do is refuse to participate in these exchanges. He neither returns nor interferes, but instead dies and disappears from the plot of the play that bears his name.

His disappearance, however, provides the play with its final chance to confront its residual humanism with an image of its own alterity – in the shape of Timon's enigmatic tomb inscription. The very last thing we hear about him is the report by a soldier who, instead of discovering the man, only finds Timon's grave:

> Who's here? Speak, ho! No answer! What is this?
> *Timon is dead, who hath outstretched his span:*
> *Some beast read this; there does not live a man.*
> Dead, sure; and this his grave; what's on this tomb
> I cannot read. The character I'll take with wax;
> Our captain hath in every figure skill,
> An aged interpreter, though young in days. (V.4.2–10)

Timon's grave inscription presents a multiple riddle. The soldier who discovers it is illiterate, thus not part of the privileged élite. Yet only for those, whom Timon has rejected, can the inscription have been made. That it comes as a negative is symbolic: it presents the reversed image of an identity that had desired to be a negative of Athens' civilization – and failed. As a double negation (and a failed refusal of communication), however, it is easily 'interpreted' and translated into the terms in which Athenian humanism wishes to think, also of itself. Alcibiades, the skilful captain, reads out Timon's farewell curse:

> *Here lie I, Timon, who alive all living men did hate,*
> *Pass by and curse thy fill, but pass and stay not here thy gait.* (V.5.70–1)

Spookily like a nineteenth-century German-speaking scholar, he then translates the multiple contradictions into a smooth and unified explanation:

> These well express in thee thy latter spirits.
> Though thou abhorred'st in us our human griefs,
> Scorned'st our brains' flow and those our droplets which
> From niggard nature fall, yet rich conceit
> Taught thee to make vast Neptune weep for aye
> On thy low grave, on faults forgiven. Dead
> Is noble Timon, of whose memory
> Hereafter more. (V.5.72–9)

It acknowledges Timon's misanthropic antihumanism, yet at the same time, by invoking Renaissance humanist set-pieces such as nature and classical gods, turns Timon exactly into what he refused to be until the last: humanist symbolic capital in the shape of 'noble Timon', not a proper person but a representative figure. Alcibiades' speech even contains a self-referential nod in the direction of Shakespeare's play itself, which forms part of the conspiracy not to let Timon escape the clutches of a civilized interpretation. Many scholars have followed his lead by explaining away Timon's strategy as a form of madness or mistaken extremism. It is only in his ultimately self-destructive opposition, however, that his character finds a viable, though extremely uncomfortable, position where it can be authentic without conforming to civilized norms that are as essentialist as they are hollow.

Pericles, Prince of Tyre – alien encounters

If Timon is a torn antihumanist figure who fails to become a posthumanist alien, Pericles is an alien from the start. Despite his privileged status as an aristocrat and ruler, he is alien geographically, socially and most damningly in his treatment of his wife and child. He is alien too in the way his character and its adventures are constructed. Only twenty years after the first production of the play, which was most likely authored by Shakespeare and George Wilkins, Ben Jonson condemned it as 'some mouldy tale ... and stale / As the Shrieve's crusts, and nasty as his fish – / Scraps out of every dish / Throwne forth, and rak't into the common tub' (Jonson, 1934, pp. 179–80). What he objects to is the blatantly intertextual nature of the episodic play, its recycling and paratactic assembly of established stories of adventure and mishap, something that even the play's first printed version in the corrupt Quarto edition of 1609 (it was, like *Timon of Athens*, not included in the First Folio) acknowledged in the play's subtitle, 'With the true Relation of the whole Historie, / aduentures, and fortunes of the said Prince: / As also, / The no lesse strange, and worthy accidents, / in the Birth and Life, of his daughter / MARIANA' (Shakespeare, 1990, p. 10).

What Jonson's new neoclassical thinking abhorred, the jumbling together of plots and characters, had been common and popular before. Shakespeare and his collaborator indeed freely pilfered from Chaucer's contemporary John Gower, who had himself retold the well-known classical story of Apollonius of Tyre solving a riddle at great personal risk. For Jonson, *Pericles* lacks integrity and authenticity, yet his neo-classical criticism of early modern *bricolage* also reminds us that not all protagonists in Renaissance plays, indeed only a small minority, match the essentialist notion of budding individuality that later periods loved to project into them. The present chapter thus prefers the terms 'figure' and 'character' for them.

Before we encounter the figure of an Apollonius who has become a Pericles, Shakespeare and his co-author indeed put intertextuality itself on the stage: the poet Gower introduces the story. In the same way that *Timon of Athens* ends with a waxen negative of a message, *Pericles* starts with an echo of an echo. This reminder of the transmitted nature of what we are going to see indeed recurs at the start of each act.

Rather undramatically, the narrator Gower also gives away the riddle that Pericles has to solve in Act I when he comes from his native Tyre to Antioch to woo the daughter of its ruler, Antiochus:

> *I am no viper, yet I feed*
> *On mother's flesh which did me breed.*
> *I sought a husband, in which labour*
> *I found that kindness in a father.*
> *He's father, son, and husband mild;*

I mother, wife, and yet his child:
How they may be, and yet in two,
As you will live, resolve it you. (I.1.65–72)

The riddle, which has cost numerous suitors their lives, concerns
the incestuous relationship of Antiochus and his daughter. Yet it is more
than just a conventional romance device (taken up, for instance, in *The
Merchant of Venice*). It is too obvious to really represent the encryption
of a secret and has far more general implication than the simultaneous hiding and showing of family relations gone wrong. Incest, Freud
reminds us, threatens the core of civilization by endangering it not
merely genetically, but also in its closest nucleus of community.[11] The
family was also the cornerstone of Renaissance thinking. A corrupt
family at the heart of a state thus signalled the collapse of all civilized
values, from the individual to the political. Pericles, the alien at the
court of Antiochus, encounters the alien in the shape of incest exactly
where he wishes to found his own family and dynasty. It is not by accident that Antiochus merely bears the name of the city he rules and his
daughter lacks a name altogether. Their crime renders them unfit to be
full characters.

Yet Pericles also becomes tainted by what he discovers, indeed even
before he does so. When he accepts that failure to solve the riddle
will lead to his death, he thanks Antiochus, 'who hath taught / My
frail mortality to know itself' (I.1.42–3). *Nosce te ipsum*, know thyself,
the classical dictum, was also a cornerstone of early modern human
self-conception. Here, however, it is provided by someone who stands
outside civilized humanity altogether. He might not be the only one,
though, for if Antiochus is a bad riddler, Pericles is an incompetent
reader. When he encounters Antiochus's daughter, 'clothed like a bride'
(I.1.7) (and therefore possibly veiled), he rhapsodies:

See where she comes, apparelled like the spring,
Graces her subjects, and her thoughts the king
Of every virtue gives renown to men;
Her face the book of praises, where is read
Nothing but curious pleasures, as from thence
Sorrow were ever razed, and testy wrath
Could never be her mild companion.
You gods that made me man and sway in love,
That have inflamed desire in my breast
To taste the fruit of yon celestial tree
Or die in the adventure, be my helps,

As I am son and servant to your will,
To compass such a boundless happiness. (I.1.13–25)

In his naive and premature conventional praises, he mistakes the character of his intended so radically that one has to question Pericles' self-definition. His status is further undermined by his promiscuous way of finding symbolic family relations himself. In the speech just quoted he calls himself 'son and servant' to the gods. After Antiochus' brief interjection 'Prince Pericles – ', he instantly declares, 'That would be son to great Antiochus – ' (I.1.26–7). His integrity, in short, is questionable, and this shows also when it comes to announcing the solution to the riddle.

Discovering that it would be highly inopportune to do so, Pericles hides behind vague formulas. Indeed a double game of pretence ensues when Antiochus realizes that Pericles knows his secret and promises him forty more days to come up with the solution. Neither of them acts honestly, and Pericles even engages in an act of sophist speculation that makes truth meaningless altogether: 'If it be true that I interpret false, / Then were it certain you were not so bad' (I.1.125–6).[12] To knowing himself and the world, crucial humanist tenets, he shows himself alienated. Indeed he alienates himself even further when, rather than facing his new enemy Antiochus, he flees from Antiochus' potential wrath. Yet not even a melancholy stay in his native Tyre seems sufficient. He needs to go to a third place, Tarsus. Both the discovered incest and his failure to address it adequately have also destabilized Pericles' normality by making his home alien to him, too, a home on which his identity as a prince depends.

This also becomes clear in the speech he makes to his advisor Helcanus, to whom he entrusts the safety and government of the city of Tyre: 'But in our orbs we'll live so round and safe / That time of both this truth shall ne'er convince: / Thou showed'st a subject's shine, I a true prince' (I.2.120–2). The universes of the two socially very different men are both imagined as equally ideal and equally closed-off from reality. Instead of showing himself as a ruler, Pericles desires to reinvent himself as a figure that is autonomous to the degree of becoming monadic, but only succeeds in mistaking his role.

And things get even worse. After helping Tarsus to cope with a famine, he is shipwrecked in Pentapolis. Although destitute, when he hears that the daughter of Pentapolis' king Simonides is available, he instantly sees himself as a suitor once again. He clearly has not learned from his previous experiences. The narrator Gower introduces this new adventure with a cynical reference to human self-confidence: 'where each man / Thinks all is writ he speken can, / And to remember what he does / Build his statue to make him glorious' (II.Chorus.11–14). Pericles only seemingly shows humbleness by referring to himself as 'A man, whom both the waters and the wind / In that vast tennis-court, hath made the ball / For them to play upon' (II.1.58–60). His conceit gives it away as exactly the self-stylization and self-textualization that Gower identifies with human hubris.[13]

Romance convention decrees that he wins the tournaments and Simonides' daughter's Thaisa's heart. Yet Thaisa, too, behaves in a dubious way. She tells her father in a letter that she will marry none but Pericles: 'Now to my daughter's letter. / She tells me here she'll wed the stranger knight, / Or never more to view nor day nor light' (II.5.14–16). Renaissance women, particularly aristocratic ones, did not choose their own husbands, and they certainly did not blackmail their fathers, at least not in the idealized world of romances. Further noteworthy here is yet another form of indirect communication: after the imprint in *Timon of Athens* and the riddle of the opening of *Pericles*, we now have a letter, a rather impractical device for a daughter who sees her father every day. All these forms of communication are prone to misunderstanding, misinterpretation or downright abuse. Yet, as Gower states, the self-perception of human beings becomes increasingly textual exactly at a time when humanism expects it to assert its essential 'nature'. The very play bears witness to this in its patchwork structure.

When Simonides offers his daughter to Pericles – he indeed shows him Thaisa's letter and urges him to become her 'schoolmaster' (II.5.39) – Pericles at first politely declares himself unworthy. When Simonides then accuses him of having bewitched his daughter and being a traitor (i.e. wishing to destabilize his rule), yet another game of mutual pretence takes place:

SIMONIDES Ay, traitor.
PERICLES   Even in his throat, unless it be the king,
           That calls me traitor, I return the lie.
SIMONIDES [*aside.*]
           Now, by the gods I do applaud his courage. (II.5.53–6)

Who are we supposed to trust in this charade? Who is traitor to whom, who is prince and who is king? Identities become alienated from themselves exactly at the moment when both the conventions of marriage negotiations and of state policy require authenticity.[14] The game of mutual deception continues after the arrival of Thaisa and includes her:

SIMONIDES   Yea, mistress, are you so peremptory?
           (*aside*) I am glad on't with all my heart.
           – I'll tame you, I'll bring you in subjection.
           Will you, not having my consent,
           Bestow your love and your affections
           Upon a stranger? (*aside*) Who for aught I know
           May be (nor can I think the contrary)
           As great in blood as I myself. (II.5.71–8)

No character is to be trusted, and yet on their mutual trust depend political and personal fates. It is therefore perhaps more than yet another romance convention, that of coincidence, that parts Thaisa and Pericles in yet another convenient storm. Thaisa had just given birth on board ship, and the sailors superstitiously demand the removal of her lifeless body. Pericles, despite being prince, allows himself to be outvoted, another sign of his unstable identity.

Things become entirely incredible, though, when he soon afterwards also loses his newborn daughter Marina. Afraid for her fragile health, he leaves her at Tarsus with the governor Cleon and his wife Dionyza, whose gratitude he thinks he can count on ever since he has helped them in the earlier famine. Yet, once again, Pericles' judgement proves deficient. When Marina grows into a beautiful girl, Cleon and Dionyza fear her as a competitor for their own daughter and plan to murder her. Marina is saved by another coincidence: pirates kidnap her and sell her into a brothel in Mytilene.

While it was common to leave one's sons with foster parents to strengthen aristocratic connections, it was rarer to do the same with girls. Losing one's wife, especially in childbirth, was also not uncommon. Yet keeping one's offspring together was vital for dynastic and non-dynastic families alike.[15] Pericles once again carelessly scatters his identity, here that which rests on his family and lineage.

Marina, too, proves an alien in more than one environment. First she is an unsuitable foster child, then an extremely unlikely prostitute whose services to her customers consist of persuading them to give up their sinful ways. A virgin in a brothel might symbolize the victory of innate human goodness and strength in the face of adversity – and thus confirm humanist ideals. Marina's story, however, smacks more of Catholic saint's legends of old and is used by the play for several scenes of lewd jokes and thereby turned from a model case to an eccentric one. Thus, the bawd in her brothel comments on her: 'She's able to freeze the god Priapus and undo a whole generation' (IV.6.12–13). Pandar, the pimp, indeed simply calls her unusual attitude a disease, 'green sickness' (IV.6.21), which was diagnosed in women as a sign of sexual frustration.

The third alien in this trinity is Thaisa who is washed up on the shore of Ephesus, revived and enters the temple of Diana as a priestess. Again, her decisions are questionable. As the wife of a prince, it would be her duty to seek him out or at least return to his country. As a wife and mother it would be her obligation to attempt a reunion with her family. Yet she immediately gives up any of these options when she learns of the shipwreck. The choice of Diana as the deity she worships is telling. As the goddess of hunting and chastity, she represents the very opposite of Thaisa's former identity. In the same way that Pericles turns himself into an isolated wanderer and Marina becomes an unlikely virginal prostitute, Thaisa also becomes an alien from her former self, and all three selves were by no means established identities, but mere flat, underdeveloped characters.

Diana, the goddess that Pericles also swears by, is associated with femininity and fickleness – rather than the firmness and masculinity that he ought to represent as a ruler. In a strange gesture that makes him resemble Timon of Athens, he vows to turn himself into the resemblance of an uncivilized barbarian by not cutting his hair until his daughter is married:

> Till she be married, madam,
> By bright Diana whom we honour all,
> Unscissored shall this hair of mine remain,
> Though I show ill in't. (III.3.28–31)

Looking impressive was required of an ideal Renaissance man, as was attested by Hoby's translation of Castiglione's *Il Corteggiano*. Pericles once again falls short of contemporary ideals.

It is in fact divine intervention, that of the goddess Diana, and not human capability that leads the chaotic plots of the plays to a satisfactory, if implausible conclusion. But before that, Pericles' fate seems to take a further turn for the worse: after returning to Tarsus, he is told by Cleon and Dionyza that Marina is dead. His reaction is again typical: he removes himself further from the ideal of a prince and ruler:

> He swears
> Never to wash his face nor cut his hairs.
> He puts on sackcloth and to sea he bears

A tempest which his mortal vessel tears,
And yet he rides it out. (IV.4.27–31)

Pericles' identity has in fact been at sea throughout the play. There is
no stability in his character. Neither does it know a fixed location. If the
humanist ideal is man resting in the centre of a universe that he himself has, if not completely created, at least meaningfully charted, then
Pericles is the very opposite.[16]

Yet, contrary to Timon, who violates the norms by doing the opposite
of what is required (such as seeking isolation and solitude rather than
sociability), Pericles' rule-breaking is as undirected as his journeys. In
this he is the analogue of the play's ramshackle episodic and intertextual structure. Things happen in it as they happen to him. Humanist
measures, rules and centres have become unstable and dislocated. One
location is as good as another, and everywhere tragedy may strike in
the same way as a happy end might be miraculously achieved. Indeed
the narrator Gower describes Pericles' attitude after learning of the
death of his daughter as his determination to 'bear his courses to be
ordered / By Lady Fortune' (IV.4.47–8). He has given up any claim to
self-determination, a central tenet of Renaissance humanism.

Indeed the play has two happy ends rather than one. The first
reunites Pericles with Marina; the second father and daughter with
Thaisa. When Pericles meets Marina in the house of the nobleman
Lysimachus where she has been working as a private tutor after being
thrown out of the brothel, he instantly notices her resemblance to
his wife, Thaisa. What could easily have turned into another incest
story to match the play's opening is, however, quickly and somewhat
surprisingly, turned into a perfect recognition. After all the mistaken
identities and characters in the play, now all identifications work: the
name Marina, that of her nurse Lychoria, and finally and most significantly the name of the father, Pericles himself, bring about not merely
a partial family reunion but also the establishment of proper order in
which Pericles can be a ruler with a dynastic line and Marina a princess
rather than a servant:

You think me an impostor. No, good faith.
I am the daughter to King Pericles,
If good King Pericles be. (V.1.167–9)

One does not have to be a Lacanian to identify the name of the father
here with the name of the law. Yet it is a law that has not remained

unbroken throughout the play; in fact it had been suspended by the very agent who ought to have represented it.[17]

Working through / with / against humanism from within

Lacanian recognition as misrecognition also applies to the principle that is supposed to guarantee symbolic stability in *Pericles* as in *Timon of Athens*,[18] and Marina's sly afterthought 'If good King Pericles be' not merely relates to the question if prince Pericles is alive or not, but also if he is himself, if symbolic power and its human representative have achieved the identity that the concept of the two bodies of the king both postulates and turns into a paradox (cf. Kantorowicz, 1970). That symbolic certainty does not bear the signature of Pericles is attested when even the reference to his own name and paternity prove insufficient to convince him. After first declaring 'this is Marina!', he instantly continues his interrogation with 'What was thy mother's name? Tell me but that, / For truth can never be confirmed enough' (V.1.189–91). Truth indeed should only need confirmation once. But just like the identities in the play, its stability is in doubt. Hence the need for another confirmation – and another happy end. Already the recognition of – and by – his daughter had noticeably changed Pericles and seemingly reintegrated him into the harmonious order of things. He now realizes his uncivilized appearance and claims to hear the music of the spheres, an expression of universal harmony: '– Give me my robes. [*They do so.*] I am wild in my beholding. / O heavens bless my girl! But hark, what music? / [...] The music of the spheres' (V.1.211–12, 216).

As has already been stated, it takes divine intervention to turn the fragmented plot of the play into a whole. Interestingly enough, what the goddess Diana demands of Pericles is once again textual, a repetition of his misfortunes, a retelling of the complicated tales of separation and alienation:

> DIANA   My temple stands in Ephesus. Hie thee thither,
> And do upon mine altar sacrifice.
> There when my maiden priests are met together,
> ... before the people all,
> Reveal how thou at sea didst lose thy wife.
> To mourn thy crosses with thy daughter's, call
> And give them repetition to the life. (V.1.227–33)

When Pericles does Diana's bidding, Thaisa, who officiates as a priestess, hears his – and her own – story from his mouth: 'Voice and favour! / You are, you are, O royal Pericles!' (V.3.13–14), and faints. Her outcry doubles Pericles again – twice – into voice and favour and into a double exclamation of his identity. Yet repetition, as in the case of truth above, undermines that which it is meant to confirm. When Thaisa gains consciousness again, she therefore asks: 'Are you not Pericles? Like him you spake, / Like him you are' (V.3.32–3). Resemblance is all she can confirm, in the same way as Pericles throughout the play merely resembled a ruler and prince (in the same way as Timon tried to resemble a hermit).

Thaisa's identity is equally dubious: 'The voice of dead Thaisa!' (V.3.34) is all that Pericles is able to recognize, a voice rather than a person, and a memory rather than a presence. In fact it requires Thaisa's presentation of a ring to convince Pericles fully. And even then, the sequence of misrecognition and doubt – which ironically echoes the game of deception that was their courtship – is not yet at an end. When Pericles' regent Helicanus hails his new-found queen, she bluntly replies, 'I know you not' (V.3.49). It once again requires text and its repetition, an echo of the play's overly intertextual nature,[19] to set things right, or as right as they can be in a play of misguided and mistaken identities:

> PERICLES You have heard me say, when I did fly from Tyre
> I left behind an ancient substitute.
> Can you remember what I called the man?
> I have named him oft.
> THAISA. 'Twas Helicanus then. (V.3.50–4)

The game of repetitions is not yet at an end. Pericles instructs another lord, Cerimon, to 'deliver / How this dead queen relives?' (V.3.63–4). The story gains credibility in the retelling, contrary to common sense where retelling, as in the case of the interpretation in *Timon of Athens*, is always prone to error, falsification and abuse. While Pericles finally changes his appearance into that which corresponds to his role ('And now this ornament / Makes me look dismal will I clip to form, / And what this fourteen years no razor touched'; V.3.74–6), Thaisa once again defines identity and value (now of Marina's betrothed, Lord Cerimon) by words and text: 'Lord Cerimon hath letters of good credit, sir' (V.3.78). Letters of good credit are references, other people's opinions put down in the susceptible form of writing. 'Credit' also echoes the financial status of the person thus described and takes us back to *Timon of Athens* where Timon's credit so drastically diminished.

If Pericles fails to learn in the play that bears his name,[20] neither do others, most noticeably his wife. Identities are perilous, since they rely on (often false) reports, words and statements not only made up by others but also made up in inauthentic words and quotations, just like the fabric of the play itself. As an exposition of early modern identity it denies more than it confirms. Self-determination is only rarely in evidence (even Marina's in the brothel is dubious in its irony and wiped away when she is simply made to marry Cerimon). Self-knowledge is equally often mistaken, as is the proper recognition of others, as the drastic mistake of believing Cleon and Dionyza to be friends and allies proves. *Nosce te ipsum*, the basic tenet of humanism, refuses to function in this play, and as a consequence, the self-determined mapping of the social sphere as well as the world becomes a hazardous game. It is ruled neither by human ingenuity nor by a benevolent or vengeful Christian God, but instead by a fickle pagan goddess. In this, the play conforms to Renaissance modes of reiterating the classics, but it crosses out any claims to a plausible humanism it might contain.

If *Timon of Athens* demonstrates the despair of a character about merely being a figure in a discursive network that attributes identities and values according to the glossy but ultimately meaningless medium of gold and simultaneously this very character's inability to leave his status as a figure behind, *Pericles* shows the failure of figuration proper. Pericles is all things to everybody. Yet as the symbolic figurehead that ought to guarantee political identity and stability as well as the dramatic integrity of the play, he not only proves the impossibility of bringing identity together in a plausible character but also demonstrates actively but unwittingly that figuration requires signification, text, tales and their repetition, in other words, intertextuality, in the same way as any desired identity and authenticity is undermined by these ingredients.[21]

For a humanist reading, this is at best a failure and at worst a catastrophe. For Shakespeare's contemporaries, ironically, it proved no problem; indeed it perhaps contributed to their enjoyment of the play.[22] For posthumanist approaches it offers *Pericles*, even more than *Timon of Athens*, as evidence of a thinking through and thinking beyond the supposed essentials of an emerging humanism already and exactly at a time when these were first formulated.[23]

Notes

1. F. D. Hoeniger's Preface to the Arden edition of *Pericles*, for instance, calls the play 'far from happy and clear', 'a most uneven and puzzling text', and

admits that 'No one would include *Pericles* among Shakespeare's masterpieces' (Shakespeare, 1990, p. vii). Suzanne Gossett (Shakespeare, 2004, p. 1) is more generous. There she calls it 'an anomaly in the Shakespeare canon' and 'a uniquely damaged text', but also stresses that it 'is one of Shakespeare's most popular plays' (p. 2). The Introduction to the Arden edition of *Timon of Athens* labels it 'a peculiar and to some unpalatable play' and emphasizes 'many loose ends and insufficiently integrated episodes' (Shakespeare and Middleton, 2008, p. 1). All further references to the plays given in the text are to the last two editions.

2. 'Deutschland ist Hamlet!,' 'Germany is Hamlet!', is the opening line of Ferdinand Freiligrath's patriotic poem 'Hamlet' of 1844.

3. Jacob Burckhardt, whose study *Civilization of the Renaissance in Italy* of 1860 had been influential in shaping the idea of a Renaissance humanism, was in fact Swiss (cf. Davies, 1997, pp. 15–20).

4. Its genre (tragedy, morality play or satire) is disputed (cf. Slights, 1977).

5. Marx's theories are seen as responses to humanism both by proponents of his so-called antihumanism and his supposed posthumanism (cf. Davies, 1997, pp. 11–13; and Badmington, 2000, pp. 4–5).

6. For examples of this approach to posthumanism via science fiction, see Badmington (2004) and Bukatman (2000, pp. 98–111).

7. That it was associated with excess in Shakespeare's time is elaborated in Miola (1980).

8. Indeed, as Clifford Davidson stresses, 'Traditionally, Timon had been known in the Renaissance as the image of a more or less unmotivated misanthrope who was believed to have lived in the Athens of Socrates, Plato, and Aristophanes' (Davidson, 1980, p. 184).

9. This dilemma recurs in several Shakespeare plays, for example, in *Coriolanus*, in which the eponymous protagonist exclaims in futile protest: 'Rather say, I play / The man I am' (III.2.14–17).

10. '[M]oney has no price. In order to form part of this uniform relative form of value of the other commodities, it would have to be brought into relation with itself as its own equivalent' (Marx, 1976, I, p. 189).

11. The first chapter of Sigmund Freud's *Totem and Taboo* is called 'The Horror of Incest' (Freud, 1985).

12. While historicizing the language of treason, Steven Mullaney also points out the excessive and subject-destabilizing power of the riddle: 'But these riddles, prophecies, or amphibologies involve something other than treason lying or disguising itself. They exceed and usurp the intentions of the traitor himself, bifurcating choice and intentionality' (Mullaney, 1988, p. 121).

13. Annette C. Flower confirms my view even though she tries to state the opposite when she claims that 'Pericles comes through the storm affirming only his essential mortality', but proves throughout her essay that Pericles simply switches from one disguise to another (Flower, 1975, p. 32).

14. The link between misrecognition (of gifts, obligations and roles) in connection with political power and authority is the theme in Mullaney (2000).

15. Marianne Novy sees this slightly differently (2000).

16. Elizabeth Biemann is thus doubly mistaken when she tries to subject Pericles to a Jungian reading in which Pericles is an example of 'delayed individuation' and the archetypal representative of the *puer aeternus*. Rather, he is a

completely unstable character assuming different and equally unconvincing roles whenever he encounters a new textual and intertextual scenario (Biemann, 1990, pp. 19, 37).

17. Robert Grainger wishes to interpret the reunion of Pericles and Marina in Jungian terms as a healing of a damaged psyche, yet even he has to admit that they are 'united *by* story' (2008, p. 103; his emphasis).

18. 'It is not a question of knowing whether I speak of myself in a way that conforms to what I am, but rather of knowing whether I am the same as that of which I speak' (Lacan, 1977, p. 165).

19. T. G. Bishop sees this at work even in the play's structure when he states: 'In *Pericles, Prince of Tyre* Shakespeare deliberately set out to resuscitate a dramatic style some twenty years out of date, and thereby made transmission and revival the central concerns of the play' (1996, p. 93).

20. Howard Felperin also notices Pericles' misconception of himself, but is a little too optimistic when he writes: 'Although his claim to self-knowledge is premature (the state he describes will not be realized until the last act), he speaks and behaves like the protagonist of a morality play. Pericles is presented as a kind of Everyman' (2002, p. 117). Yet Pericles is not an Everyman. As prince of an exotic city he is clearly marked as a special character.

21. This conforms, in fact, remarkably well to the definition of the posthuman in terms of cybernetics by N. Katherine Hayles as 'an informational material entity' (Hayles, 1999, p. 11).

22. Hayles, whose literary examples are all postmodern rather than early modern, again provides an interesting parallel when she reiterates in her conclusion that 'the prospect of becoming posthuman both evokes terror and pleasure' (1999, p. 283).

23. Neil Badmington's cautionary demand, 'Posthumanism ... needs theory, needs theorizing, needs above all to reconsider the untimely celebration of the absolute end of "Man"', would therefore have to be supplemented by: 'It needs history, too' (Badmington, 2003, p. 10).

Works cited

Badmington, Neil (2003) 'Theorizing Posthumanism', *Cultural Critique* 53, Posthumanism (Winter), pp. 10–27.

Badmington, Neil (ed.) (2000) *Posthumanism*, Readers in Cultural Criticism, Basingstoke: Palgrave, now Palgrave Macmillan.

Biemann, Elizabeth (1990) *William Shakespeare: The Romances*, TEAS, 478, Boston: Twayne.

Bishop, T. G. (1996) *Shakespeare and the Theatre of Wonder*, Cambridge Studies in Renaissance Literature and Culture 9, Cambridge, New York and Melbourne: Cambridge University Press.

Buck, August (1990) 'Einleitung', in Giovanni Pico della Mirandola, *De hominis dignitate: Über die Würde des Menschen*, trans. Norbert Baumgarten, ed. August Buck, Philosophische Bibliothek 427, Hamburg: Felix Meiner Verlag, pp. vii–xxvii.

Bukatman, Scott (2000) 'Postcards from the Posthuman Solar System', in Badmington (2000), pp. 98–111.

Davidson, Clifford (1980) '*Timon of Athens*: The Iconography of False Friendship', *The Huntington Library Quarterly* 43.3 (Summer), pp. 181–200.

Davies, Tony (1997) *Humanism*, The New Critical Idiom, London and New York: Routledge.

Erasmus, Desiderius (1970) *The Praise of Folly*, trans. Hoyt Hopewell Hudson, Princeton, N.J.: Princeton University Press.

Felperin, Howard (2002) 'The Great Miracle: *Pericles*', in David Skeele (ed.), *Pericles: Critical Essays*, Shakespeare Criticism, New York and London: Garland, pp. 114–32.

Flower, Annette C. (1975) 'Disguise and Identity in *Pericles, Prince of Tyre*', *Shakespeare Quarterly* 26.1 (Winter), pp. 30–41.

Foucault, Michel (1988) *Madness and Civilization: A History of Insanity in the Age of Reason*, trans. Richard Howard, New York: Vintage.

Freud, Sigmund (1985) *The Origins of Religion, Totem and Taboo, Moses and Monotheism and Other Works*, trans. James Strachey, ed. Albert Dickson, The Pelican Freud Library 13, Harmondsworth: Penguin.

Grainger, Robert (2008) *Theatre and Relationships in Shakespeare's Later Plays*, Oxford: Peter Lang.

Greenblatt, Stephen (1980) *Renaissance Self-Fashioning: From More to Shakespeare*, Chicago and London: University of Chicago Press.

Hayles, N. Katherine (1999) *How We Became Posthuman: Virtual Bodies in Cybernetics, Literature, and Informatics*, Chicago and London: University of Chicago Press.

Hoeniger, F. D. (1990) 'Preface', in Shakespeare (1990), pp. i–lxxxix.

Jonson, Ben (1934) 'Ode (to himself)', in H. J. C. Grierson and G. Bullough (eds), *The Oxford Book of Seventeenth Century Verse*, Oxford: Clarendon Press, pp. 179–80.

Kantorowicz, Ernst H. (1970) *The King's Two Bodies: A Study in Medieval Political Theology*, Princeton, N.J.: Princeton University Press.

Lacan, Jacques (1977) 'The Agency of the Letter in the Unconscious or Reason since Freud', *Écrits: A Selection*, trans. Alan Sheridan, London: Tavistock, pp. 146–78.

Marx, Karl (1976) *Capital: A Critique of Political Economy*, trans. Ben Fowkes, 3 vols, Harmondsworth: Penguin.

Miola, Robert S. (1980) 'Timon in Shakespeare's Athens', *Shakespeare Quarterly* 31.1 (Spring), pp. 21–30.

Mullaney, Steven (1988) *The Place of the Stage: License, Play, and Power in Renaissance England*, Chicago: University of Chicago Press, 1988.

Mullaney, Steven (2000) '"All That Monarchs Do": The Obscured Stages of Authority in *Pericles*', in David Skeele (ed.), *Pericles: Critical Essays*, Shakespeare Criticism, New York and London: Garland, pp. 168–83.

Novy, Marianne (2000) 'Multiple Parenting in *Pericles*', in David Skeele (ed.), *Pericles: Critical Essays*, Shakespeare Criticism, New York and London: Garland, pp. 238–48.

Shakespeare, William (1976) *Coriolanus*, ed. Philip Brockbank, The Arden Shakespeare, 2nd edn, London: A & C Black.

Shakespeare, William (1990) *Pericles*, ed. F. D. Hoeniger, Arden Edition of the Works of William Shakespeare, London and New York: Routledge, [1963].

Shakespeare, William (2004) *Pericles*, ed. Suzanne Gossett, The Arden Shakespeare, Third Series, London: Arden Shakespeare.

Shakespeare, William, and Thomas Middleton (2008) *Timon of Athens*, ed. Anthony B. Dawson and Gretchen E. Minton, The Arden Shakespeare, Third Series, London: Cengage Learning.

Slights, William W. E. (1977) '*Genera mixta* and Timon of Athens', *Studies in Philology* 74.1, pp. 39–62.

8
Surviving Truth (*Measure for Measure*)

Mark Robson

In a short but luminous piece written for an Italian newspaper in 1983, 'Translating Kafka', Primo Levi considers the famous final sentences in Kafka's *The Trial*, which he had recently translated. The novel's last words are like 'una pietra tombale', a tombstone, he says (Levi, 1986, p. 142). The English translation of the novel concludes with: 'it was as if the shame of it must outlive him'. Kafka's German reads: 'es war, als sollte die Scham ihn überleben' (Kafka, 2002, p. 312). What does this sense of *überleben*, to outlive, to survive, to live on or live beyond, mean here? For Levi, who translates this as 'e fu come se la vergogna gli dovesse sopravvivere' (Levi, 1986, p. 142), there is nothing enigmatic in the phrase, even if there are many possible and contradictory elements and events in the narrative that might be thought to prompt K.'s shame. There is no mystery because Levi recognizes something in K. that he feels he knows, and this knowledge is to do with the nature of the tribunal that passes judgement on K. rather than that of the judgement itself. As Levi expresses it at the end of his piece: 'È finalmente un tribunale umano, non divino: è fatto di uomini e dagli uomini, e Josef, col coltello già piantato nel cuore, prova vergogna di essere un uomo' (p. 143) ['It is in the end a human, not a divine, tribunal: it is made up of men and by men, and Joseph, with the knife already planted in his heart, feels ashamed of being a man'] (Levi, 1991, p. 109; translation modified).

The relation between the works of Shakespeare and the definition of the human and of humanism has been restated in many forms. The location of the emergence of what we now think of as the modern subject in the early modern period proposed most obviously by certain forms of historicism – particularly in the early stages of new historicism and cultural materialism – has been countered and extended in a resurgence of a humanist reading to be found in texts by critics as diverse as Harold Bloom (1999) and A. D. Nuttall (2007), as well as objected to by those who see the historical claim itself as dubious. Others, notably Joel Fineman and Cynthia Marshall, have sought to complicate the pattern of temporal succession that underpins this notion of emergence, drawing in particular upon Lacanian psychoanalysis (cf. Robson, 2010). And, as in many other areas of literary and cultural studies, early modern studies has also witnessed a turn towards the animal.

At the heart of all of these definitions is a relation between the human individual, the 'world' in which that human is located (whether we think of this in terms of the natural world or some form of social being or human collectivity) and – at the risk of sounding needlessly vague – something else. This something else is most clearly at stake in tragedy, where it appears in the form of God, or gods, or some other signifier of the transcendental such as Fate, Destiny, Fortune, Nature and so on. Later, this will appear as History. There is thus an articulation of the worldly existence of the human (and the non-human) with the super- or sub-human, where this latter category is seen to be determinedly beyond human control. Where Hamlet may perceive a divinity that shapes our ends, and Gloucester can imagine gods who merely sport with human life, Romeo and Juliet can be seen – if we accept the reading of the play offered in the Prologue – as sacrifices to forces that remain determinately beyond them. It is precisely in the recognition of this 'beyond' that the tragic element of tragedy is often seen to lie.

It is not perhaps as obvious how all of this works in genres other than tragedy. Particular problems are presented by a play such as *Measure for Measure*, although this play has been read as especially open to a political reading in which the worst forms of 'Shakespeare's' conservatism are apparent. Thus it becomes a seminal example for both Jonathan Dollimore's and Kathleen McLuskie's essays in *Political Shakespeare* (1994). With Dollimore, critics including Richard Wilson (1996), Leonard Tennenhouse (1986) and Jonathan Goldberg (1983) read the play as a prime example of Foucault's theses on the emergence of the carceral state in *Discipline and Punish*, stressing structures of display, surveillance, power and largely contained transgression. The play has also been repeatedly scoured in order to make its religious dimension yield up something of its author's fidelities, including Nuttall's intriguing reading in terms of Gnosticism (Nutall, 2007, pp. 262–76).

In a more formalist mode, the generic status of the play has also elicited much attention, as well as a certain amount of critical irritation. While some, such as Robert Watson, are happy with the compromise of calling it a tragicomedy, Frank Kermode sees in the play a broken-backed decline from a promising tragic opening half through to a somewhat confused and unconvincing – and, crucially for Kermode, simply uninteresting – comic resolution (Kermode, 2000, pp. 142–64). Watson's take is more forgiving, attributing the bifurcation of the play to two competing principles: sex and death. This is thematized explicitly in the play, he suggests, drawing from this dual impulse, first, a vision of sexuality that is fundamentally comic and generative, that is, that heads towards the happily procreative marriages that the ending conjures through its focus on family and state; and, second, he counterposes to this a tragic vision centred on the individual which subverts any comic promise (Watson, 1994, pp. 103–32). Reading the play either positively or negatively, what most critics agree on is its fundamental impurity of form.

The generic and formal difficulties are impossible to ignore, but these are only some of the many problems that *Measure for Measure* poses. To begin with only one of the most immediate, the significance of the title remains far from evident. What does this phrase 'Measure for Measure' actually mean? The apparent resonance, as all of the editors note, is with the biblical passage to be found in Matthew's Gospel, as part of the Sermon on the Mount: 'Judge not, that ye be not judged. For with what judgment ye judge, ye shall be judged: and with what measure ye mete, it shall be measured to you again'. This chapter of the Gospel develops this sense of measure in explicitly ethical directions: it is here that judgement is related to hypocrisy, here that giving and receiving are established as fundamental elements in the relation between humans and God ('Ask, and it shall be given you'), here that destruction and life are set in balanced opposition, and that Jesus warns of false prophets in sheep's clothing.[1] Various critics have attempted to see in this a suggestion that the pleas for mercy at the end of the play made by Isabella in particular are to be read as an endorsement of a New Testament ethical stance, opposing it to the Duke's use of the idea of the measure in ways which come much closer to the Old Testament Talion law of an eye for an eye. But is this division quite as stark as some would have us see it? The Sermon on the Mount contains a vision of judgement in which it is not only the act of judgement but also the mechanism of judging that is at stake. To make a judgement is to invite judgement. But equally the model of judgement becomes the model according to which you will be judged, in a quasi-pre-echo of the categorical imperative. And the result or measure of that judgement will similarly be redoubled. In each case there is a form of doubleness or repetition at play, an economic relation that slides into a staging of the ethics or politics of response and responsibility.

This queasy evocation of judgement in the title and its extension and revision in the course of the play exemplifies the curious logic that the notion of measure evokes, for measure is always a matter of attempting to sense or master both sameness and difference. We measure in order to know what the relation is between one thing and another, between one moment and another, between one and another where 'another' always marks two possibilities, that it will be another one (and thus the same) or that it will be an other that is different from the one. Measuring is thus always a matter of sharing (holding in common, asserting that there is some common quality or property) or sharing out (dividing) according to the finding of or the failure to find a common measure. This raises the possibility of being able to identify the difference between two forms of difference: 'difference between' and 'difference within'.[2]

But what might also usefully be taken account of here is the fact that the act of measuring – even the simple invocation of the measure or of the need for a measure – implies a relation to the unknown. While measuring may be carried out for the sake of confirmation, this need for confirmation in fact expresses a doubt, a wrinkle in certainty, a sense that the measure may reveal an unlooked-for dissimilarity rather than the reassurance of another encounter with the known, or else an equally troubling identity or resemblance where it was not expected to occur. A moment of strangeness or of the strangely familiar hovers, uncannily, and this opens the possibility of thinking of the text in terms of event. But the notion of event is always shadowed by the threat of the monstrous which lurks in the promise, the trace of the predictable in the unforeseeable aspect of true futurity. Finitude remains, ineliminably. Death, unsurprisingly then, is frequently thought to be the common measure, as that which is proverbially the great leveller; death – as it is put by the Duke in *Measure for Measure* – 'makes these odds all even' (III.1.41) in a collapse of difference into identity.[3] There remains something strange in this evocation of death, as so often in Shakespeare. Strange beyond measure. As Nicholas Royle proposes, '"strange" would perhaps be Shakespeare's word for "uncanny", unheimlich' (Royle, 2009, p. 4; for some of the implications of this see Royle, 2003).

Human finitude must be carefully disentangled from death, which might too easily be taken as a property or possession (to the extent that it can be thought as a concept at all). It is this very exappropriability, as Derrida might invite us to call it – marking the possibility of loss of that which was never possessed as if it were one's own – that renders finitude 'common'.[4] Finitude offers a form of ontological equality, that which exposes the vulnerability of the human rather than grounding it in an essential quality or capacity. It is this sense of community and the common that Jean-Luc Nancy evokes in his elaboration of the 'inoperative' or 'unworked' community (*la communauté désœuvrée*). As Martin Crowley has proposed, this lack of qualification fruitfully opens the possibility of a politics of finitude which takes as an enabling presupposition just this ontological equality, marking a common exposure to finitude that becomes the basis for a politics of *l'homme sans* (Crowley, 2009). (Parenthetically, it is this logic of presupposition [*Voraussetzung*] that also underpins Heidegger's opening of the existential analysis of death in *Being and Time*.)

The Duke's moment of equalization comes at the end of the remarkable speech in which Claudio is advised to be 'absolute for death'. The word 'absolute' rings throughout the play: it is his absolute power that the Duke grants to Angelo in the first act and Angelo is himself described as absolute in the last. But there are several instances in the play of those who are unable to reach this state of absoluteness. The character of Barnardine may be read as the key to a certain form of resistance to the Duke's connection of death and measure. Described in the play as 'A man that apprehends death no more dreadfully but as a drunken sleep: careless, reckless, and fearless of what's past, present, or to come' (IV.2.125–7), Barnardine's failure to allow death to be the point of judgement enacts a refusal to obey order, both temporal (allowing this to be heard in all its senses) and divine. Rather than accepting the judgements of others, whatever sovereign rights they may lay claim to, Barnardine believes in notions of consent and resists rhetorical power: 'I will not consent to die this day, that's certain ... I swear I will not die today for any man's persuasion' (IV.3.47–8 and 51). Performativity punctures persuasion.

Building on this rejection of temporal sequence and succession, Kiernan Ryan argues for a form of utopian Marxism inspired by Benjamin, Marcuse and Bloch, in which Shakespeare's plays are not referred endlessly back to a moment of origination that is always to some extent known and thus predictable, but instead are read in terms of that which opens a future (Ryan, 2001). Ryan cites Marcuse approvingly:

> The critical function of art, its contribution to the struggle for libera-
> tion, resides in the aesthetic form ... The encounter with the truth
> of art happens in the estranging language and images which make
> perceptible, visible and audible that which is no longer, or not yet,
> perceived, said and heard in everyday life.

Strangeness and estrangement at the level of form and language opens
a space for perception of the unperceived. Ryan then reinforces this idea
of the potential of form – and thus formalism – with Bakhtin's slightly
more terse formulation: 'Form serves as a necessary bridge to new, still
unknown content' (cited in Ryan, 2001, p. 229). Strangeness of form
leads to a collapsing and reimposition of a form/content distinction; it
is possible to discern a new content – identifiably unknown – through
the bridge provided by, or that simply is, form.

A consideration of form might seem at first sight to be curiously
unhelpful in reading a play that so obviously frustrates attempts to
make it cohere. Certainly those who have looked for purity of form
have often found Shakespeare's plays recalcitrant. Voltaire's characterization of these plays as 'dunghills', in which the valuable jewels are
besmirched with excremental lapses of taste, the comic befouling the
tragic, and vice versa, is only extreme in its expression of a recurrent
sense that Shakespeare's plays almost all contain elements that probably
shouldn't be there. Voltaire's organic analogy points up a failure for
the drama to be sufficiently organic. *Measure for Measure* is certainly
a strange play. But are there not elements of strangeness in all of
Shakespeare's plays? Isn't this exactly what we have come to expect
from Shakespeare, that the plays will continue to deliver themselves of
a strangeness that cannot be thought or wished away? This is not to fall
back into a form of bardolatrous wonder at the richness or profundity of
the mind that created these texts as 'poem unlimited' (even if it runs the
risk of domesticating strangeness precisely in the act of identifying it).
Rather, it is to suggest that there are moments at which the encounter
with the unknown that these plays so often stage will always resist and
demand readings that cannot be entirely predicted, that invoke that
something else with which we must always struggle.

Indeed, such moments are explicitly thematized in this and other
Shakespeare plays. Take a passage such as this one from Act V, for
example:

ANGELO   My lord, her wits I fear me are not firm.
            She hath been a suitor to me for her brother

	Cut off by course of justice–
ISABELLA	By course of justice!
ANGELO	And she will speak most bitterly and strange.
ISABELLA	Most strange, but yet most truly will I speak.
	That Angelo's forsworn, is it not strange?
	That Angelo's a murderer, is't not strange?
	That Angelo is an adulterous thief,
	An hypocrite, a virgin-violator,
	Is it not strange and strange?
DUKE	Nay it is ten times strange.
ISABELLA	It is not truer he is Angelo
	Than this is all as true as it is strange.
	Nay, it is ten times true, for truth is truth
	To the end of reckoning. (V.1.34–47)

Truth is truth. To the end of reckoning. What does this mean exactly? It all hinges on the word 'strange', which acts as a marker of credulity. When Angelo suggests that Isabella will speak 'strange', he means 'strangely' and thus it is the nature of the discourse itself that is to be considered 'strange', but this is countered by the commonplace of strange but true which shifts attention back to the substance of the discourse. From here, it is the relation between the competing discourses and truth that emerges. The intensification that occurs through the use of 'strange' five times in six lines culminates in the 'strange and strange' which echoes similar uses earlier in the play ('home and home', IV.3.141). This is then multiplied by the Duke. But Isabella enacts an elision of the distinction between the strange and the true so that what she says is said to be 'as true as it is strange', that is, the intensity of its strangeness equals the intensity of its veracity. The Duke's 'ten times strange' is matched and cancelled by Isabella's 'ten times true'. And yet, does this equation really work? For Isabella is actually suggesting something more here: strangeness is relative, she says, truth is not. Where Angelo sees her speech as bitter and strange, she asserts that what she says is simply true. The strangeness lies not in the manner of her speaking, but in that of which she speaks. It is his behaviour that harbours strangeness, and it is this that makes her speech strange. In other words, what she says is not relative but absolute; his actions are definable for her in terms of an absolute moral standard.

And yet, to think about truth in these terms might suggest that it is possible to know securely the 'limits of truth'. To get the measure of truth, it is necessary to know where it begins and ends, where its borders lie. It is a short step from here to consideration of what determines and terminates truth, that is, it is always (too) easy to move towards the relation of truth and finitude.

'To the end of reckoning' both reinforces and inflects this sense of finitude. Reckoning implies calculation, enumeration, computation or an account; in the early modern period, this sense of the account could also mean the bill, the sum owing or due, especially in an inn or tavern (one of the many theories regarding the death of Christopher Marlowe is that he was killed in a quarrel over the reckoning). But there is also a particular sense of the reckoning as a name for rendering an account of one's life or conduct to God at death or judgement. This is to be found in Shakespeare: in *Henry V*, Williams proposes that the King will have a 'heavy reckoning to make' if the cause for which they have gone to war is not good (Shakespeare, 1982, IV.1.130). *Henry V* also gives us a sense of reckoning as anticipation or expectation (IV.1.279). And elsewhere in the same play we also find reckoning as a judgement of equivalence, if somewhat comically, as Fluellen proposes that: 'The pig or the great or the mighty or the huge or the magnanimous are all one reckonings, save the phrase is a little variations' (IV.7.15–17).

The problem of measure as reckoning in *Measure for Measure* is largely focused on the character of Claudio. One of the most striking scenes is the debate between Claudio and Isabella in III.1:

CLAUDIO   Death is a fearful thing.
ISABELLA   And shamèd life a hateful.
CLAUDIO   Ay, but to die, and go we know not where,
             To lie in cold obstruction, and to rot,
             This sensible warm motion to become
             A kneaded clod; and the delighted spirit
             To bathe in fiery floods or to reside
             In thrilling region of thick-ribbèd ice,
             To be imprisoned in the viewless winds
             And blown with restless violence round about
             The pendent world, or to be worse than worst
             Of those that lawless and incertain thought
             Imagine howling – 'tis too horrible.
             The weariest and most loathèd worldly life
             That age, ache, penury, and imprisonment
             Can lay on nature is a paradise
             To what we fear of death.
ISABELLA   Alas, alas!

CLAUDIO   Sweet sister, let me live.
         What sin you do to save a brother's life,
         Nature dispenses with the deed so far
         That it becomes a virtue.
ISABELLA   O you beast!
         O faithless coward, O dishonest wretch!
         Wilt thou be made a man out of my vice? (III.1.119–41)

What emerges in this exchange between siblings is a distinction between
two conceptions of 'life'. It is tempting to think of this as a debate
over what tends to be called 'quality' of life, in other words, over the
experience of living. For Isabella, life can become too hateful to be end-
ured; for Claudio, the most hateful life is preferable to death. Yet this
opposition between two conceptions of life is not strictly adhered to:
Isabella stresses shameful life, and Claudio refers not to death as such
but instead to 'what we fear of death'.[5] In other words, both refer us to
matters of perception rather than to the thing itself, as if recognizing the
profound complication of the itself when one speaks of either death or
life. Is there such a thing as life or death itself? Better to qualify or mediate,
better to remain (however apprehensively) at the level of apprehension:
shame and fear become placeholders for life and death, and both can be
experienced in an embodied or psycho-somatic manner. In Shakespeare's
texts, Ewan Fernie suggests, shame is presented as 'a painful rehearsal for
the dissolution of death or an experience of dreadful metamorphosis,
and yet ultimately a liberation from the illusions of pride into truth.
Shakespearean shame turns out to be the way to relationship with the
world outside the self' (Fernie, 2002, p. 1; for a reading that links to
conscience rather than shame explicitly, see Lukacher, 1994). As he goes
on to say, shame is 'ultimately an experience of mortality' (Fernie, 2002,
p. 110). But is there also in this play, as in Kafka, a sense that this shame
may outlive mortality, that there is a 'shamèd life' beyond life, which
lives on (life) like a parasite?

    The crucial moment in any staging of this scene between siblings
comes in the metrical disruption – the rupture of the measure – that
threatens to appear and then does. Isabella's 'Alas, alas!' rounds out
and neutralizes Claudio's invocation of the fear of death by supplying
the necessary syllables without offering a counter-argument. And 'Alas'
does more than simply mark time: it comes into English through Old
French (then *a-lasse* now *hélas*) from the Latin *lassus*, meaning 'weary'.
So Claudio's invocation of 'The weariest and most loathèd worldly
life' gives way to repeated expression of Isabella's weariness. But his

next line – 'Sweet sister, let me live' – cannot itself be so easily sweet-ened. If we accept the notion of the verse as conforming to a full line in which the missing syllables are to be supplied by silence (in which we would read the idea that 'the rest is silence' in a musical mode), then there are still several possibilities for the actor or reader as to where that silence comes in the line.[6] There are three 'natural' places: a pause before he speaks, a caesura indicated by the comma, or space for a response that never comes and which leads him to continue to his attempted justification. This measure of four unvoiced syllables, equal in length in each case, is filled differently depending on where it falls. If it comes at the beginning of the line, it marks his and our thinking time, in which he chooses his response to her 'Alas'. If it falls after 'sister', then this is the word that rings out in his appeal. If at the end, then it is 'live' that fills the pause that follows. But it isn't clear what each understands by 'live'.

What Isabella seems to wish to avoid is any coming to terms with death. In a French idiom that Derrida exploits in several places, *s'expliquer avec la mort* means both coming to terms with death and explaining and unfolding oneself (to oneself) in relation to death (cf. Boothroyd, 2000). As one of the voices proposes in Derrida's *On Touching – Jean-Luc Nancy*, shame enters into an economy of life, death and living on:

> I pray that one day you'll outlive me. But this prayer already shames me, as if I were also admitting that I'm afraid – afraid of being a survivor and bearing death. Because, to admit to one last resignation, I expect the only chance of a reconciliation with death, I mean to say my own, from the good fortune thus promised of no longer seeing those whom I have loved – like myself, more than myself – die. (Derrida, 2008a, pp. 3–4)

> je prie pour qu'un jour tu me survives. Mais cette prière déjà me fait honte, comme si j'avouais aussi une peur, la peur de survivre et de porter la mort. Car pour avouer une ultime démission, la seule chance d'une réconciliation avec la mort, je veux dire avec la mienne, je l'attends de la chance ainsi promise de ne plus voir mourir les êtres que j'aurai aimés – comme moi-même plus que moi-même. (Derrida, 2000, p.13)

Derrida attempts to deal with death, to come to a deal with death, that is, to enter into an economic relation with death such that it would be possible (for him, for us) to know which would be the worst, death or survival. Death is an escape from the fear that survival may be harder than bearing witness to death; death thus presents itself as an escape from a dying that always already shadows love from the moment of encounter with the one who is loved, since one must always die before the other. But this is only possible by giving that burden of survival, of living on, to the loved other, and the debt that must then be paid is shame.

In the dialogue with Claudio, Isabella seems to lack a comprehension of death as loss, thinking of it in terms simply of the weariness of worldly life; or else to lack sufficient sisterly love for Claudio to wish to spare him death. Or she truly believes that a shamed life is not worth living, and does not believe (contra Kafka) that this shame can meaningfully live on after death. Or she wishes to spare him the pain of survival, attempting (contra Derrida) to do so without fear or shame. Or she does not see as credible Claudio's suggestion that it is in her power to allow him to live; the 'choice' that Angelo has given her is not a real one, since there can be no rational decision in favour of prolonging the life of Claudio's earthly body at the expense of her eternal soul. Nature, which Claudio calls up, is not the frame for the values that she considers since the 'sin' he urges her to is not against nature. To write her attitude off as simply the expression of a Christian paradox – death as necessary to the movement beyond mortal life into the life eternal, and therefore neither to be lamented nor feared – misses the clear conclusion that Isabella must recognize: her brother's sinful behaviour must condemn him to damnation, not simply extinction. Surely she should wish to delay his entry into this damned state rather than speed him to it?

As I began to suggest a little earlier, perhaps the key to understanding this is to think about the nature of the 'life' that she associates with him. At the conclusion of the passage that I quoted from III.1, she describes Claudio as a 'beast', ending with the suggestion that he wishes to be 'made a man' which suggests either that he is not a man yet or that he has ceased to be one and must be made so anew.[7] It is his human presence, then, that is at stake, but this judgement about the nature of human life – of what separates it at once from the bestial that is thought to be beneath it and the celestial that is projected beyond it – must itself be open to judgement, if the title's echo of the Gospel is to have any purchase on the play's action.[8] Isabella seemingly locates this final judgement – conventionally enough – beyond the human realm (unlike Joseph K.), and thus has no fears for its consequences.

But what are we to make of the all-too-human judgements that those in the play, and those in the audience, might be tempted to make about her?

At the risk of taking a swerve that will have to remain almost wholly telegraphic, this might be phrased in other terms, and most tellingly as: 'Is there a measure on earth?' This is perhaps the ethical question per se. In particular, it opens up that space that ethics has repeatedly tried to fill, that emptiness that arrives in a movement of withdrawal, the withdrawal of the gods or of the God that condemns human beings to ponder their place in the world and beyond it. This question arises in a hunger for certainty, to know, finally, how to live. And knowing how to live must always be learned in the face of death (cf. Derrida, 2005; trans. Derrida, 2007). But this question, which arises from a desire for certainty, is also at the root of a version of philosophical relativism usually associated with Protagoras, and discussed at length in Plato's *Theatetus*.[9] The discussion that follows from the proposition that 'Man is the measure of all things [παντων χρηματων μετρον ανθρωπος]' suggests that there is no absolute standard of experiential 'measurement' (Aristotle, 1990, X, 1053a–b). This continues into a debate about perception and judgement that will be reawakened under the name of sense-certainty many times. In Book X of Aristotle's *Metaphysics*, Protagoras' claim that man is the measure of all things is taken to refer only to the scholar or 'man of perception', thus also making measure a matter of *aisthesis*. It is here perhaps, in this intersection of Plato and Aristotle, that the kernel of the 'aesthetic' interest of the measure finds its jumping-off point. This slipping away of the absolute standard for the judgement of experience is frequently seen as attributable to the apparent unknowability of the gods themselves in the strand of pre-Socratic Greek thought that Protagoras represents. As it is expressed in one of his best-known phrases: 'As to the gods, I have no means of knowing either that they exist or that they do not exist. For many are the obstacles that impede knowledge, both the obscurity of the question and the shortness of human life.'[10] This difficulty is thus bound up both with the nature of the knowledge sought, of its knowability, and with human finitude. The matter of human transience is taken up by Seneca in *De brevitate vitae*, and becomes part of a tradition that leads to an extended meditation in the first half of Derrida's *Aporias*.

What Derrida moves us towards in this text is an encounter with one of the most powerful attempts to rethink this question of measure. Friedrich Hölderlin's poetry, and its reading by Heidegger, will allow for a final step.[11] Heidegger's insistence that man is 'capable' of death leads to an insistence on finitude as a process that lasts a lifetime, a dying, that is, rather than a death. What Heidegger calls 'dwelling' is thus inseparable from finitude, but in his reading of Hölderlin it also becomes inseparable from poetry precisely to the extent that poetry may be thought of as a kind of measuring. In ' … Poetically Man Dwells … ', Heidegger tells us:

> Only man dies – and indeed continually, so long as he stays on this earth, so long as he dwells. His dwelling, however, rests in the poetic. Hölderlin sees the nature of the 'poetic' in the taking of the measure by which the measure-taking of human being is accomplished.

> Nur der Mensch stirbt – und zwar fortwährend, solange er auf dieser Erde weilt, solange er wohnt. Sein wohnen aber beruht im Dichterischen. Das Wesen des "Dichterischen" erblickt Hölderlin in der Maß-Nahme, durch die sich die Vermessung des Menschenwesens vollzieht. (Heidegger, 2000, p. 200; trans. Heidegger, 1975, p. 222; Hölderlin, 2004, pp. 788–93)

Again, this might be related to the structure of judgement that we have already seen: to make a judgement is to inaugurate a series of judgements, in which not only the decision made but the means by which it is made are opened up to further judgement. Hölderlin's poems, as read by Heidegger, attempt to get the measure of the act of 'measuring' human being. The nature (*Wesen*) of the poetic is related to the nature of being human (*Menschenwesen*). That this should be a matter of poetry is, Heidegger admits, 'strange':

> [I]t strikes us as strange that Hölderlin thinks of poetry as a measuring. And rightly so, as long as we understand measuring only in the sense current for us. In this sense, by the use of something known – measuring rods and their number – something unknown is stepped off and thus made known, and so is confined within a quantity and order which can always be determined at a glance. Such measuring can vary with the type of apparatus employed. But who will guarantee that this customary kind of measuring, merely because it is common, touches the nature of measuring? (Heidegger, 1975, p. 224)

> Indessen befremdet es doch, wenn Hölderlin das Dichten als ein Messen denkt. Und das mit Recht, solange wir nämlich das

Messen nur in dem uns geläufigen Sinne vorstellen. Da wird mit Hilfe von Bekanntem, nämlich den Maßstäben and Maßzahlen, ein Unbekanntes abgeschritten, dadurch bekannt gemacht und so in eine jederzeit übersehbare Anzahl und Ordnung eingegrenzt. Dieses Messen kann sich je nach der Art der bestellten Apparaturen abwandeln. Doch wer verbürgt denn, daß diese gewohnte Art des Messens, nur weil sie die gewöhnliche ist, schon das Wesen des Messens trifft? (Heidegger, 2000, p. 203)

The strangeness inheres, then, in our familiar understanding of measuring, even if Plato and Aristotle may have prepared us for the move into poetics by emphasizing *aisthesis*. The key here is to take account of the work that the notion of the unknown is doing here. If measuring is about rendering the unknown known, then this common practice will tell us little about the nature of measuring itself, it will simply give us measurements. In the same way, judgements that do not involve reflection on the nature of judgement itself can give us only a series of decisions, not the metajudgement of which the Gospel warns us. This process of measuring is about imposing limits or borders (*Grenzen*), and also enacts a kind of normalization, since *gewöhnlich* implies common in the sense of ordinary or everyday more than the 'held in common'. But Heidegger finds in Hölderlin's poetry something that goes beyond this transformation of the unknown into the known, and this becomes definitive of the true poet:

Yet the poet, if he is a poet, does not describe the mere appearance of sky and earth. The poet calls, in the sights of the sky, that which in its very self-disclosure causes the appearance of that which conceals itself, and indeed as that which conceals itself. In the familiar appearances, the poet calls the alien as that to which the invisible imparts itself in order to remain what it is – unknown. (Heidegger, 1975, p. 225)

Allein, der Dichter beschreibt nicht, wenn er Dichter ist, das bloße Erscheinen des Himmels und der Erde. Der Dichter ruft in den Anblicken des Himmels jenes, was im Sichenthüllen gerade das Sichverbergende erscheinen läßt und zwar: als das Sichverbergende. Der Dichter ruft in den vertrauten Erscheinungen das Fremde als jenes, worein das Unsichtbare sich schicket, um das zu bleiben, was es ist: unbekannt. (Heidegger, 2000, p. 204)

What Hofstadter translates as 'alien' is *Fremde*, the same word used to denote the strangeness (*befremdet*) of thinking of poetry as measuring, and it is this that the poet calls forth from within familiar (*vertraut*, something of which we have knowledge) appearance. This is a reconciliation or resignation as much as a sending or imparting (*sich schicken*) of the invisible to the strange or alien, in other words, it is a resignation of the invisible to remaining beyond measure by virtue of its invisibility. Since measuring is always a matter of perception, the invisible cannot be accounted for by it other than through displacement.[12] There is again a topography to this, just as measuring is earlier described in terms of placing within limits: *bleiben* frequently calls for location, in asking where something is, as well as that it remain what it is. The confusion to be avoided is taking one form of measure for another. As Fenves puts it, Hölderlin's poetry exhibits a recurrent refusal to allow us to take the 'measure of man' for 'the non-human – and, to this extent, nontechnological – technical measure of poetry' (Fenves, 1999, p. 40). There is no common, absolute measure that could find its place on earth.

And thus it is fitting that in a play that hovers continually around questions of judgement and decision in its delineation of the problems of defining life, of power over life, death and birth, sovereignty and the absolute, the resolutions of the final scene ultimately resolve nothing. They remain beyond measure, satisfying neither law nor justice, indifferent to the difference between them. Isabella's silence at the end of the play marks an opening to survival, to living on, *überleben*, which overflows the bounds of the play itself. But what is this life after life to be? Any 'decision' that could be made would exhibit its violence all too markedly, all too remarkably, endlessly evoking doubt and postponing its measuring of the human into a space and time with all the appearance of the posthuman.

Notes

1. I have drawn on the Geneva Bible for the wording alluded to here. Frank Kermode also cites the less well-known lines from Romans 2.1: 'Therefore thou art inexcusable, O man, whosoever thou art that judgest: for wherein thou judgest another, thou condemnest thyself; for thou that judgest doest the same things' (Kermode, 2000, p. 146).
2. This is a deliberate echo of Barbara Johnson's work, in which she stresses that 'difference between' habitually reveals itself as 'difference within', thus neutralizing the work of binary opposition (Johnson, 1980). As Geoffrey Bennington points out, however, this choice in favour of 'difference within' in fact runs the risk of simply displacing that binary logic into an opposition of 'difference between' and 'difference within' (Bennington, 2008).

3. All references are to Shakespeare (1991). Immediately after the death of Antony, Cleopatra similarly suggests that now 'the odds is gone' (Shakespeare, 1994, IV.16.68). I am grateful to Nicholas Royle for reminding me of this passage.
4. This notion of exappropriation appears starkly, for example, in Derrida's account of his relationship to the French language (Derrida, 1998).
5. On death 'as such', and the enormous supposition that such a statement involves, see Derrida, 1993.
6. This way of reading and performing Shakespeare's verse is that popularized by the director John Barton, and is still much used in workshops with actors by major theatres in the UK.
7. To avoid the risk of opening a reading that cannot be adequately handled here, I will set aside the path that would link the questions of sovereignty raised by the Duke's instruction that Claudio be absolute for death and this identification as a beast. Derrida's seminars that bring together precisely these terms are beginning to be published. As I write, two volumes have appeared in French (Derrida, 2008b, 2009a). The first has been translated by Geoffrey Bennington (Derrida, 2009b).
8. In this, it is as if Isabella had anticipated Heidegger's now much-disputed claim that animals cannot experience death as death, just as they do not have language. Claudio's death, then, would not be the death of a man, and thus not death 'as such' (cf. Heidegger, 1959, p. 215; trans. Heidegger, 1971, p. 107). See also Derrida, 1993, pp. 35–42. On the relation between animality and speech and its consequences for humanism, see Robson, 2011.
9. Cf. Plato, 1987. The discussion of Protagoras's phrase begins at 152a. This text also contains the suggestion that this phrase was the first sentence of a book entitled Truth.
10. The word used for human life here is *bios* not *zoe*. This is the wording given in Diogenes Laertius (1991, pp. 51–2). See also the section on Protagoras in Diels and Kranz (1992, DK 80).
11. Heidegger is not, of course, the only one to explore this in relation to Hölderlin, and his thought here merits a more sustained analysis. See, for intriguing examples, Marx (1987) and Levin (2005).
12. Measuring is thus related to spacing. On the work of poetic meter in Hölderlin and its consequence for grounding the limit of philosophy, see Fenves (1999).

Works cited

Aristotle (1990) *Metaphysics*, trans. Hugh Tredennick (Loeb edn, 1935), Cambridge: Harvard University Press.
Bennington, Geoffrey (2008) 'La Chienne', *Deconstruction Is Not What You Think, and Other Short Pieces and Interviews*, Createspace, pp. 55–72.
Bloom, Harold (1999) *Shakespeare: The Invention of the Human*, London: Fourth Estate.
Boothroyd, Dave (2000) 'Of Ghostwriting and Possession: Translating "my father", or *s'expliquer avec la mort*', in Joanne Morra, Mark Robson and Marquard Smith (eds), *The Limits of Death: Between Philosophy and Psychoanalysis*, Manchester: Manchester University Press, pp. 198–219.

Crowley, Martin (2009) *L'homme sans: Politiques de la finitude, postface de Jean-Luc Nancy*, Paris: Lignes.

Derrida, Jacques (1993) *Aporias: Dying – Awaiting (One Another at) the 'Limits of Truth'*, trans. Thomas Dutoit, Stanford: Stanford University Press.

Derrida, Jacques (1998) *Monolingualism of the Other, or, the Prosthesis of Origin*, trans. Patrick Mensah, Stanford: Stanford University Press.

Derrida, Jacques (2000) *Le toucher, Jean-Luc Nancy*, Paris: Galilée.

Derrida, Jacques (2005) *Apprendre à vivre enfin: Entretien avec Jean Birnbaum*, Paris: Galilée/Le Monde.

Derrida, Jacques (2007) *Learning to Live Finally*, trans. Pascale-Anne Brault and Michael Naas, Hoboken: Melville House.

Derrida, Jacques (2008a) *On Touching – Jean-Luc Nancy*, trans. Christine Irizarry, Stanford: Stanford University.

Derrida, Jacques (2008b) *Séminaire La bête et le souverain: Volume I (2001–2002)*, ed. Michel Lisse, Marie-Louise Mallet and Ginette Michaud, Paris: Galilée.

Derrida, Jacques (2009a) *Séminaire La bête et le souverain: Volume II (2003–2004)*, ed. Lisse et al., Paris: Galilée.

Derrida, Jacques (2009b) *The Beast and the Sovereign*, vol. 1, trans. Geoffrey Bennington, Chicago: University of Chicago Press.

Diels, Hermann, and Walther Kranz (eds) (1992) *Die Fragmente der Vorsokratiker*, Zürich: Weidmann.

Diogenes Laertius (1991) *Lives of Eminent Philosopers*, vol. 2, trans. R. D. Hicks (Loeb edn, 1925), Cambridge: Harvard University Press.

Dollimore, Jonathan (1994) 'Transgression and Surveillance in *Measure for Measure*', in Jonathan Dollimore and Alan Sinfield (eds), *Political Shakespeare: Essays in Cultural Materialism*, 2nd edn, Manchester: Manchester University Press, pp. 72–87.

Fenves, Peter (1999) 'Measure for Measure: Hölderlin and the Place of Philosophy', *The Solid Letter: Readings of Friedrich Hölderlin*, ed. Aris Fioretos, Stanford: Stanford University Press, pp. 25–43.

Fernie, Ewan (2002) *Shame in Shakespeare*, London: Routledge.

Goldberg, Jonathan (1983) *James I and the Politics of Literature*, Baltimore: Johns Hopkins University Press.

Heidegger, Martin (1959) *Unterwegs zur Sprache*, Pfullingen: Günther Neske.

Heidegger, Martin (1971) *On the Way to Language*, trans. Peter D. Hertz, New York: Harper.

Heidegger, Martin (1975) *Poetry, Language, Thought*, trans. Alfred Hofstadter, New York: Harper.

Heidegger, Martin (2000) ' … dichterisch wohnet der Mensch', *Gesamtausgabe*, vol. 7: *Vorträge und Aufsätze*, Frankfurt am Main: Vittorio Klostermann, pp. 191–208.

Hölderlin, Friedrich (2004) *Poems and Fragments*, trans. Michael Hamburger [dual language edn], London: Anvil.

Johnson, Barbara (1980) *The Critical Difference: Essays in the Contemporary Rhetoric of Reading*, Baltimore: Johns Hopkins University Press.

Kafka, Franz (2002) *Der Proceß, Kritische Ausgabe*, Frankfurt am Main: Fischer.

Kermode, Frank (2000) *Shakespeare's Language*, London: Penguin.

Levi, Primo (1986) 'Traddure Kafka', *Il fabbricante di specchi: Racconti e saggi, Terza edizione ampliata*, Torino: La Stampa, pp. 141–3.

Levi, Primo (1991) *The Mirror Maker*, trans. Raymond Rosenthal, London: Minerva.

Levin, David (2005) *Gestures of Ethical Life: Reading Hölderlin's Question of Measure after Heidegger*, Stanford: Stanford University Press.

Lukacher, Ned (1994) *Daemonic Figures: Shakespeare and the Question of Conscience*, Ithaca: Cornell University Press.

McLuskie, Kathleen (1994) 'The Patriarchal Bard: Feminist Criticism and Shakespeare: *King Lear* and *Measure for Measure*', in Jonathan Dollimore and Alan Sinfield (eds), *Political Shakespeare: Essays in Cultural Materialism*, 2nd edn, Manchester: Manchester University Press, pp. 88–108.

Marx, Werner (1987) *Is There a Measure on Earth? Foundations for a Nonmetaphysical Ethics*, trans. Thomas J. Nenon and Reginald Lilly, Chicago and London: University of Chicago Press.

Nuttall, A. D. (2007) *Shakespeare the Thinker*, New Haven: Yale University Press.

Plato (1987) *Theaetetus*, trans. Harold North Fowler (Loeb edn, 1937), Cambridge: Harvard University Press.

Robson, Mark (2010) '"An empty body, a ghost, a pale incubus": Shakespeare, Lacan and the Future Anterior', *Shakespeare Yearbook* 19, pp. 55–74.

Robson, Mark (2011) 'HUM (-an, -ane, -anity, -anities, -anism, -anisation)', in Andy Mousley (ed.), *Towards a New Literary Humanism*, Basingstoke: Palgrave Macmillan, pp. 181–96.

Royle, Nicholas (2003) *The Uncanny*, Manchester: Manchester University Press.

Royle, Nicholas (2009) *In Memory of Jacques Derrida*, Edinburgh: Edinburgh University Press.

Ryan, Kieran (2001) '*Measure for Measure*: Marxism before Marx', in Jean E. Howard and Scott Cutler Shershow (eds), *Marxist Shakespeares*, London: Routledge, pp. 227–44.

Shakespeare, William (1982) *Henry V*, ed. Gary Taylor, Oxford: Oxford University Press.

Shakespeare, William (1991) *Measure for Measure*, ed. N. W. Bawcutt, Oxford: Oxford University Press.

Shakespeare, William (1994) *Antony and Cleopatra*, ed. Michael Neill, Oxford: Oxford University Press.

Tennenhouse, Leonard (1986) *Power on Display: The Politics of Shakespeare's Genres*, London: Methuen.

Watson, Robert N. (1994) *The Rest Is Silence: Death as Annihilation in the English Renaissance*, Berkeley: University of California Press.

Wilson, Richard (1996) 'Prince of Darkness: Foucault's Shakespeare', in Nigel Wood (ed.), *Measure for Measure*, Buckingham: Open University Press.

Part III
Hamlet, 'Posthumanist'?

9
(Post-)Heideggerian *Hamlet*

Laurent Milesi

The critical assumption behind this chapter is that *The Tragedy of Hamlet, Prince of Denmark* revolves around scenes whose parallel wording turns them into fateful, ironic counterparts unbeknownst to the characters, as befits the essence of a tragedy.[1] Most crucially, the play hinges on an 'existential distance' between Hamlet's famous 'to be or not to be' soliloquy and his less conspicuous inflection of the question of being as 'Let be' in the final scene, a dramatic philosophical twist that inevitably comes too late for its untimely hero. Between these two poles *Hamlet* repeatedly interrogates the significance of '(no)thing', 'being' and 'man', among other 'concepts', implicit or explicit, whose *germanity*,[2] that of the Wittenberg student of philosophy/theology and even 'theory'[3] in a play about brotherly duels, this *essay* proposes to investigate in order to read the hero's tragic evolution as a shift from a Heideggerian problematic of being and existence to a Derridean qualification of ontology and substitution of 'desistance' instead. In a final move, or twist to the Renaissance drama, we shall enquire into the posthumous, as much as posthuman, nature of a tragedy famously known since Derrida's *Specters of Marx* for its untimely effects of *revenance* by exhuming its ghostly dead in the light of Nicolas Abraham's imaginary epilogue, 'The Sixth Act'.

Who's there? A thing or nothing?

Shakespeare's arguably most existentialist play opens with a call for an identity to be revealed in the form of a question whose resolution was delayed from the First to the Second Quarto:[4]

First Sentinel	Stand, who is that?
Barnardo	Tis I. (*Hamlet* [1Q], 1.1)

181

BARNARDO	Who's there?
FRANCISCO	Nay, answer me. Stand and unfold yourself.
BARNARDO	Long live the King!
FRANCISCO	Barnardo?
BARNARDO	He. (*Hamlet* [2Q], I.1.1–5)

This symptomatic suspense, doubled by the possible ambivalence of Barnardo's 'He' as opposed to the more straightforward "'Tis I', is not only in keeping with the prevalent theme of dilatoriness in the play but also puts into perspective how even the most emblematic line from the Prince's soliloquy in Act III.1, 'To be, or not to be, that is the question' (56), was so thoroughly recast, from 1Q's more affirmative 'To be, or not to be – ay, there's the point' (7.105 – cf. [2Q] 65: 'ay, there's the rub'). More generally, the rapid succession of yes-no hesitations in Hamlet's speech in the First Quarto gave way to a more dilated set of alternatives anchored to a deconstructive 'perchance' (i.e. a 'maybe' rather than a secure ontology of being) in the better known variant:

> To die, to sleep – is that all? Ay, all.
> No, to sleep, to dream – ay, marry, there it goes ... (*Hamlet* [1Q], 7.116–17)

> ... To die – to sleep,
> No more ...
> ... To die, to sleep;
> To sleep, perchance to dream – ay, there's the rub ... (*Hamlet* [2Q], III.1.60–1, 64–5)

Unlike Gertrude, to whom the phantasmal Ghost fails to appear and who therefore remains visually unaffected by the phenomenology of the 'apparition' – compare her reply to Hamlet's 'Do you see nothing there?': 'Nothing at all; yet all that is I see' (*Hamlet* [2Q], III.4.132–3) – Hamlet suffers the ontological pangs of both spirit and flesh, the inhuman and the human:

QUEEN	If it be,
	Why seems it so particular with thee?
HAMLET	Seems, madam? Nay, it is. I know not 'seems.' (*Hamlet* [2Q], I.2.74–6)

HAMLET	O that this too too sullied flesh would melt,
	Thaw and resolve itself into a dew ... (*Hamlet* [2Q], I.2.129–30)

Unlike Wallace Stevens's 'The Emperor of Ice-Cream', where 'Let be be finale of seem. / The only emperor is the emperor of ice-cream', and unlike Gertrude for whom the phantom registers only the 'apparition of the inapparent'[5] and therefore *is not*, the Prince does not count himself king of those phenomena that he sees freezing and melting before his very eyes.

Hamlet Senior's ghost had appeared even before the play began and is therefore the prime mover without which the tragedy would not have happened, keeping it tensed between phenomenology and ontology, inessential *phainesthai* and tangible essence. Witness the early exchange between Barnardo and Horatio, where 'nothing' can be given a retrospective twist of paradoxical *double-entendre* if reread in conjunction with Hamlet's question to the Queen seen above but also with his later ironic description of kinghood – just as Barnardo's 'He' pointing to himself can be made to sound ambiguous in the light of a third party's apparition:

HORATIO	What, has this thing appear'd again tonight?
BARNARDO	I have seen nothing. (*Hamlet* [2Q], I.2.24–5)

HAMLET	... The King is a thing –
GUILDENSTERN	A thing, my lord?
HAMLET	Of nothing. (*Hamlet* [2Q], IV.2.27–9)

In this Danish setting, one should not forget the Scandinavian meaning of 'thing' as a (political) gathering or assembly (cf. the Icelandic Althing, germane to the *res publica* or public thing), and in the context of Hamlet's essential thinking and existential doubts, Descartes's view of the self as a *res cogitans* or 'thinking thing' recalled in Heidegger's *Being and Time*. From the 1930s onwards Heidegger came to understand *das Ding* as a manifold or assemblage, before resurrecting the Old High German cognate sense of 'assembly' seen above. Heidegger's definition as 'a something not nothing' to the basic questioning 'What is a thing?', which 'brings the whole world into play' (cf. Inwood, 1999, pp. 214–15; s.v. 'thing') – cf. Hamlet's 'The play's the thing / Wherein I'll catch the conscience of the king' (II.s.800–1) – can be tacitly heard against the Prince's ironic assertion that the King is a thing of nothing, an assemblage of non-entity, a being of not-being, since in his eyes he merely has the semblance of royalty.

Likewise, the inaugural 'Who's there?', as well as the original 'there's the point' [1Q] / 'rub' [2Q] sequel to 'To be or not to be', can be made to resonate as a Germanic, germane, Hamnletian (from Wittenberg) question preceding the Heideggerian 'imperative' *es gibt Sein* – or, here, *es gibt Da-sein*, which Derrida, in 'Les fins de l'homme', sounded as a 'donner le là' (Derrida, 1972, p. 160), the latter becoming similarly disarticulated and displaced as 'il y a là cendres' in *Feu la cendre* once the *est* of man has cooled into post-human *restes*, the ends of man at the beginning of a play which opens on questi(oni)ng the spectre, a spectral hauntology destabilizing a speculative, even specular, ontology and closes with hardly anybody 'remaining' onstage, and whose temporality, as Derrida later showed in *Specters of Marx*, could run backward in untimely fashion.

Untimeliness revisited

Recalling, after critics like Ricardo Quinones in *The Renaissance Discovery of Time*, the impact of the Renaissance invention of the clock, a mechanism that could at last fraction time into discrete 'present' instants, Wylie Sypher states that 'Hamlet stands on a boundary between a world where time was a natural and indivisible flow ... and the post-Renaissance world with its sense of punctual, mechanical time' (Sypher, 1976, p. 68). Borrowing French historian Gaston Roupnel's concept of 'punctiform time', Sypher goes on to note that 'Hamlet's experience is punctiform, episodically distributed through acts that do not, until the end, cohere into action' (p. 69), a view that is consonant with our earlier observation that the play is structured, unbeknownst to the characters, by a set of discrete recalls or counterpoints whose consequence is what Derrida called an 'untimeliness and disadjustment of the contemporary' (cf. Derrida, 1994, p. 99).

If time is notoriously 'out of joint' in *Hamlet*, which is evidenced in its hero, unsure of his own humanity and subjectivity, and whose hour is for most of the play the hour of the Other, being either too rash or too slow to act and respond to the present, contemporary instant,[6] so is essence and existence, which trope between being and non-being, being and seeming, an oscillation that correlates with (not) seeing and seeming.[7]

This prompted Terence Hawkes to 'read *Hamlet* backwards', Orpheus-like, against the temporal grain of an implacably linear tragic plot:

> In search of *Telmah*, we can begin by noticing the extent to which looking backwards, re-vision, or reinterpretation, the running of events over again, out of their time sequence, ranks, in fact, as a fundamental mode of *Hamlet*. (Hawkes, 1985, p. 313)

Hawkes then posits subsequence and posteriority as presiding over the unfolding of this posthuman drama, placed under the sign of a hauntology whose spectres, Derrida famously reminded us, may have several times and tenses: 'It is a proper characteristic of the specter, if there is any, that no one can be sure if by returning it testifies to a living past or to a living future' (Derrida, 1994, p. 99). For Hawkes, the play within the play – or replay of a replay – of *The Mousetrap* would mark the Prince's most recursive moment as its 'tropic' (cf. III.2.232) functioning is the turning point of *Telmah*'s a posteriori temporality (Hawkes, 1985, p. 317).[8]

The tragedy's dénouement cannot be triggered off until Hamlet finally becomes reconciled with time's indomitable passage, in the sequence ending with 'Let be' whose addition from the first to the second quarto invites the view, not merely out of 'misplaced ingenuity',[9] that there is more to it than the hero's recognition of a dramatic interruption, albeit in a play full of such 'abridgments' and stoppages; that at stake is the final acceptance of existence's intimate bond with a suprahuman temporality:

> If it be now, 'tis not to come; if it be not to come, it will be now; if it be not now, yet it will come. The readiness is all. Since no man, of aught he leaves, knows aught, what is't to leave betimes? Let be. (V.2.216–20)

From ek-sistence to desistance

Ewan Fernie has alerted us to the philosophico-theological import of Hamlet's trajectory from the 'To be or not to be' dilemma to his final 'Let be':

> No one to my knowledge has placed Hamlet's crucial transition from 'To be, or not to be' (3.1.58) to 'Let be' in the context of the rich history of indifference and letting-be in the history of ideas in the Western tradition ... In philosophy, the later Heidegger appropriated this theological tradition [of the medieval German mystic Meister Eckhardt and of Hans Urs von Balthasar] in his own crucial notion of *Gelassenheit*. (Fernie, 2005, pp. 204–5)[10]

What Fernie does not note – and that we wish to emphasize within our view of the tragedy as hinging upon ironic counterpoints – is that Hamlet's celebrated about-face in relation to being in V.2.215–20 is somehow anticipated not only by Hamlet himself as early as I.5.116: 'So be it.', but also, more incongruously, by the Ghost's 'Brief let me be' (I.5.59), to which in turn one can then hear Polonius's 'I will be brief' as an ironic half-echo (II.2.92, two lines after recalling with his usual pontificating pomposity the proverbial 'brevity is the soul of wit'). *Hamlet* boasts a few other 'briefs', such as Ophelia's ''Tis brief, my lord' (III.2.148) about the Prologue of the play-within-the-play, and no doubt this vein of brevity is meant to heighten the problematic of the untenable fleetingness of the present instant, which makes any action, especially Hamlet's, hard to time right. Oscillating therefore between rashness and dilatoriness (cf. III.4.107: Hamlet about himself to the Ghost: 'tardy son', following his impetuous killing of Polonius behind the arras earlier in the scene), thus never getting or managing to set the time right (cf. I.5.196–7), Hamlet would finally reconcile himself with (the inevitability of the passing of) time and being when he eventually 'lets be'.

Recalling Derrida's observation in *Specters of Marx* that 'the phenomenal form of the world is spectral' and that 'the phenomenal *ego* ... is a specter' (Derrida, 1994, p. 135), Fernie notes that in *Hamlet* 'It is a question not of "to be" and "not to be" ... but of *being-in-between*' (Fernie, 2005, p. 193). Such an *inter-esting* 'being-in-between' could be Hamlet's near-final 'Let be', then his 'But let it be' (V.2.343) at point of death, especially if one hears in them a more Germanic *lassen* (+infinitive), a 'middle voice' in between active (making – Hamlet's many 'let me's' earlier – even *poiein*: Hamlet as performative, poetic punster) – or here 'acting' (Hamlet's role in providing the play-within-the-play) – and passive (letting: no longer rash or dilatory, waiting for his fate as a mortal being). One may also look back to Hamlet's earlier ambiguous 'I'll make a ghost of him that lets me' (I.4.85) analysed by Avi Erlich and recalled by Marie-Dominique Garnier in her witty development on 'let' and letters in the play, featuring the hero's name, as in IV.6.10: 'I am let to know it is' (cf. Garnier, 2003). To adapt Derrida's remark on Cixous's poetics of *kommen lassen* (Derrida, 2006, pp. 66–7, 80), Hamlet's ultimate acceptance of *Gelassenheit* ('releasement'; cf. Heidegger, 1992; trans. Heidegger, 1966),[11] therefore turns 'making be' into 'letting be', an affirmative passivity akin to the impassivity of the Greek stoics, yet as a way of retaining an involvement with beings (*sicheinlassen*; cf. Heidegger, 1993, p. 125; see also Inwood, 1999, pp. 116–18, s.v. 'letting and releasement'), while freeing oneself from the question of existence. Undergoing a Blanchotian *désastre*, or tragic fall from a heroic star (*astre*) 'too much in the sun' (I.2.67), the Prince is more Ham*let* than ham, a Lacanian *hommelette* that cannot face up to himself until too late.

Thus, how one should envisage this newly resolved letting-be becomes perhaps the main question here, if only since this afterthought has been construed to account for Hamlet's self-sacrificing decision to take up the wager of a duel whose odds he knew were heavily stacked against him. Can Heidegger's more contemporary *Gelassenheit,* or thinking as the renouncing of willing,[12] be let to conveniently translate Hamlet's 'Let be' since the Prince wilfully accepts the challenge, even preventing the ever-faithful Horatio from intervening and thus interfering with the course of Fate? Or should one look beyond Heidegger's critique of humanism and anthropocentrism towards a more radical disjunction of being, temporality and existence, as in Derrida's notion of *désistance*? (Derrida, 1989, esp. the section on *'Ge-stell',* pp. 15–25).

In another less well-known reflection on *Hamlet,* Derrida writes of the experience of deconstruction in a way which can be compared with his approach to desistance – itself a coinage in response to Lacoue-Labarthe's *désistement* as the new 'question of the subject' (Derrida, 1995, p. 25) – and how the latter might then be seen as the condition of tragedy:

> perhaps deconstruction would consist ... in ... deconstructing, dis-locating, displacing, disarticulating, disjoining, putting 'out of joint' the authority of the is. (Derrida, 1995, p. 25)

Perhaps the *dé* dislodges [the *ester*] radically. (Derrida, 1989, p. 23)[13]

Later, commenting on Lacoue-Labarthe's '(de)constitution', Derrida points out that the 'de' in 'desistance' should likewise not be heard 'as a negativity affecting an originary and positive constitution' but rather as the mark of this movement of *de*sistance whereby the 'subject' *'is nothing other than* the formation of this movement' (Derrida, 1989, p. 17). Bent upon redressing a family wrong, Hamlet the tragic *sub-ject* desists from being *geworfen* and his 'let be', poised between activity, passivity and impassivity, and proffered soon after the scene of Ophelia's *inhumation,* heralds the coming of the posthuman subject for whom existence is no longer the question.

In Derrida's new, radically altered *coup de dé, 'Désistance* is the ineluctable' (p. 1), in the sense of what has already happened before happening, not unlike Blanchot's *désastre* and the radical affirmation of passivity in the face of (the experience of) death: 'Something began before me, the one who undergoes the experience. I'm late' (p. 2). The disjointed time of the subject of tragedy comes too late, posthumously, in a play that had already started before him and perhaps still needs to be teased out and satisfactorily resolved centuries after him.

Post-scriptum: posthumous, posthuman Hamlet

> One must stop pretending to know what is meant by 'to die' and especially by 'dying.' One has, then, to talk about spectrality. You know very well who pronounces the sentence 'The time is out of joint:' Hamlet, the heir of a specter concerning which no one knows any longer *at what moment* and therefore *if* death has happened to him. (Derrida, 1995, p. 30)

Taking his cue from the King rebuking Hamlet for his 'unmanly grief' and over-protracted mourning, Derrida notes that 'the question of mourning, which is the very heart of any deconstruction, carries beyond the human (or the viril) the only possibility of interrogating the human (or the viril) as such' (p. 21). Likewise, in 'Desire and the Interpretation of Desire in *Hamlet*', Lacan emphasizes that Shakespeare's tragedy is, from first to last, a play about mourning, although, as Richard Kearney rightly observes, Fortinbras-the-son 'ensures that Hamlet-the-son has the proper mourning and burial that Hamlet the father never received' (Kearney, 2005, p. 165).[14]

What could be more powerful and more uncanny than a returning ghost, more inhuman or 'beyond the human' still, if not the quasi-spectral comeback of the slain Prince risen from the dead to confront his ghostly sire yet again? This tour de force forms the basis for the post-revelations known as 'The Phantom of Hamlet' or 'The Sixth Act', preceded by the short essay 'The Intermission of "Truth"', the post-humously published fictional supplement imagined by psychoanalyst Nicolas Abraham in order to bring to light, as much as lay to rest, the Ghost's falsehoods and the inconclusiveness of Shakespeare's tragedy (Abraham, 1994). Waged on the premise that the Ghost's would-be revelations are nothing but fallacious, deceitful subterfuges to egg the Prince on for his own vengeful purposes and which account for his 'fits of indecision', that his untold secrets (since he is 'forbid to tell' them [I.5.13–14]) are in fact 'phantom secrets' concealing more truthful ones yet to be penetrated, Abraham's supplementary act creates a phantom text full of *coups de théâtre* in a posthumous relationship with Shakespeare's original play.[15]

Whereas Shakespeare's Hamlet could never get a timely grip on his actions, Abraham's is said to have had a visionary moment in which he could envisage a surreally distant future in which souls would be loosened or 'psycho-analysed' of their burdensome sins:

... One day, he spiced
His play of wit with antic prophecy,
As though the future he could read in dreams:
Before another thousand years have passed
A learned doctor in Vienna [i.e. Freud] will
Unlock dark treasures within our souls.
Then others, spurred on by his blazing light,
Will contemplate our trouble-coiled century,
Inventing all ... (Abraham, 1994, pp. 191–2)

The '[w]ell-timed' ghost of old King Hamlet reappears but, unlike ghostly apparitions, now does so in noontide's broad daylight, being thus himself 'too much in the sun', as if to make a natural light out-shine the more murky phenomenal light of the phantom who, knowing that the Prince would be restored to life and therefore to the throne, has now returned precipitously to try and discredit his son. Young Fortinbras's guess of the Ghost's deeper motives unleashes a series of (for some) hardly credible disclosures or '[a]bsurd ... phantoms of the mind', while in the meantime Hamlet – whose first words are 'To be or not to be ... Derisive fate. / He that is not, is – he that is, is not. / Am I alive?' (cf. later: 'Dead as I am') – returns to the living congregation (and at first does not see this 'ghost of a ghost'). Thus we learn that Hamlet Senior won his unmanly duel against old Fortinbras by using a sword poisoned by Polonius, and then festered to death not so much from the 'vial' of a similar substance poured into his ear by Claudius in his sleep but from his brother's venomous word of how he had 'vio-lated' the secret of old Hamlet's unnatural action thanks to Polonius's enlightenment. Developing the gravedigger's hint that every fool knows that young Hamlet was born the day when the old King overcame old Fortinbras (V.1.139–40, 142–3), 'The Sixth Act' makes Hamlet the son of Gertrude and old Fortinbras's union, hence the Ghost's former attempt to manipulate the Prince and now his speaking ill of a bastard son whom the Queen would sometimes call Orpheus, that is, blending Ophelia's name with that of the Greek mythological hero Orpheus, who symbolizes the loss of desire through looking backwards. (Ophelia herself expiated her father's double dealings through her suicide, her suspicions being confirmed by the garland of Polonius's venomous plants, or 'wreath of poison', that adorned her deathbed in the river.)

Then the same contriving Polonius would have anointed Laertes's sword with the unctuous poison of his son's renown as swordsman to make Hamlet doubt. In the words of young Fortinbras,

> The story opens with a wager. With a wager it nearly ended ... Of the two duels, fought thirty years apart, the second must include the first. Hamlet was skilled but Laertes won ... (Abraham, 1994, p. 199)

This is soon followed by Hamlet 'speaking in the voice of THE GHOST' – cf. earlier: 'And now ... we have changed places' – who keeps accusing Claudius. 'The Sixth Act' ends on Prince Hamlet being restored to the throne of Denmark and making a plea to share the lands of the Union with young Fortinbras '[a]s we spoke the truth about our forebears'. *Wo Es war soll ich werden*, or all was not well but ends well, even in a tragedy in which, at the end of a truly phenomenological or 'epochal' posthumous act (since its aim is 'to reduce the phantom'), the unconscious is brought out into full light to unravel the mysterious riddles that had haunted and resisted generations:

> Having reflected on all these things, I realized that this analysis might result in another play – nearly as dramatic – directed by the desire to resuscitate the 'dead' ghost, to 'cure' him, to allow him finally to cease being a phantom: to die happy, in the end, at having been understood, in his *surmounted* truth. (Abraham, 1994. p. 190)

Abraham's fictional exhumation makes apparent what we have always surmised and been haunted by: that, beyond his crises of identity and his tragic fate, Hamlet lives on – and never quite 'gives up the ghost'. His 'posthumanity' (both posthumous and posthuman) stems from the '*non-contemporaneity with itself of the living present*' that unhinges every action in the play but without which there would be no sense in asking the question 'where' or 'what tomorrow?'[16]

Notes

1. In '*Telmah*' Terence Hawkes had already noted the 'mirror reflection of phrases' in the play (Hawkes, 1985, p. 311).
2. See *OED*, s.v. 'german, germane' and 'German' for the related etymologies.
3. Since *theoria* originally designated the ability to see the divine manifestation and then report it, Hamlet the philosopher can be said to be the main 'theorist' of sorts in the play, in the context of his *father*'s spectral apparition.

4. Both the Arden volume of the second quarto (1604–5), ed. Harold Jenkins, and the more recent edition featuring the first quarto (1603) and the first folio (1623), eds Ann Thompson and Neil Taylor, have been consulted and will be referred to when variants differ significantly for interpretive purposes, as 2Q, 1Q and 1F respectively.
5. To borrow the title of the fifth, final section of Jacques Derrida's *Specters of Marx* (Derrida, 1994).
6. See Jacques Lacan (1982, esp. pp. 18–19). A parallel may be established with Lacan's discussion of the sophist 'solution' to the riddle of the prisoners in 'Logical Time and the Assertion of Anticipated Certainty', which deploys the drama of subjective assertion and of being as temporalization in three stages of observation, understanding and conclusion (decision), and ends on the following syllogism:

   1. A man knows what is not a man;
   2. Men recognize themselves among themselves as men;
   3. I declare myself to be a man for fear of being convinced by men that I am not a man. (Lacan, 2006, p. 174).

7. As well as with spectrality's interruption of specularity in what Derrida calls the 'visor effect' (Derrida, 1994, pp. 6–7).
8. One should perhaps also note that the play within the play is composed in *verse* of rhymed couplets, from Latin *vertere*: to turn, for which the Greek *trope* would be an equivalent.
9. Thus we wish to take issue with Harold Jenkins's dismissive editorial footnote in the Arden edition of the play (Shakespeare, 1982, p. 407).
10. The idea behind the present chapter was first formed without an awareness of Fernie's thesis, which was brought to my attention by Catherine Belsey, to whom I wish to express my gratitude.
11. *Gelassenheit* was first published in 1959, on the basis of a 1955 lecture and a dialogue written in 1944–5, 'Ein Gespräch selbstdritt auf einem Feldweg', where it is said to lie outside the difference between activity and passivity, or, anticipating the spirit of Derridean differance, to harbour in itself a higher form of activity (see Heidegger, 2007, esp. pp. 108–9).
12. For some excellent developments of the connection between *Gelassenheit* and Non-Willing as a more Primal Willing, see e.g. John D. Caputo (1987, *passim*) and esp. Davis (2007).
13. Cf. also p. 2: desistance 'puts off (from itself) any constitution and any essence', and p. 23: desistance 'calls for an "otherwise than Being" (otherwise than *ester*) … which would be neither "Heideggerian" nor "Levinasian"'.
14. Kearney's excellent essay reviews four significant critical attitudes about Hamlet's phantoms: the psychoanalytic paradigm of phantom-as-unconscious (Lacan, Abraham, Green), the existential paradigm of phantom-as-failure (Kierkegaard), the deconstructive paradigm of phantom-as-erasure (Derrida) and the theological paradigm of phantom-as-conscience (Girard).
15. See also Royle (2003, pp. 277–88), especially his contrastive analysis of Abraham's theory of the phantom and Derrida's conception of the spectre, which we cannot enter here.
16. Cf. Derrida (1994, p. xix). The slight tampering with Derrida's original questioning is meant to reflect the title of a series of exchanges with Elisabeth

Roudinesco about the future-to-come (cf. Derrida and Roudinesco, 2004). In one of those, reminiscing over *Specters of Marx*, Derrida incidentally hints at the 'unstable limit between "making-die" and "letting-die"' (p. 90), a border which would trace a faultline between Shakespeare's actual tragedy and, in the light of its unresolved tensions, its posthuman laying to rest in Abraham's posthumous 'Sixth Act'.

Works cited

Abraham, Nicolas (1994) 'The Phantom of Hamlet *or* The Sixth Act *preceded by* The Intermission of "Truth"', in Nicolas Abraham and Maria Torok, *The Shell and the Kernel*, vol. 1, ed., trans. and intr. Nicholas T. Rand, Chicago and London: University of Chicago Press, pp. 187–205.

Caputo, John D. (1987) *Radical Hermeneutics: Repetition, Deconstruction, and the Hermeneutic Project*, Bloomington and Indianapolis: Indiana University Press.

Davis, Bret W. (2007) *Heidegger and the Will, On the Way to 'Gelassenheit'*, Evanston: Northwestern University Press.

Derrida, Jacques (1972) *Marges de la philosophie*, Paris: Minuit.

Derrida, Jacques (1989) 'Desistance', in Philippe Lacoue-Labarthe, *Typography: Mimesis, Philosophy, Politics*, ed. Christopher Fynsk, intr. Jacques Derrida, Cambridge, Massachusetts: Harvard University Press, pp. 1–42.

Derrida, Jacques (1994) *Specters of Marx: The State of the Debt, the Work of Mourning, and the New International*, trans. Peggy Kamuf, intr. Bernard Magnus and Stephen Cullenberg, New York and London: Routledge.

Derrida, Jacques (1995) 'The Time Is Out of Joint', trans. Peggy Kamuf, in Anselm Haverkamp (ed.), *Deconstruction is/in America*, New York and London: New York University Press, pp. 14–38.

Derrida, Jacques (2006) *H. C. for Life, That Is to Say ...*, trans., with additional notes, Laurent Milesi and Stefan Herbrechter, Stanford: Stanford University Press.

Derrida, Jacques, and Elisabeth Roudinesco (2004) *For What Tomorrow ... A Dialogue*, trans. Jeff Fort, Stanford: Stanford University Press.

Fernie, Ewan (2005) 'The Last Act: Presentism, Spirituality and the Politics of *Hamlet*', in Ewan Fernie (ed.), *Spiritual Shakespeares*, Abingdon: Routledge, pp. 186–218.

Garnier, Marie-Dominique (2003) '*Hamlet*: Selected Letters between Derrida and Deleuze', *Oxford Literary Review* 25 (*Angles on Derrida, Jacques Derrida and Anglophone Literature*, ed. Thomas Dutoit and Philippe Romanski), pp. 63–77.

Hawkes, Terence (1985) 'Telmah', in Patricia Parker and Geoffrey Hartman (eds), *Shakespeare and the Question of Theory*, New York and London: Routledge, pp. 310–32.

Heidegger, Martin (1966) *Discourse on Thinking*, trans. J. M. Anderson and E. H. Freud, New York: Harper & Row.

Heidegger, Martin (1992) *Gelassenheit*, Pfullingen: Neske.

Heidegger, Martin (1993) 'On the Essence of Truth', *Basic Writings*, ed. David Farrell Krell, rev. edn, London: Routledge.

Heidegger, Martin (2007) *Gesamtausgabe III. Abteilung: Unveröffentliche Abhandlungen (1995)*, vol. 77: *Feldweg-Gespräche* (1944/5), Frankfurt: Klostermann.

Inwood, Michael (1999) *A Heidegger Dictionary*, Oxford: Blackwell, 1999.

Kearney, Richard (2005) 'Spectres of *Hamlet*', in Ewan Fernie (ed.), *Spiritual Shakespeares*, Abingdon: Routledge, pp. 157–85.

Lacan, Jacques (1982) 'Desire and the Interpretation of Desire in *Hamlet*', in Shoshana Felman (ed.), *Literature and Psychoanalysis. The Question of Reading: Otherwise*, Baltimore and London: Johns Hopkins University Press, pp. 11–52.

Lacan, Jacques (2006) 'Logical Time and the Assertion of Anticipated Certainty', *Écrits* (The First Complete Edition in English, trans. Bruce Fink, in collaboration with Heloïse Fink and Russell Grigg), New York and London: Norton, pp. 161–75.

Royle, Nicholas (2003) *The Uncanny: An Introduction*, Manchester: Manchester University Press.

Shakespeare, William (1982) *Hamlet*, The Arden Shakespeare (second quarto, 1604–5), ed. Harold Jenkins, London: Methuen.

Shakespeare, William (2006) *Hamlet: The Texts of 1603 and 1623*, The Arden Shakespeare, third series (first folio, 1623), ed. Ann Thompson and Neil Taylor, London: Arden.

Sypher, Wylie (1976) *The Ethic of Time: Structures of Experience in Shakespeare*, New York: The Seabury Press.

10
Loam, Moles and *l'homme*: Reversible *Hamlet*

Marie-Dominique Garnier

> Unities only exist for our intellect. Each individual has an infinity of living individuals within itself.
> (Nietzsche, 1867, trans. in Pearson, 1997, p. 138)

> Become clandestine, make rhizome everywhere, for the wonder of a nonhuman life to be created. (Deleuze and Guattari, 1987, p. 191)

Becoming Gilles Shakespeare

Voltaire's arrogant claim that he was the first to point out to the French the 'few pearls' in the 'enormous dunghill of Gilles Shakespeare's plays' yields in retrospect the singular pearl of William Shakespeare's frenchified first name – a William warped into a Gilles. Jumping ahead of its time, Voltaire's reconfiguration of Shakespeare as a 'Gilles dressed in ragged strips' (Voltaire, 1963, pp. 10–12; cit. in Wilson, 2007, pp. 268–9, nn. 34 and 40) productively resonates against the host of striped Gilles of late twentieth-century French philosophy – a Gilles Deleuze, a Jacques Derrida, a Foucault or a Félix. Voltaire's statement and the volte-face it invites to perform offer a proto-example of what Gilles Deleuze and Felix Guattari have conceptualized as a line of flight, as a principle of transverse, a-historical connectivity.

From *Gilles* Shakespeare to Gilles Deleuze and back runs an improbable line of flight, the chance coincidence of names becoming neighbours in an early, retrofitted, counter-historical assemblage of pre-s and posts. From the Voltairian figure of the village clown 'in ragged strips' emerges more than a coincidence between partially overlapping names, more than the serendipitous force of an improper translation. A *'gille'*, according to the *Littré* dictionary, possesses the mobile contours of a character in medieval lore, a jester or beguiler – named after the figure of *'Gilles le niais'*, 'as he was often nicknamed in French' – a connection lamely echoed in *Hamlet's* boy players or *'little eyases'* (II.2.317) imported from the French *'nyas / niais'*.[1] *'Gilles'* performs as a reversible, 'wily', name, applying as it does both to beguiler and beguiled – a figure of 'guiles' and 'wiles'.

From one 'Gilles' to the next (and back) runs a transverse force, sent or addressed in a non-linear, non-historical fashion. A force, in the smooth space of Deleuze and Guattari's plateaus, exists in relation to a *nomos*, to the nomad's or no man's land that 'lies between two striated spaces' in which it acts as 'a non-communicating force or a force of *divergence* like a "wedge" digging in' (Deleuze and Guattari, 1987, p. 384). The 'wedge' of Shakespeare's writing, once the author's monumental name is revised into a stray 'Gilles' Shakespeare, triggers off, machine-wise, an open-ended series of post-nominal adjacencies that look ahead (or aside, or back) towards the productive *jacqueries (*or jacques-and-gilleries) of post-humanist philosophy.

What follows interrogates posthumanism from the mobile position of Deleuze and Guattari's philosophy of the *nomos*, a term here addressed in relation to names, reopening yet once more the Shakespearian question of what is in or in the vicinity of a name, 'wounded' or not. In the literal, unstable vicinity of 'man' roams the 'name'. A posthuman name waits, reversibly, to be caught by its mane – arrested or captured, not interpreted. *Names* belong to the same verbal plateau as the *'nomos'* – a term Deleuze and Guattari's elaborate on in the 'Treatise on nomadology' of *A Thousand Plateaus*:

> The *nomos* came to designate the law, but that was originally because it was distribution, a mode of distribution. It is a very special kind of distribution, one without division into shares, in a space without borders or enclosure. The *nomos* is the consistency of a fuzzy aggregate: it is in this sense that it stands in opposition to the law or the *polis*, as the backcountry, a mountainside, or the vague expanse around a city ... Smooth or nomad space lies between two striated spaces ... affirming a non-communicating force or a force of divergence like a 'wedge' digging in. (Deleuze and Guattari, 1987, pp. 381–4)

Based on Emmanuel Laroche's philological study of the Greek root *nem-*, Deleuze and Guattari's reconceptualization of the space of the *'nomos'* swerves from received acceptations of the term in connection with the law. Deleuze and Guattari's revision relocates the term in the vicinity of numbers and numerical organization:

> The *nomos* is fundamentally numerical, arithmetic ... Nomad organization is indissolubly arithmetic and directional; quantity is everywhere ... The numbering number is rhythmic, not harmonic ... number is always complex, that is, articulated ... The complex or articulated number comprises not only men but necessarily weapons, animals, and vehicles ... However small the unit, it is articulated. (Deleuze and Guattari, 1987, pp. 390–1)

Touching ground

What is at stake in this chapter is a revision of the concept of 'man' from a position which pries open the 'name' and show its degree of articulatedness – 'however small the unit'. A name can be reappraised from a differential, posthuman angle, rechanneled towards a *nomos*, affected with divergent forces. Deleuze and Guattari's 'vague expanse' fits *Hamlet*'s opening location, the vagueness of its gaping 'ground' – semantically groundable as much as grindable. Meanings as well as parts happen to be relievable on Elsinore's 'platform before the castle' – a stage or proto-plateau. Ground rather than 'land' (cf. De Grazia, 2007) is peddled as a vague answer to the play's hammered and haunting question: 'Who's there?': 'Friends to this ground' (I.1.17). From a prosodic angle, the syllables of 'who's there' emit airy, h-bound signals that dismantle the stability of signs, resist the groundedness of ground. Not only is air displayed in the open weave of textuality – 'the erring spirit' (I.1.153) is 'as the air, invulnerable' (I.1.142); 'the air bites shrewdly ... it is an ... eager air' [I.4.1–2) – it filters through the chinks of a semantically unrelated series of h-words, muted or voiced: 'hour', 'heart', 'honest', 'haste', 'hear' – a proliferating, fluid assemblage of recombinable sound particles shaken loose from the sonorous plateau of Shakespeare's proper name. 'Wedges' rather than words dig or tunnel through the *nomos* of the play's opening scene, grinding its soundtrack to air-borne molecules and unstable particles, such as the subterranean and skin-deep 'mole' to come – a Deleuzian, subterranean animal as well as a perfect instance of vagueness. Margreta De Grazia has shown how the mole had become interchangeable with the name of its milieu, as 'in 1600, *mole, mould, moulde* and *moule* could refer to both the burrowing mammal and the earth in which it burrowed' (De Grazia, 2007, pp. 29–30) – a philological proximity which conduces her to argue in favour of a similar linkage between '*homo*', man, and its mouldy milieu, and to unearth the classical *homo/humus* association.

What this chapter addresses, however, is not the connection between 'moles' and mould, nor a reading of *Hamlet* based on what De Grazia terms 'homonymic clusters' and 'semantic overlays' linking man and clay, human and *humus*. Besides semantic clusters and overlays, *Hamlet* circulates non-semantic relays and heterogeneous aggregates, of the reversible, *mole/loam* kind: effects pertaining to non-linguistic signals rather than signs, going against the grain of linearity and chronology. *Hamlet* is amenable to 'relieving' and 'relievable' readings, requiring both a sense of *relief*, an attention to salient moments, as well as a 'relieving' game involving the displacement of pieces, of interstitial, chiral molecules.

Between who?

In *Hamlet without* Hamlet, Margreta De Grazia sets out to resist the type of character-oriented narrative imposed on *Hamlet* since Coleridge, in order to redirect critical attention to 'the subject of the land' and to related issues of inheritance. Based on the classical 'attachment of persons to land, human to *humus* (De Grazia, 2007, p. 3), her analysis revives the Hebrew etymology of 'the name of the first man, called not after his father but the dust from which he was fashioned, *adamah*, the Hebrew word for clay' (p. 3). Such a dislodging of filiation in favour of a pulverulent or loamy outside comes in support of Deleuze and Guattari's own views – in support of the claim they make against arborescences and family trees. Thirty pages later, however, De Grazia's study returns to the subject-bound narrative of inheritance and personal promotion, concluding that 'in a semantic setting in which human and *humus* are cognate, ambition for land is a form of self-aggrandizement' (p. 34). She concludes:

> The play dramatizes one conflict over land after another: Fortinbras I and Hamlet I over crown lands, Hamlet I and Claudius over the garden kingdom, Gonzago and Lucianus over the 'bank of flowers' or 'estate', Norway and Poland over 'a patch of ground', the boy and adult companies over the commercial stage, the crown and the Church over the churchyard, Laertes and Hamlet over Ophelia's flowered body, and the actor who plays Hamlet and any actor whose role challenges Hamlet's command over the stage. (De Grazia, 2007, p. 43)

If matters of inheritance and the threat of dispossession are vital issues in *Hamlet*, if indeed the play urges its readers and audiences to hear a connection between 'being diseased' and 'being diseized' (p. 157), one may wonder why *Hamlet* persistently questions the solidity of land and throws discredit on solid states of matter – why it grinds 'land' into 'ground' and 'loam'. Across the textual platform run a ceaseless series of fluxes – of troops, of waves and wet graves, complete with a river and Rhenish wine – the adjective itself being akin to the Greek root ρευ-, to flow. Twice, *Hamlet* shows traces of its 'Rhenish' lining, in the first act, as the King 'drains his draughts of Rhenish down' (I.4.10), and in the graveyard scene, as the clown reminisces about Yorick, who 'poured a flagon of Rhenish on [his] head once' (V.1.154–5).

De Grazia's initial statement that, in this play, 'flesh and earth repeatedly coalesce through overlaps of sound and sense, as they do in the name of the first man' (p. 3), paves the way for a nomadic rereading of *Hamlet*, once the 'name of the first man' is understood to operate as *nomos* rather than as 'proper' name: as a verbal field submitted to a wedging, heterogeneous programme, provided '*humus*' is freed from a 'land-owning' or proprietary line of thought. Neither ground nor soil are, 'properly' speaking, owned. Retranslated in Deleuzian terms, 'the ground of smooth space' differs from 'the land of striated space' (Deleuze and Guattari, 1987, p. 412).

Nothing in *Hamlet* points to the emergence of a home or human abode inviting to homecoming. Hamlet's several homecomings (from Wittenberg, from the verge of the cliff, from the flipside of the arras, or from the voyage to England) all point to a critique of the possibility of a 'home' – a word circulated in vacuous fashion by Polonius, who advises Gertrude to 'lay home' to Hamlet (III.4.1). A 'ham-', one might argue, is the opposite of a home. Hamlet-the-proper name, whose letters Shakespeare reshuffled from Saxo Grammaticus' original *Amleth*, is peddled as a variable, multi-directional name, breakable into moles, grindable into '*ams*' and '*lets*' and other disenfranchized outlets. In what could be described as a pre-machinic, typo-prone spelling environment, the name and the way it is spelt are set at large, free to roam between etymologies and roots. Before the *OED*'s third entry, in which 'ham' is akin to home, *ham 1* and *ham 2* release pre-modern, nomadic acceptations. A ham (ham n. 1) is 'the hollow or bend of the knee' – the juncture or joint, one of the play's leitmotivs as well as the key condition of articulation. In the second dictionary entry, a 'ham' is a pasture or meadow enclosed with a ditch. Far from being a home, a 'ham' is a *nomos*. The following quotation from the *OED* is of particular relevance:

> *1617, Minsheu, Ductor*: a Hamme or a little plot of ground growing by the rivers or Thames side, commonly crooked or beset with many willow trees or osiers.

At the end of the second chapter of *Hamlet without* Hamlet, Margreta de Grazia notes how tempting it has been to 'connect the landless Hamlet with the humble unit and land whose name he shares' (De Grazia, 2007, p. 44), and adds, after quoting Minsheu's Dictionary, that the terms used here are 'uncannily apposite to *Hamlet*'s most famous landscape', by which she means the willow trees and osiers. The term 'crooked', however, is just as important as the willows and osiers. As is 'ground'. A 'ham' is a plot of 'ground', not land.

Between Hamlet's 'we'll shift our ground' (I.4.155), his desire to find 'grounds more relative' (II.2.560) and the question asked in the graveyard 'upon what ground?', *Hamlet* 'grinds' ground to 'fine dirt' (V.1.93) – a grinding process to which the proper 'name' can also be subjected. Hélène Cixous's 2004 rewriting of *Hamlet*, published in partial form as *The Blind Fiancée or Amelait* (in Segarra, 2010) fragments the proper name into the less than coherent, heterogeneous pair of syllables '*âme/lait*'. In Cixous's text, in answer to her fictional Mole's invitation to 'tell, tell, tell, tell', Amelait responds in schizoid terms: 'I would and I would not like. I'm unstrung, twisted. I want and I do not want what I want ... I croak like a rat' (Cixous, in Segarra, 2010, p. 271).

Letters without post: from Chronos to Aion

Hamlet has persistently been read in humanist terms, as a text recording 'human promptings' (Kay, 1991, p. 231). Critics insist on finding in it a novel attention to 'the notion of an interior life that can never be accurately represented by word or deed' (p. 234), to the effect that 'the English language of his day had not developed names for two of *Hamlet*'s most striking characteristics; it did not include the words "aside" or "soliloquy"' (p. 234). Commenting on the rush of new words introduced in *Hamlet* – 'more than six hundred of these words, many of them not only new to Shakespeare but also – *compulsive, fanged, besmirch, intruding, overgrowth, pander, outbreak, unfledged, unimproved, unnerved, unpolluted, unweeded* ... – new to the written record of the English language', Stephen Greenblatt concludes that 'something must have been at work in Shakespeare, something powerful enough to call forth this linguistic explosion', something which can only be accounted for by 'some more personal cause for his daring transformation both of his sources and of his whole way of writing' (Greenblatt, 2004) – by which is implied the real-life linear chronology of *Hamlet*'s composition which the critic places between the deaths of Shakespeare's son and father (Greenblatt, 2004). But why should linguistic explosions be accounted for by 'personal causes'? One word is missing from Greenblatt's list: 'groundling', a frequenter of the 'ground' of a theatre, is of particular interest here.

Against this linear strain, a number of critics have noted the counter-chronological effect of a play in which 'the beginning comes last' (Wilson, 2007, p. 228) and events run 'out of their time sequence' (Hawkes, 1986, p. 96). Following Terence Hawkes's 'Telmah' which explored backtracking ('running events out of their time-sequence') as a fundamental feature of *Hamlet*, my previous essay devoted to crooked disarticulation of the proper name '*Hamlet* Letters' (cf. Garnier, 2003) traced the play's dissemination of chiral verbal particles, its spate of reversible 'let' and 'tell'. Similarly folded in *Hamlet*'s textual machine, *loam* and *mole* form (crookedly) exchangeable sides, chiral halves of an improbable *l'homme* in a (mock, lawless) act of translation.

Akin to *Hamlet*'s chiral inversion is the question of polarity and polarizing, for which the play provides an early tutorial in its treatment of the name of Polonius and of phonetically adjacent terms including 'Poland', the 'pole / polack' assemblage (II.2.63; V.2.355; IV.4.21–23) and the 'sledded Polacks' (I.1.63) or 'pole axe'. Poland is both *nomos* and name – 'a little patch of ground that hath no profit in it but the name' (IV.4.19). A 'field', according to the *OED*, is what the 'proper' name 'Poland' literally means – except that 'meaning' here boils down to mean-ing in the sense of being intermediate, wedged in, intercalated. Poland's being-in-the-middle (of Europe) holds, in other words, meaning and polarization in check. Fortinbras's last speech associates the name of Hamlet to the figure of the (battle) field: 'such a sight as this becomes the field, but here shows much amiss' (V.2.355–6). 'Here' operates a final reterritorialization, a polarization (not found in the initial 'who's there?') enhanced by the cloying effects of phonetic aggrandizement machined from the loud name of Fortinbras, rendered in the linear, non-reversible proliferation of the syllables of his 'own' name: for, forth, fort and four, including the fourfold term 'quarry' ('this quarry cries on havoc', V.2.312) and the four-stress hallmark of the character's half-lines, such as 'Where is this sight?' or 'Go, bid the soldiers shoot' (V.2.315, 357). What seems to prompt Hamlet to action is a mere particle of sound, a Leibnizian *petite perception*, released or triggered from Fortinbras's catching name, the force of an adverbial 'forth' ('O from this time forth', IV.4.65).

If humanism thrives on linear temporality and teleology, its critique will logically seek a resistance to *telos*. Deleuze and Guattari militate among other things against what they call 'a very inadequate conception of causality':

> The human sciences, with their materialist, evolutionary, and even dialectical schemas, lag behind the richness and complexity of causal relations in physics or even in biology. Physics and biology present us with reverse causalities that are without finality but testify nonetheless to an action of the future on the present, or of the present on the past (....). It is necessary from this standpoint to conceptualize the contemporaneousness or coexistence of the two inverse movements, of the two directions of time (...) as if the two waves that seem to us to exclude or succeed each other unfolded simultaneously in an 'archeological', micropolitical, micrological, molecular field. (Deleuze and Guattari, 1987, p. 431)

'Two directions of time' or 'inverse movements' seem to affect the temporality and readability of *Hamlet* – the one-sided temporality of Chronos and the divided, twofold reversible time Deleuze conceptualized, in the wake of the Stoics, as Aion in *The Logic of Sense* – a dual form of time, a time of pure becoming unfolding in two directions, to which *Hamlet*'s reversible particles perhaps belong. Aion, Deleuze adds, can be approached as the time of the actor:

> The actor is not like a God but like an 'anti-God'. God and actor are opposed in their reading of time ... The God is Chronos: the divine present is the circle in its entirety ... The actor's present, on the contrary, is the most narrow, the most contracted, the most instantaneous, and the most punctual. It is the point on a straight line which divides the line endlessly, and is itself divided into past-future. The actor belongs to the Aion: instead of the most profound, the most fully present, the present which spreads out and comprehends the future and the past, an unlimited past-future rises up here reflected in an empty present which has no more thickness than the mirror. The actor or actress represents, but what he or she represents is always still in the future and already in the past ... The actor strains his entire personality in a moment which is always further divisible

in order to open himself up to the impersonal and pre-individual role. (Deleuze, 1990, p. 150)[2]

Imp, impersonal, imp/post/hume

Although difference is inscribed at every level in the play (between the man of many metals, Fortinbras and Hamlet, between a father and a son, between Denmark and Norway) *Hamlet* resists alterity through procedures of alteration resorting to short-circuits and syllabic promiscuity – 'as if a machinic phylum, a destratifying transversality moved through elements, orders, forms and substances, the molar and the molecular, freeing matter and tapping forces' (Deleuze and Guattari, 1987, p. 335). Characters or subjects give way to what Deleuze and Guattari have defined as the proper name:

> The proper name does not designate an individual: it is on the contrary when the individual opens up to multiplicities pervading him or her, at the outcome of the most severe operation of depersonalization, that he or she acquires his or her true proper name. The proper name is the instantaneous apprehension of a multiplicity. The proper name is the subject of a pure infinitive comprehended as such in a field of intensity. (Deleuze and Guattari, 1987, p. 37)

Shakespeare's 'cellular' language explores the juncture or the 'interim' between Saxon and Latinate flows, challenging the 'cells' of closure-bound sense-making procedures and twisting them into a game of cellular reduplication with minimal differences – an example of which can be seen at work in Hamlet's use of the Latinate term 'imposthume'. The term captures unstable, uncouth forces in *Hamlet*, as the 'imposthume of much wealth and peace, that inward breaks and shows no cause without why the man dies' (IV.4.27–9). 'Imposthume' can be read from a molar angle, taken to mean an abscess, a hidden sore with no apparent symptoms, a silent disease. But as an unstable molecular compound which 'inward breaks', it also releases, once broken into parts, the force of each of its particles: an 'imp', a 'post', a 'post-hume'. An altered form of 'apostem' infected at its core with an extra 'h' which the *OED* terms 'erroneous' (but how erroneous is it?), the word releases viroid energies: instilled at a turning point in Act IV, it liberates the necessary energy to 'spur' Hamlet's 'dull revenge'. An archaic, premodern term for an aposteme, 'imposthume' jumps ahead of its time – behaving as a timely yet timeless signifier or post-signifier, an intempestive or 'untimely' term in the Nietzschean sense. Its initial syllable, reiterated in a number of similar 'imp-words' ('impress', 'impart', 'impartment', 'import') across the play, yields a metamorphic, impish principle – the first dictionary entry for imp being a young shoot, a scion, a slip ready to rhizome along, either as a vegetal being or as a creature belonging to no human genealogy.

An 'imp' beckons in *Hamlet*, inviting to non-linear reading modes, offering a degree of resistance to the stratifications of 'the language of the West'.[3] Taking its cue from the jumping skulls repeatedly thrown out of the common grave, *Hamlet*'s uncouth textuality invites to comparable acts of jumping – not to interpretive conclusions, but from one experimental, pre/post-modern word or 'word-event' to the next, in a series of local, disconnected moves which retain a connection with an outside, between two temporal uses of an adverb: 'jump at this dead hour' (I.1.66) and 'jump upon this bloody question' (V.2.390). Proper names in Shakespeare's text possess the power to jumpstart reading. The 'character' of Yorick, for example, functions less as a sign than as a signal, a phonetic jaw-drop maintained in place with a literal, graphic hook which connects it to its phonetic neighbour in *Hamlet*'s plateau of asignifying resonances: 'unyoke' (V.1.45), uttered in the thin interim between 'Marry, now I can tell' and 'Mass, I cannot tell'. Beyond the scene's humanist, topical reflection on life's vanity and the inevitability of grinning death and falling jaws, the gaping, yoking initial Y in Yorick's Scandinavian name acts as a nomadic event which redirects hermeneutics towards schizo-analysis: towards the divisive force of a wedging or an 'unyoking'. Unyoked, pried open, *Ham/let* the name, not the 'man', disseminates bits of code, irresponsive to the dialectics of being alive or dead. Its viroid pack of subsignifiers operates in 'a sonorous much more than a visual space' (Deleuze and Guattari, 1987, p. 382), a gaping space.

In such a gaping, nomadic space, the temporality of the 'post' ceases to operate in a linear way – Hamlet's 'post' being suitably relocated in the middle of what is 'imposthume' (a term able to grow from its active middle). *Hamlet* disrupts the linear temporality of the 'passage', a term used both for the projected killing of Claudius and for Hamlet's removal from the 'stage' in the last scene. 'To pass', the verb, occurs in the first of Hamlet's shorter speeches, in answer to the dialectics of what seems and what is, in a statement which deserves to be read at least twice, although it has become a critical banality to interpret it as a humanist defence and illustration of the character's inner self:

I have that within which passes show –
These but the trappings and the suits of woe. (I.2.85–6)

Grammatically and prosodically, 'that within which' admits several readings, depending on whether 'within' evolves towards nominalization (either as a 'within', a self or interiority, or as a pronoun followed by an adverb, 'that within') or whether a pause is implied, wedged in halfway through the syntagm (that / within which), a second reading which transforms Hamlet's stable inner identity into a *'nomos'*: a locus of cross-circulation in which the only possible subject of the verb 'to pass' is 'show'. Pass, in this second reading, no longer means 'surpass' but simply go through: 'show' or 'showmanship', the force of dramaturgy, 'passes' through the subject of Hamlet, transforming it into a multiplicity, to the effect that, to quote Deleuze and Guattari, 'space and that which occupies space tend to become identified' (Deleuze and Guattari, 1987, p. 488) (or, to quote De Grazia's earlier analysis, the 'mole' is both container and contained in the 'mould').

Your rats your rations your rats rations[4]

Between the striated space of militarized Norway and the opposed polarities of Poland, Denmark, one might argue, liberates smooth, stammering 'marks' and 'fuzzy aggregates' (Deleuze and Guattari, 1987, p. 328) such as *Hamlet*'s near-redundant 'damned Dane' (V.2.304) or the series linking *Den-mark / market / march / Marcellus* (the one who marks the ghost) (I.1.6–9). Another monosyllabic series cuts across several animalized scenes in the play, such as the rat-ridden centre of Act III, when mice displace men. The mouse that refrained from stirring in the opening dialogue returns in the *Mouse-trap* as well as in the rat Hamlet mistakes Polonius for, in a textual context which rings the changes on quasi-similar but heterogeneous syllables: a rat / arras / rash (III.4.23–32). What occupies space (an imagined rat) and the backdrop that constitutes that space (the 'penetrable stuff' of the 'arras') become, in Deleuzian terms, identified. An additional, stray rat of sorts might be heard pattering in and out of the middle of Ho*rat*io's rational-sounding, humanistic name – a name less than solidly attached to a character who makes his partial entrance in *Hamlet* only as 'a piece of him', and happens to resonate, much later, in Gherasim Luca's stammered verse. With such mobile 'pieces' and name parts, one might argue, Shakespeare invents or machines a *nomos*-bound *logos*.

In an essay on '*Hamlet* and Counter-Humanism', Ronald Knowles comments on Shakespeare's use of the term 'machine' – which, Knowles recalls, 'is the first recorded instance of the word used in this way

(*OED* 4c)'. Knowles analyses the 'character' of Hamlet from the angle of 'Shakespeare's inner psychological perspective' and concludes that Hamlet fails to sustain his newly found, emotive subjectivity, since 'his mind is shaped by rhetoric':

> Rhetoric provides not just knowledge, but *how* knowledge was assimilated and understood: it provides a cognitive structure which enforced the Western censure of emotion. Consequently, in desperation, Hamlet ponders on dissolution of mind and body: 'O that this too too sullied flesh would melt' (I.2.129). But Hamlet's body actually undergoes a kind of reification when we hear, '*whilst this machine is to him*' (II.2.122–123). Hamlet is imprisoned with rhetoric the enemy within. (Knowles, 1999, p. 1064)

This is not at all how 'machine' is understood from a Deleuzian-Guattarian position. There is no incompossibility between Hamlet's signature as a 'machine' and his desire to 'melt'. No 'reification', to borrow Knowles's term, is implied in the word 'machine', which as a 'late-modern', Deleuzian-Guattarian philosophical object harbours infinitely mobile, fluctile, non-binary arrangements. *Hamlet* 'machines' Hamlet, as both character-and-play form a resonant series and cross thresholds of 'deterritorialization', or deconstruct the semantic barrier between a 'piece' and a '*pièce*', between player and play. A 'machine', besides referring to the 'human' frame, branches onto a continuum in which the word may signal a machination, a military engine, a ship, an apparatus, a combination of parts, as well as a contrivance for the production of stage effects, a piece of stagecraft. 'This' machine oscillates between the 'body' of Hamlet and the body of *Hamlet*, the collective force of a nomadic name. A machine, in Deleuzian-Guattarian terms, is a matter of 'flows'. It knows no 'reification', contrary to what Knowles implies – only 'melting'.

To M.E.L.T., to T.H.A.W.

Melting or 'unsinewing' affect the 'mettle' of man as well as the ontological underpinning of being. Between the metallic paraphernalia of Fortinbras's sonorous name, which sows the seeds of a proto-technical nightmare in the Heideggerian sense, and the steeled, helmeted figure of Hamlet the elder, Prince Hamlet's several disquisitions on 'melting' revise the politics of the 'mettle' of man. Between the territory-bound figures of the men of state, men of 'remembering' (Old Hamlet, Young Fortinbras), stands the line of flight of Hamlet, whose programme, 'to melt, thaw' (I.2.129–30), shuffles and 'posts' the letters of his 'own' yet disowned name, in a series of double-axis, chiral, left to right and top to bottom rotations: MLET / MELT, HAM-T / THAW.

Shakespeare's disassembly line follows what Deleuze and Guattari have called an abstract machine or 'diagram' which 'knows only traits and cutting edges ... which draw one another along, form relays, and meld in a shared deterritorialization: particles-signs' (Deleuze and Guattari, 1987, p. 142). Hamlet's strange solidifying, in Fortinbras's words, into a 'soldier', retains the possibility of escaping the 'code' of a return to solid state, to the kind of immobile, territorial, State-informed corps Fortinbras stands for. The zone of uncertainty or proximity between the two ends of what 'sold' means (paying in 'sols', coins, or welding, soldering, forming an alloy) somehow return Hamlet to a malleable, soldering metal. Hamlet's wish that 'this too too sallied flesh would melt, thaw, and resolve itself into a dew' is literally 'resolved' in the end, in both senses: as resolution and as repeatable process of re/solving without end – a dissolving, a soldering, a (ha)melting.

For the cryptic 'melting' and 'thawing' harboured in the proper / improper, loose name of Hamlet the character, *Hamlet* the play resorts to a verb in the infinitive: 'to post', used in the context of Gertrude's speedy betrayal, of her posting to 'incestuous sheets'. Positioned on the edge of a line, as a cliff-hanging infinitive, used in the context of chiasmic inversion ('O most wicked *sp*eed, to *p*ost, I.2.156), to 'post' operates as a variable verb, suspended between effects of speed, postal redirections and literal migrations – at a short distance from Hamlet's offer to 'change that name' with Horatio. The 'posted' letters of Hamlet's mobile name rewrite the 'proper' name on a foldable surface, the type of surface Deleuze and Guattari have termed a 'plateau'.

'Be', and being, also undergoes a posting process. Against Claudius's use of 'behaviour' (II.1.5) Hamlet circulates 'haviour' [I.2.81). 'To be or not to be' confronts two literal series, stringing, on the one hand, a series of alliterative bs (such as 'bear', 'bare', 'bare bodkin') chirally affected and reversed into an equally prolific string of 'ds' ('death', 'fardel', 'dread'). One of the effects of Hamlet's soliloquy is to produce a crossover, a mutant flow from one series to the next – to form, in Deleuze and Guattari's words, a 'post-signifying regime of signs' in which 'a sign or packet of signs detaches from the irradiating circular network and sets to work on its own account, starts running a straight line, as though swept into a narrow, open passage' (Deleuze and Guattari, 1987, p. 121).

Hamlet on a plateau

Whether on the platform of Elsinore or on a stage, names participate in the leveling process, in the making of a *nomos*. Uncouth juxtapositions warp words and names into chance, impersonal formations: out of Rome and off the well-defined map of the 'Roman street', one happens to jump into the less stable, *nomos*-oriented country of 'romage' (I.1.107–16). Tellus (III.2.138) strangely takes up Ophelia's previous 'tell us' (127). 'Ossa', the mountain Hamlet claims he would pile upon Olympus in a bout of rivalry against Laertes in the graveyard scene, becomes literally and cross-linguistically a signifier of the graveyard, a mountain of bones or '*os*'. Another nomadic table forms between the culturally well-mapped geography of Ossa and the plethoric, loud-mouthed figure of Osric (after the Latin '*os*' for mouth). As in the case of the earlier molecular 'mole', Shakespeare's asymmetries produce folds or involutions able to resist the rooted power of etymologies. A non-organic, machinic skeleton articulates one end to the next, plugging onto the signifier 'Ossa' the lateral, liquid force of Osric's comic fluidifications – mouth and mountain forming a heterogeneous assemblage in which the parasitic presence of the foreign, French particle '*os*' – 'bone' can be heard.

Similar effects seem to be programmed in the play's disarticulation of the name of Lamord, which a number of critics have explored, mainly for its deadly association with '*la mort*' (Ferguson, 1985). Spelt with a final 'd', however, Lamord is also a name with a bite to it – after the French '*mordre*', to bite. Out of such a name leaks the possibility of a rhizoming series which sends its letter-deep roots back towards one of the play's earlier remarks: 'the air bites (I.4.1), inviting not only to read backwards but also to read twice – as biting implies a coming home, a hold, as well as a cleaving, tearing process. A biting syllable connects, laterally, the names of H*am*let and L*am*ord in a viral assemblage, a 'pack' or 'multiplicity'. If the 'bras', the strong, military or meretricious ('brass') arm of Fortinbras proves stronger than Hamlet's hand, the ruling organ in the play's array of body parts is the 'mouth', or, to bring up the name of 'Lamord' once more, what 'bites'. A mouth is never there by itself. Twice, within a few lines, the same phrase 'not from his mouth' is used by Horatio in the last scene, referring to Hamlet's mouth and to a posthumous 'mouth whose voice will draw on more' (V.2.371). A notable textual variation occurs in this line, some editions preferring 'no more' to 'on more' (cf. Shakespeare, 1937, p. 156), which gives the sentence another twist – more bite, in the reversible sense of the word. '*Draw* on / no more' grafts itself on Hamlet's previous request that Horatio '*draw* [his] breath in pain to tell my story' (V.2.327). In the context of so many (final) drafts, *Hamlet* calls for additional breathings. The h-inspired, breathing line formed by the names of Hamlet/Horatio follows the folds of a dual trajectory, aspired and expired.

L'homme into loam

The failed attempt to seal off graves, bodies and meanings, to plug or block the 'ends' of man, comes as close as can be to the question of humanism in connection with *humus*, the substance in which human-ism finds its pseudo-etymological roots. *Hamlet*, however, comes up with a non-Latin word for it, a term both glutinous and apt to flow, with the help of its liquid initial: loam – 'of earth we make loam; and why of that loam whereto he was converted might they not stop a beer-barrel?' (V.1.180–2). Loam (also found in *Richard II*'s 'men are but gilded loam', [I.1.179]) is a variation on lime – the sticky, clayey substance that per-vades the 'limed soul' of Claudius (III.3.68), and as such seeps through the play. Opposed, yet close, to the '*limes*' of the limit, 'lime' and in particular 'loam' form a literal deterritorialization of '*l'homme*', one of the names of man. If 'loam' operates as a device, a minimal machine (a stopper), as a proto-Deleuze and Guattari machine it works mostly by breaking down.

Nothing is stopped by Hamlet's use of 'loam', which, like the term 'bunghole' (a 'bung' being a stopper as well as a hole), calls for trans-verse connections (beyond the French connection that lawlessly retunes loam as *l'homme*). Rather than build on the biblical *topoi* of dust and vanity, 'loam' creates a focus of linguistic instability, in which 'man' (the clayey, loamy principle of the early verses of Genesis) flows with the fluid force of beer out of a barrel, or with the equally fluid force of 'the wind' or the 'winter's flaw' (V.1.186) – a flaw or a flow, if one fol-lows Hamlet's invitation 'but to follow' (V.1.176). The 'dust' or solid 'earth' at the root of '*humus*' and 'human' are revised into flows, in a scene prosodically ridden with liquid consonants (as in Hamlet's 'but to follow him thither with modesty enough, and likelihood to lead it'). Loam is generated in a speech that, on the page, combines prose and verse – four lines of verse formatted as a visual block, graphically performing as a textual stopper in the mouth of prose.

Hamlet's 'moles' and their chiral counterpart 'loam' bring humanism close to ground (neither land nor *humus*) – making it, in both senses, touch ground. Loam – a possible cross-linguistic substitute for *l'homme* – does not belong with the 'molar or rigid segments that always seal, plug, block the lines of flight' (Deleuze and Guattari, 1987, p. 223). It makes them flow, between the lines, between languages.

Posts and stops: from *Hamlet* to Henry Miller

Henry Miller's *Hamlet Letters* began as an epistolary exchange with Michael Fraenkel, a correspondence spanning four pre-war years (1935–8) which, according to plan, should have filled one thousand pages – a proto-version of *A Thousand Plateaus*, as it were, at least for its arbitrary engagement with numerical size. When reverting to the circumstances of writing, Miller wonders:

> Was it not the fact that we suddenly agreed to write a thousand pages, not one more, not one less, which clinched the idea? Where was Hamlet then? The thousand pages were more important than *Hamlet* itself. *Hamlet*, that is to say, hath neither beginning nor end. The whole world has become *Hamlet* and what we say will neither add nor subtract from the subject. (Miller, 1988, p. 19)

The letter exchange failed to reach its planned size and was never published in toto – as successive editions, whether British, French or American, failed to bring together both sides of the correspondence. In one of the first letters addressed to his co-writer, Henry Miller states that he is out to 'waylay the ghost and strangle it', to 'reveal the lingering effects of Hamletism and thus to scotch it'. Yet a perceptible Hamletian strain infiltrates Miller's writing in other instances, such as in the statement that 'when one is a hero to himself he feels under no obligation to act' (p. 35). Miller embarks on a redefinition of man in vegetal terms:

> The fascination for the animal side of our nature leads us to ignore, or despise, the plant in us ... If man is ever going to become himself, MAN, and not something different, he will have to stand outside the realm of Idea and, growing more and more satisfied with himself, vegetate ... My plan, then, is to stop evolving ... The weed exists only to fill the waste spaces left by cultivated areas. It grows between, among other things. (Miller, 1988, p. 53)

'Growing between', intercalated growth, the need to glorify the weed and the *nomos*, the 'waste spaces' in which weed grows (as opposed to cultivation and arborescences) figure prominently in the introduction to Deleuze and Guattari's *A Thousand Plateaus* – in their opening defence of the rhizome which is 'composed not of units but of dimensions or rather directions in motion' and 'has neither beginning nor end' (Deleuze and Guattari, 1987, p. 21). What has neither beginning nor end, one might add, can be, with little or no loss, reversed – and the 'post' of linearity turned inside out, into Miller's 'stops':

> For when Shakespeare talks it is empty prattle to me, but when he nods, when he dreams, then do I follow him … You close your eyes and put your fingers on a stop – anywhere – and then, because of a vibration inaccessible to the understanding of man, millions of other stops suddenly spring up out of the brake of the Unconscious … As every organ stops bowels forth its secrets there comes about a limitless confusion in which truth and untruth are drowned, and in the surrender to the flux, to the welter of eternal transformation, there is born at the same time an illogical harmony and agreement which simply says – I AM. To the brink of this abyss Hamlet refused to draw near. Tightly and proudly he held himself – held back the gift of surrender. (Miller, 1988, p. 88)

In and out of Miller's 'stop' flows the vibration, the reversible force to resist the solidifications of the 'post', of posting and posthumanism. Against Miller's judgement that Hamlet 'held back the gift of surrender', one could add that Henry Miller's own initials (H / M, as well as the 'AM' he chose to capitalize) recirculate, in helter-skelter fashion, the letters of Hamlet the name – turned *nomos*.

Notes

1. A number of dated (though not outdated) philological enquiries on the name of Hamlet open up what from a Deleuzian perspective belongs to a rhizoming rather than to a 'root'- or 'stem'-oriented approach: Kemp Malone, among other philologists, cites one of the Old English derivations of the name of Hamlet, based on *'hamelod'* meaning 'foolish, crazy', and quotes A. Nordfelt and Detter who derive 'the Hamlet tale from the Roman tale of Brutus and … look upon the name *Hamlet* as a translation of the Latin *brutus'* (Malone, 1928, p. 258).
2. Further research would be required linking Deleuze and Shakespeare via Marcus Aurelius, a late Stoic figure, quoted in *The Logic of Sense*, as well as indirectly imported into the subtext of *Hamlet* (in the 'noble-dust of Alexander' (V.1.197), which, as Ronald Knowles shows, is found 'in the Stoic context of Marcus Aurelius where the dust of Alexander is likened to that of his groom' (Knowles, 1999, p. 1047).

3. The phrase is from Derrida's essay 'Les fins de l'homme', which conveys impersonal echoes, floating traits which seem to import their marks from *Hamlet*'s Denmark, and to peddle the trembling name of Shakespeare: 'Man is the proper of Being, which right near to him *whispers in his ear*; Being is the proper of man, such is the truth that speaks, such is the proposition which gives the there of the truth of Being and the truth of man ... Is not this security of the near what is *trembling* today, that is, the co-belonging and co-propriety of the name of man and the name of Being, such as this co-propriety inhabits, and is inhabited by, the language of the West ? ... But this *trembling* ... was already requisite within the very structure that it solicits. Its *margin was marked* in its own (*propre*) body' (Derrida, 1982, pp. 133–4; my emphasis).
4. Cf. Luca, 1973, p. 87–94; quoted in Deleuze and Guattari, in the context of redundancies and stammering language (1987, p. 132).

Works cited

Ansell Pearson, Keath (1997) *Viroid Life, Perspectives on Nietzsche and the Transhuman Condition*, London and New York: Routledge.

Cixous, Hélène (2010) *The Blindfolded Fiancée or Amelait* (2004), scenes 5 and 6, trans. Judith G. Miller, in M. Segarra (ed.), *The Portable Cixous*, New York: Columbia University Press, pp. 257–77.

De Grazia, Margreta (2007) *Hamlet without* Hamlet, Cambridge: Cambridge University Press.

Deleuze, Gilles (1990) *The Logic of Sense*, ed. Constantin V. Boundas, New York: Columbia University Press.

Deleuze, Gilles, and Félix Guattari (1987) *A Thousand Plateaus: Capitalism and Schizophrenia*, trans. Brian Massumi, Minneapolis: University of Minnesota Press.

Derrida, Jacques (1982) *Margins of Philosophy*, trans. Alan Bass, Chicago: University Press of Chicago.

Ferguson, Margaret (1985) '*Hamlet*: Letters and Spirits', in Patricia Parker and Geoffrey Hartman (eds), *Shakespeare and the Question of Theory*, New York and London: Routledge, pp. 292–309.

Garnier, Marie-Dominique (2003) '*Hamlet*: Selected Letters – between Derrida and Deleuze', *The Oxford Literary Review* 25 (Thomas Dutoit and Philippe Romanski (eds), *Angles on Derrida, Jacques Derrida and Anglophone Literature*), pp. 63–77.

Greenblatt, Stephen (2004) 'The Death of Hamnet and the making of *Hamlet*', *New York Review of Books* 21 October (available online at: http://www.nybooks.com/articles/archives/2004/oct/21/the-death-of-hamnet-and-the-making-of-hamlet/

Hawkes, Terence (1986) *That Shakespehearian Rag*, London and New York: Methuen.

Kay, Dennis (1991) *Shakespeare, His Life, Work and Era*, London, Sidgwick and Jackson.

Knowles, Ronald (1999) 'Hamlet and Counter-Humanism', *Renaissance Quarterly* 52.4, pp. 1046–69.

Luca, Gherasim (1973) *Le Chant de la carpe*, Paris: Soleil noir.

Malone, Kemp (1928) 'More Etymologies for Hamlet', *Review of English Studies* 4.15 (July), pp. 257–69.

Miller, Henry (1988) *Hamlet Letters*, Santa Barbara: Capra Press.

Nietzsche, Friedrich Wilhelm (1988) *Teleologie seit Kant* [1867], in C. Crawford, *The Beginnings of Nietzsche's Theory of Language*, Berlin and New York, Walter de Gruyter, pp. 238–67 [trans. Ansel Pearson, 1997, p. 138, n. 13].

Shakespeare, William (1992) *Hamlet, A Norton Critical Edition*, ed. Cyrus Hoy, New York: Norton.

Shakespeare, William (1998) *The First Quarto of Hamlet*, ed. Kathleen O. Irace, Cambridge: Cambridge University Press.

Voltaire (1963) 'Lettres philosophiques XVIII'; 'Lettre à d'Argental (1776)', reprinted in 'Voltaire: A Shakespeare Journal', *Yale French Studies* 33.5, pp. 10–11.

Wilson, Richard (2007) *Shakespeare in French Theory, King of Shadows*, London and New York: Routledge.

11
'This?': Posthumanism and the Graveyard Scene in *Hamlet*

Ivan Callus

'The Shakespearean Collection': novelty, posthumanism and death

In 1991 the Royal Doulton Company, which manufactures tableware, glassware and china collectables, discontinued 'The Shakespearean Collection'. The collection, launched in 1982, featured a range of six character jugs depicting well-known characters from the plays – Hamlet, Macbeth, Othello, Henry V, Romeo – as well as the playwright himself.[1] As with all portraiture, ascribing identity is difficult unless the subject is straightforwardly recognizable. Recognition is consequently prompted through cues in the jugs' design which, if unsubtle, contribute to the charms of grotesquerie that make the jugs what they are. The jug depicting Macbeth, for instance (Doulton Number D6667), helpfully sets in the handle three unprepossessing faces, evidently those of the witches. Indeed, the design of Royal Doulton's character jugs is rather less restrained than the Company's heritage, built on the work of artists like Charles J. Noke, George Tinworth or Mark V. Marshall, may lead one to expect. This is clear also in the jug in the collection that depicts the head of William Shakespeare (D6689). The figure of the Globe Theatre is set at the foot of the handle; closer inspection shows that the handle is shaped as a quill, that the Globe is cast as an inkwell and that a theatrical mask adorns either point of Shakespeare's collar. Clearly, jug art is less conservatively hagiographical than the art of the bust, which memorializes famous heads too but does so with rather more classical leanings and with less inclusiveness towards figures from literature or popular culture.

Other jugs depicting Shakespeare that are not part of the collection extend the disinvestment in restraint which is part of jug poetics. One example has two handles rather than one, with each carrying three different figures of characters from the plays on either side of the Bard's head (D6933). Another (D6938), like the one in the collection, has the handle shaped as a quill set in an inkwell, the difference being this jug's smaller size and the inclusion of two books with burgundy covers serving as a stand for the inkwell. Yet another, issued in 1999 as the company's Character Jug of the Year in commemoration of the four-hundredth anniversary of the Globe's opening, has the handle 'fashioned from the masks of Comedy and Tragedy, as well as a replica of the Globe Theatre' itself (D7136; cf. Dale, 2008, p. 386). This allusive exuberance jars with the sparer statuettes that helped earn Royal Doulton its 'legacy of excellence' (cf. Whittecar and Rimpley, 2002; and Eyles, Irvine and Baynton, 1994, pp. 59–62), including the vellum figures designed by Charles Noke of Henry Irving in the roles of Cardinal Wolsey and Shylock, of Ellen Terry in the role of Queen Catharine and Portia (introduced in 1893) and of Shakespeare himself (introduced in 1899).[2] However, for the purposes of this chapter, which focuses on posthumanism in the graveyard scene in *Hamlet* through some reflections on faces and skulls, on heads and beheading, on figuration and disfiguration, and on familiarity and (mis)recognition, the jugs in 'The Shakespearean Collection' make a suitable, if unexpected, gift. As I hope to show, there is relevance in the unusual incipit they prompt and the foils they provide.

Unfortunately, the collection fell shy of depicting Yorick, who will be important in this chapter's argument. Royal Doulton has produced various figures of jesters, but the catalogues designate them merely as 'Jester' or 'Jack Point' and do not specify Yorick in the role.[3] Nevertheless, the alternative sitting on my desk, a 7¼" jug produced between 1982 and 1989 which instead portrays Hamlet, is telling enough (D6672). It shows the hero's head and a bit of neck. Lined and heavy-featured, the ruddy face is too middle-aged to be in keeping with how one might imagine 'young Hamlet' (I.1.169).[4] However, it will perhaps just do if we prefer to believe the suggestion in the graveyard scene that he is thirty. In keeping with jug design, the art is not minimalist. The hero is shown in the hand-to-chin stance of cogitation; further contributing to the jug's busy design is a 'chapfallen' (V.1.182) and disproportionately small skull nestling beneath Hamlet's healthier left cheek. Additionally, Hamlet has an Osric-like gaucherie in his wearing of headgear (V.2.79–91). He bears a black, flamboyant hat on his blonde hair, a generous interpretation for which might presume allusion to the 'sable-plumed hat' that became 'conventionalized' after John Philip Kemble's first performances in the role in the late eighteenth century (cf. Hapgood, 1999, p. 108). And this Hamlet appears to have been very assertive about logoed-up self-absorption. The headgear bears his initial, *H*, prominently brocaded on the front of the cap. The letter is also monogrammed on the jug's handle, which is shaped in the figure of a sheathed dagger and with the hat's plume – *blanc* rather than *sable* – twined around the hilt. We cannot be in doubt therefore. 'This is I, Hamlet the Dane', the jug is saying (V.1.246–7).

With recognition established (one could also remember, of course, the expedient of turning the jug over to read its name on the base, beneath the Royal Doulton backstamp), let us see what might be taken from the improbable reference to character jugs in a posthumanist context. Posthumanist futures, we know, have scant use for yesteryear's knick-knacks. Their designs and textures follow not the intimacy of ceramic art but, as Rosi Braidotti demonstrates, the edge and purpose of the meta*l*morphic (Braidotti, 2002, ch. 5). Nevertheless, an amenability to posthumanist capture can be discovered in these homely jugs, at least in the Hamlet example. To show that, let us first recall that at its most fundamental, and away from 'the technological unconscious' or 'the technological sublime' or 'the prosthetic aesthetic' or considerations

Illustration 11.1   Toby Jug, *Hamlet*, Royal Doulton Number D6672, photograph Joseph Mangion

of 'enhanced humanity', the *post-human* – hyphenation, here, carries significance – is only ever, and most directly, about death (see Powell, 2008; and Nye, 1994). Death dominates Hamlet, both character and play. And few scenes in the history of theatre are more nakedly focused on death than the graveyard scene in *Hamlet*. Death remains the focus as Hamlet moves, with harrowing differences in tone and mood, from the graveside repartee involving the first gravedigger, who as Harold Bloom notes is 'the only personage in the play witty enough to hold his own with Hamlet' (Bloom, 2003, p. 5), to the pondering of Yorick's skull, to the raucous grieving that seeks to upstage what Lacan sees as the ostentatious mourning of Laertes (Lacan, 1977, p. 35). At the same time, few scenes are quite so histrionic and *loud*. Yet for all its lack of restraint (the analogy with the jugs is easily recalled here), for all its staginess, for all its endless reproduction and fixity in the popular imagination, the scene retains its delicacy, rawness and mystery. It does so partly because Hamlet has been so introspectively and singularly expressive of the generalized human encounter with ineluctable decay; partly because he is or is not unmethodically mad and free of any antic disposition in the impetuousness of his grief once the funeral cortège arrives and the fact of Ophelia's suicide is revealed; and partly because it is always instructive to reread or watch the scene again and to see how the renewed sense of its poignancy overcomes the suspicion that it might pall upon us or seem platitudinous.

There is an irony in that, for the scene can not only seem like its own cliché, but can also exemplify that other cliché, 'what oft was thought but ne'er so well express'd'. The familiarity of the quotation from Pope's *An Essay on Criticism* (1711) should not obscure the intriguing realization that this has itself become a cliché on the workings of cliché. Or, at least, it prompts reflection on the manner in which any supreme re-articulation of commonplace thought or of a truth acknowledged and understood by all can bear becoming platitudinous and grows neither tired nor tiresome in the repetition.[5] What is critical in this context is the way in which cliché can turn or take on associations with catachresis, linked by Derrida and Paul de Man with the figure of dead metaphor.[6] Cliché and catachresis, which both emerge from overfamiliarity and easy recognition, are very often co-implicated. They can be a little more than kin and quite of a kind, to adapt the words of the play's hero (I.2.65). More will be said later of such punning in the graveyard scene and beyond, of the relation between the familial and the familiar, of estrangement from them and from oneself, and of how cliché and catachresis find themselves (dis)placed there. Meanwhile, note here that the graveyard scene and particularly the episode with the skull, which contributes so much to the enduring allure of the play, stand in a little too recognizably now as a prime expression of melancholy, incomprehension and grief before death's inescapable and levelling despoliation. Only the phrase *Vanitas vanitatum omnia vanitas* is more economic in that regard.[7] The episode with the skull, then, is almost familiar enough to be a dead metaphor, a cliché. Nothing, it could be said, is more banal than a classic, and the episode has been classicized and banalized into triteness. It is so well known that refreshing its oft and commonplace thoughts on death is both impossible and imperative. It also means that any posthumanist take on the graveyard scene must meet the challenge of finding new resonances in one of literature's most familiar scenes.

It is hard to see how a character jug can help in that. Let us persist, however. We are, we know, overfamiliar with *Hamlet*. And we are even more overfamiliar with Hamlet's holding of Yorick's skull – or *a* skull, for, as will be shown, much could be made of the fact that it cannot be certain that the skull is Yorick's. The familiarity is clear also from the fact it only needs a young man to intently hold up a skull, or pretend to, for him to be an instant Hamlet. In an essay on the graveyard scene, which incidentally explains why that holding was never gender-specific, Catherine Belsey draws attention to how all over Europe, 'nineteenth-century actors who made their reputations playing the Prince of Denmark were also identified by the skull in their hands' (Belsey, 2002, p. 136). Before that, however, the scene had occasionally been perceived as burdensome on the play's effects and reputation. It was irritating to the aesthetic sensibilities of Voltaire, and David Garrick saw fit to exclude it entirely from his production of the play.[8] But the skull episode could not be suppressed. It had too many other familiar echoes. Research by Roland Mushat Frye, Belsey, Margreta de Grazia, Alain Tapié and others establishes the episode's roots in longstanding memento mori traditions and within the commonest cultural currencies – across both popular and more genteel iconographies – of the bared human cranium, by far the earliest and readiest token of death (cf. Belsey, 2001, ch. 5; Frye, 1979; De Grazia, 2007; Tapié, 2010).

It is therefore not speculative to suggest that the scene might already have appeared quite unoriginal to Shakespeare's audience, to whom other ingenious representations of skulls would not have been entirely unfamiliar.[9] There is the anamorphic skull in Hans Holbein's *The Ambassadors* (1533), a painting produced 66 years before *Hamlet*'s first staging. It defamiliarizes cranial associations and, all too literally, slants them differently. Before that Dante, in gruesome sequences in Canto 32 of the *Inferno*, depicts the skull of Archbishop Ruggieri degli Ubaldini being gnawed at by the head of an enemy, Ugolino della Gherardesca's: a punishment both original and eternal.[10] The sharper comparison, however, is with Andreas Vesalius's pioneering study of human anatomy, *De humani corporis fabrica* (1543). Vesalius there provided a number of plates in which he revealed human life bared to its inmost bone and nerve and sinew. They are marked by a dissecting detail that even nowadays appears extraordinary. To sixteenth-century eyes they would have seemed all too posthumanly exquisite, searching for the core of humanity itself (from Latin *exquirere*, to search out). The first book in Vesalius's work is devoted to the 'delineation of the bones' and the skeletal structure, with sections and plates focusing on 'Variants of skull shape', 'Three views of the base of the skull', 'Internal aspects of the base of the skull', 'Anterior aspects of the skull', and, later, representations of the occipital bone and 'dissection of the cranium' and the skull cavity (see Saunders and O'Malley, 1973). It is unlikely that Shakespeare and his audience were not aware of the famous plate, the twenty-second of that first book, bearing the figure of a skeleton contemplating a skull that rests on a tomb bearing the inscription 'Vivitur ingenio, caetera mortis erunt' (Genius lives on, all else is mortal). If he (and they) did, then the episode with the skull is derivative (as so much else in Shakespeare): a revisiting of what would already have been clichéd, both in the light of the plate and possibly also of the *Ur-Hamlet*, the source play which remains stubbornly lost. Indeed, it has been said that Vesalius's skeleton is the first Hamlet in history (cf. Henschen, 1966, p. 59; and Fehrman, 1952). Shakespeare, in other words, would have been recasting the familiar. Admittedly, what Vesalius conjures up is starker: the skeletal ponders the cranial, so that the subject is only vestigially human and, for all the anthropomorphically vital and poised arrangement of meditative bones in the illustration, already very dead, very post-human. The skull in Vesalius, however, does not quite return the look; the lines of sight do not meet. In *Hamlet* they do, at least in most enactments of the episode. Consequently the skull in Vesalius's illustration does not prompt the continuation of the cliché-quotation from Pope: 'Something whose truth convinced at sight we find / that gives us back the image of our mind.' Instead the skeleton seems to have been caught in the act of ponderingly rolling his skull (which, in fact, is another's). Vesalius's imagining of a graveyard scene, therefore, may have been starker and more reduced than Shakespeare's, which is almost too fleshed. However, if not ironic the inscription on the tombstone is arguably more hopeful than the intimation of complete oblivion in the graveyard scene, while the gaze of death is still not quite as unnervingly reciprocal as in the play, even if the plate suggests the prospect of a staring contest between a skeleton and a skull: between the skeletally posthuman and the cranially empty, to both of which the direction of perception and conscious thought is counter-intuitively imputed.

Because of these outré genealogies of the familiar, reimagining the play radically is a challenge. Our sense of Shakespeare's refashioning ingenuity but also of his borrowings is sharpened by consideration of these intertexts. Those who say that they would give anything to be able to travel back to the first-ever performance of *Hamlet* to witness audience reaction implicitly acknowledge that. Whatever we do with the play can never quite achieve originality – nor with the graveyard scene which, inexhaustible as it is, must always have seemed derivative even at its freshest. How, then, can *Hamlet* be defamiliarized? What kind of reading could lead to its well-known setpieces – the ghost on the ramparts, the play within a play, the death of Ophelia, the graveyard scene and Hamlet's address to Yorick's skull, the final duel and all the tragic deaths – conveying the elusive sense of freshness it only tenuously ever had? Is there any reading that can impossibly go beyond everything that is culturally preframed in our response to Shakespeare, thereby radically recasting for our posthumanist times our sensibilities about this play?

Hardly. Originality is in any case not expected from Shakespeare criticism. Blurbs and reviews, if they are anything to go by, applaud achievements measured in phrases like 'bold reinterpretation' or 'critical revaluation'. Revision, rethinking, rereading: these are the more realistic objectives, not originality or newness. Indeed, there is the danger that in aspiring to originality and newness what is pulled off instead is novelty. Novelty, '[t]he quality of being new, original, or unusual' (*OED*), but a quality touched by connotations of tawdry and transient originality, has instant but not enduring appeal. The suggestion that any attempt at a posthumanist reading might provide something more radical than this – something original rather than novel, something new rather than something renewed, something inaugural rather than 'rethought' – is suspect. It is unlikely that posthumanism can lay on the major new editorial or philological or historical or conceptual discovery to change that. At most it might add itself usefully to the diverse repertoire of contemporary Shakespeare criticism.

The Hamlet character jug in 'The Shakespearean Collection' therefore takes on an emblematic, cautionary presence. It is a 'novelty' in the way that so many novelties are: whimsically charming on a first encounter, but with tenuous claims on sustained appeal. No rereading or alternative reading of Shakespeare will want to end up there. Consequently the jug acts as a warning of where reinterpretation – whether on boards, in print, or in porcelain – ought not to go. But the jug is evocative of something else. People who acquire this 'collectible' may do so because of having bought into its commodification of some of the best-known Hamlet features: here, his introspection and the episode with the skull. We look at it, however, and probably feel that the cues are too heavy-hinting. Perhaps any attempt to reread *Hamlet* that wishes to lay some kind of claim, however measured or self-deluding, on newness might instead seek to defamilarize or at least reframe those very associations in the play (just like Shakespeare reframed Vesalius). In other words, it is all about recognition of familiarity and defamiliarization of what ought to be recognizable, in life *and* death – a dynamic accessibly present with the Hamlet jug, but which is more darkly apprehensible in the graveyard scene. The rest of this chapter consequently reconsiders the graveyard scene in *Hamlet* (while keeping the jug and its lessons in view, almost as in one of those Renaissance paintings depicting the practice of writing, with a skull on the desk). The most grandiose reason for that reconsideration would be that any assessment of posthumanism's purchase on Shakespeare must address arguably the best-known scene in arguably the best-known play. The more sober justification, however, arises when remembering what was indicated above. The posthuman is, at its most direct, about death. The play's emphasis on that theme, on motifs involving skulls, graves and (dis)interment, and on the sense of melancholy, absurdity and despair when confronted with others' finitude – and thence with the disjunctive temporalities of self-mourning that are confronted in Vesalius too – attaches itself most unnervingly in this scene, and in its extensions of the memento mori tradition that render it central, to rephrase one of Bloom's titles, to Shakespeare's invention of the *post*human. In doing so it tries to keep one lesson of the Hamlet character jug firmly in view. Heads and faces, headiness and defacement, truncation and bodilessness, 'firstness' and novelty are what it must (not) be about.

Truncation, beheading, recognition, (mis)identification: the graveyard scene reread

Through their design and ornamentation, character jugs disguise the fact that they mutilate. Jugs are all about heads parted from bodies.

It would be frivolous to say that this explains why the faces some-times look grotesque. The creators of 'The Shakespeare Collection', for instance, did not after all share the morbidity of Théodore Géricault. During the same period that he painted his famous *Le Radeau de la Méduse* (1819), Géricault was working on studies of decapitated heads, as well as on one of the starkest pictures of the posthuman ever depicted. *Étude de pieds et de mains* (1817–19; Musée Fabre) is a chiaroscuro composition of a pile of dismembered human limbs. The macabre arrangement is determined by the sweep of an arm that is the topmost limb in the pile. It is severed at the shoulder and encircled above the elbow by the tattered and bloodied remains of a sleeve. The crook of forearm and upper arm appears to almost embrace the lower part of a human leg, the foot of which is thrust into the foreground with an anatomical detail and directness that arrests the eye before this moves down the painting to notice that the hand rests just above another foot, less sharply distinct but easily discernible, that appears unattached to any leg.

There are many things that are unnerving in this picture. They all go beyond the shock at the casual care with which apparently butchered human body parts are arranged in still(ed) life – a *nature (humaine) morte*. There is the twin association of slaughterhouse and charnel house. There is the frisson of sensing a throbbing vitality in the limbs still, well past death but before decomposition. There is, simultane-ously, the sense that though these body parts are anatomically as precise as their analogues in Vesalius and more fleshed, they are much deader. There is the incongruity of the tender cradle of the arm which embraces, in a manner suggesting that the head of a loved one might have nestled there in life, only dismembered limbs that may or may not have belonged to the same body. There is the realization that in life these limbs, if they did not belong to the same body, were never in articulation, which brings the deliberation behind their togetherness on canvas into ruthless relief. And there is the further realization that the limbs' objectification appears so stark precisely because the absence of a head (or heads) and a torso (or torsos) renders the sense of disarticulation – of perception and sentiment as well as of corpus and corpse(s) – all too literally 'out of joint'. The arrangement, indeed, is sharply truncating of anything that might be considered whole(some). Without the trunk(s), and especially without the head(s), these limbs suspend identity. The painting is about that suspension. It portrays a state that leaves forever in abeyance questions concerning identity and identification.

I mention *Étude de pieds et de mains* here because it offers this chapter, which among other things is about portraits, a full-face study of abjectest (post)humanity without face. A further reason is its affinity and difference with Géricault's associated paintings of the guillotined heads of criminals. The heads are all very dead. But the expression on a number of them is still vitally aghast, caught in the registering of anguish and fear. They provide a disquieting reminder of what character jugs suppress.

Jugs, busts, portraiture, close-ups decapitate only in a manner of speaking and for effect, often affectionately or reverentially. But these decapitations, even on canvas, are real. And even in abjection – after their macabre defiguring of humanity expelled by and from humanity – they press their claim on recognition. Humanity itself, however, is scantly recognizable here. Identity and personality and pasts can be only incompletely gleaned from disembodied, discarded heads and limbs. What we see instead is humanity in the raw: beyond enhancement in life, death, art, science or posthuman redetermination. Character jugs,

Illustration 11.2 Théodore Géricault, *Severed Heads*, © The Nationalmuseum Stockholm, reproduced with permission

busts, portraiture distance this rawness. This happens also, say, with Lewis Carroll's *Alice in Wonderland* (1865), where the apparition of the Cheshire cat's head or the 'Off with their heads!' mantra of the Queen of Hearts never quite unsettle us enough, in their games with heads parted from bodies, to induce us to worry over wholeness. It is almost as if such stories, like jugs, sanitize what even cauterization cannot treat.[11]

And yet, as we shall see, the effects of mis/dis-identification where the acephalous and the bodiless are concerned will be cautionary for our conclusions on posthumanism. We can anticipate: before all levels of stilled life and in all attempts, off the prompts provided by human remains, to charge memory and imagination with the sense of what was once vital and whole, all that is thrust towards us is the irrecoverable. We unearth skulls, but little more; we recognize (or not) a (death's) head, and we build on that or come up against the futility of trying to. There is hardly a reading of the graveyard scene that fails to point out that dynamic. The ache of the loss of the other and the certainty of self-loss prompt sublime and commonplace thought, and we have seen how cliché comes to rest there. The theme is linked to familiar moves in poststructuralist commentaries on anamorphosis, defacement, *méconnaissance* and their relation to death, as the third section indicates. How might all this be connected, however, to posthumanism? Might the posthuman be the name, or the process, of the experience of the estrangement from what is most familiar to the human? Is *Etude de pieds et de mains* so disturbing because that estrangement is so raw: rawer, even, than Vesalius's illustrations? How, by extension, does the graveyard scene in *Hamlet*, where the hero faces (*down* and *up to*) and recognizes defacement, (dis)figuration, decomposition and death, relate (to) that? How precisely does this posthuman relation turn on the defamiliarization and scope for misrecognition of what was once most familiar, so that what is left – what is sinister – is enactment of the impossible recognition of what is at once most strange *and* best known and remembered? How is it that what occurs there is the laying bare of what had been closest in the quick of life? And how, in the end, does bare death bare life?

Clichédly. That is the answer to that last question. We have already seen that cliché dogs this inquiry, and we shall return to the problem of cliché (having, in truth, never left it). But there are the other questions to answer before we can readdress it properly, and to do so we must home in on an urgent, prior question. What does it mean to recognize a skull? 'Is't possible?'

Hamlet, we often seem to forget, does not recognize Yorick. How could he? One skull is very like another, unless one digs with the knowledge of a paleoanthropologist, say, who can distinguish the skull of a member of one species of human from another, or with the knowledge of a gravedigger, apt to think of a grave as 'his' and thereby able to be, or claim to be, familiar with and/or responsible for its contents and confident in identifying a skull. The gravedigger in this most famous of all scenes in Shakespeare – a cliché built on clichés, a dead metaphor on death that never dies – is competitively and (un)equivocatingly particular about property. When asked by Hamlet 'Whose grave's this, sirrah?', he is prompt in saying 'Mine', and cheekily proceeds with his song. When he verbally fences with Hamlet over lying in the grave and thence laying claim to it, he pertly (and forebodingly) returns with "Tis a quick lie, sir, 'twill away again from me to you.' The insolence is not mitigated by his use of the polite form, *you*, to Hamlet, who has addressed him as *thou* and *sirrah* (V.1.110–22). Hamlet might through that usage have immediately tried to keep him in his place. But it is a place from where the answer is indeed 'quick' and one which will be swapped when Hamlet leaps into the grave for his competitive mourning with Laertes. Certainly, in the sense meant by the gravedigger the grave will remain his, even if it might eventually be Hamlet's – and indeed, the play's pace is pretty smart from this point on, and Hamlet will need a grave soon. Significantly, Hamlet warily and uncharacteristically pulls back from wordplay here – 'We must speak by the card or equivocation will undo us' – and takes a different line: 'How long has't thou been gravemaker?' (V.1.134). Whereupon the answer confirms the counter-identification between the two characters: 'It was that very day that young Hamlet was born', which, we learn, is 'thirty years' ago, quite as long as the gravedigger has been 'sexton here, man and boy' (V.1.139–53).

Here the gravedigger may indeed be lying in the grave: that is, about it and from it. The supposition that Shakespeare was careless about making 'young Hamlet' all of thirty years old is less careless if we accept that someone who equivocates might also lie and deceive. We must suppose that the gravedigger does not recognize Hamlet, who presumably, as a number of critics have suggested, is still wearing his 'sea-gown', having freshly returned from England. But there is a chance the gravedigger might indeed have recognized Hamlet, and is having his play as well as his grave. And the play and the deceit might further run – just to speculate – to saying that the skull is Yorick's when it isn't. Indeed, the gravedigger does not even have to lie or to intend any mischief for what follows from that to demand scrutiny. He only has to be mistaken. For interpretation to direct itself differently, the gravedigger need only have been imprecisely taxonomic about who 'liest in't' and who he has (dis)interred there. After all, he chucks skulls around his 'grave' with the insouciance suggested in the stage direction, '*Throws up a skull*', and with an abandon and effrontery that moves Hamlet to have him down (three times) as a 'knave'. Which means, of course, that we must scrutinize the moment when the skull is handed over. It is a moment more pivotal for this chapter's purposes than Hamlet's meditations on the skull.

The gravedigger has a fine judgement of build up: 'Here is a skull now hath lien you i' th'earth three and twenty years' (V.1.163–4). As Thompson and Taylor note, 'Q2's *lyen* may suggest an echo on the punning on *lie*.' We are, indeed, already in the tease of uncertainty, and also, we know, in a place of equivocation and possibly deceit. And soon the gravedigger announces, with pointed, deliberated pauses – they had not punctuated his language up to this point – his identification (which, incidentally, is not solicited): 'This same skull, sir, was, sir, Yorick's skull, the King's jester' (V.1.170–1). Notice the repetition of 'sir', as if in eager deference, or in anticipation of the effect his ascription might provoke. Hamlet replies with only one word. 'This?' (V.1.172). The sense of wonderment on that simple word, 'This?', is dramatic. It is also innocent. It is, after all, the response of someone already described by Claudius as 'most generous and free of all contriving' (IV.7.133). The gravedigger confirms his identification. 'E'en that' (V.1.173). Hamlet must take the gravedigger's identification on trust, and does. His 'This?' does not suggest doubt over the identification. Rather it communicates the process of accommodation to the posthuman, described earlier in this chapter as the experience of the estrangement from what is most familiar to the human.

Admittedly, histories of the play in performance do not appear to suggest that Hamlet doubts the gravedigger (cf. Rosenberg, 1992; Hapgood, 1999).[12] But it is significant that Gail Kern Paster, in her reflections on 'thinking with skulls' in Hamlet and associated texts, is alive to the possibility that the skull might not be Yorick's (Paster, 2009).[13] In an essay that interestingly foregrounds posthumanist affinities and casts Holbein's ambassadors as cyborgs (p. 253), Paster writes, acknowledging Michael Neill:

> Strictly speaking, as Neill points out, we rely here on the 'gravedigger's unverifiable say-so' for the identity of this 'chop-fallen' piece of bone. In his reading, the skull is not only unverifiable but also unanswerable: the skull, being unable to speak its own name or history, can only be *given* an identity; and thus the skull identified as Yorick claims distinction only briefly, soon reasserting its 'horrible

sameness', its significance as that of an 'undifferentiated absence'. (Paster, 2009, p. 260)[14]

Whatever the case, Hamlet's taking of the skull – signalled by 'I prethee let me see it', in the First Quarto, and 'Let me see' in the Folio, neither of which appear in the Second Quarto – does not occur in confirmation but in acceptance of the identification, and in prelude to the working through of the posthuman experience as this is described above. It is as if he is 'a child learning for the first time the facts of death' (cf. Kerrigan, 1994, p. 127).

Now in one sense it does not matter, of course, whether the skull is Yorick's. The poignancy of Hamlet's reflections at this point would be only marginally diminished if it weren't, for this is a powerful meditation on generalized death and 'an elemental experience of finitude' (Belsey, 2002, p. 140). And yet it does matter too, for what Hamlet is holding up is the prefiguration of his own mortality in a reminder of the arrested life of one he knew. It is almost an instance of self-mourning, amplified in productions where Hamlet holds the skull to his own head and faces the audience. 'The one unbearable dimension of possible human experience is not the experience of one's own death, which no one has, but the experience of the death of another', writes Lacan (1977, p. 37). In the context of that autothanatographical intimation it is significant that '[i]n Saxo Grammaticus and François de Belleforest' – authors of plays that serve as sources for *Hamlet* – 'the hero returns to find his own obsequies being performed' (Thompson and Taylor, in Shakespeare, 2006, p. 409, n. 10). So in the scene's generalization of mortality and its genealogies it matters, of course, that death is particularized, that we are able to know with certainty who is being mourned. Hamlet learns that all too cruelly in the graveyard scene. The gravedigger never tells him who the grave is for. Hamlet must witness the funeral party before he realizes it. And there are also quite specific ways in which identifying the dead is telling, in which it might matter if Hamlet were not holding up Yorick's skull and he is deceived. His reflections are prompted by the memory of someone who had been dear and familiar, 'who hath bore me on his back a thousand times', who had lips that 'I have kissed I know not how oft', but who is so past recognition that the reaction now is that Hamlet's 'gorge rises at it', so that the figure is 'abhorred' (V.1.174–85) in his imagination as the mind focuses rather on 'to what base uses we may return', on 'bung-holes', 'dust', 'earth' and 'loam' (V.1.192–201). Hamlet's tendency 'to consider too curiously' at this point, which Horatio warns him about (V.1.195), is prompted thence not only by the specificity of Yorick's skull, but also by its non-specificity. In the skull, the unrecognizable form and reduced metonymy of a beloved, uproarious servant are felt keenly. And the root of *familiar*, it bears saying in this scene in which we are excavating the familiar itself, and in which the most emblematic of familiar clichés is uncovered, lies in Latin *familia*, household, and *familius*, servant. Yet the servant – if it is him at all – is now so far gone that unlike Hamlet's father, whom Hamlet scarcely recognizes anyway, he is not even a familiar. The familiar – as cliché, as household memory, or as spectre – is that which we had always known, almost too well, and yet scarcely recognize when it stares us in the face from its disfiguration. Nevertheless, attempts at recognition of what is closely *and* scarcely familiar any more press themselves upon us. The play abounds in scenes of unsure identification, most notably where Hamlet's father's ghost confounds recognition. At the points in the play where that happens, *this* seems curiously and perhaps needlessly overrepresented as a word: 'this thing' (I.1.20); 'this dreaded sight' (I.1.24); 'this apparition' (I.1.28); 'this something more than fantasy' (I.153); 'this portentous figure' (I.1.108); 'this spirit' (I.1.170). The misattribution of Yorick's skull, itself a portentous figure and here ratified by Hamlet's own and surprised 'This?', would therefore aggregate itself to those moments: reinforcing various interpretations, too many to cite here, that cast Yorick as another father figure to Hamlet. And while it is in Hamlet's hand, looking back at him even while it cannot, even while it stages the capacity for the counter-gaze that it cannot enact, the skull gives him back the very image of his mind, to recite Pope's cliché. It is a mind now set on death and perhaps already placed there ever since he spoke of his too sullied flesh, which he will not have about him for much longer. It has tended there ever since he uttered that other quotation-cliché, in the midst of a soliloquy which by definition cannot be pronounced to anyone in the play but himself, but which affords that other emblem of overfamiliarity with the play, 'To be or not to be, that is the question' (III.1.55). This example of overfamiliarity with what had been private to Hamlet confirms that the play – ironically and unknowingly to its hero, who never knows enough but whose story is too well known – is an acting out of the process of becoming-cliché, of becoming-catachresis, of becoming-general-knowledge. 'Absent thee from felicity awhile … to tell my story' (V.2.331–3) the dying Hamlet tells Horatio – and the telling has been all too successful.

There are three points to observe before moving to the posthumanist affinities of all this. The first is that as he bursts out of hiding and approaches the funeral party, just after he '[c]omes forward' (as the stage direction has it) to speak of his 'phrase of sorrow', Hamlet will shout, in a cathartically assertive moment, 'This is I, Hamlet the Dane' (V.1.247). It is an exceptional moment: one that accepts and countersigns identification, in contrast to the other instances (exemplified above) where the word *this* is tinged with uncertainty or incredulity. After this *this*, Hamlet will be more decisive, if rashly so.

The second is a cue that Hegel gives us.[15] In *Phenomenology of Spirit* (1807), in paragraphs 334–5, Hegel writes that

> the skull-bone is not an organ of activity, nor is it even a speaking movement; neither theft, nor murder, etc., is committed by the skull-bone, nor does it even in the least make a change in countenance such that it would thereby become a verbal gesture. – Nor does this *existent* even have the value of a *sign*. Countenance and gesture, tone of voice, for that matter, even a post hammered onto a deserted island, all directly proclaim that they mean something other than what they immediately *merely are*. Without further ado, they proclaim themselves to be signs since they have a determinateness in themselves which points to something else which does not distinctively belong to them. In the presence of a skull, one can surely think of many things, just like Hamlet does with Yorick's, but the skullbone on its own is such an indifferent, unencumbered thing that there is nothing else immediately to be seen in it nor to think about; there is just it itself. To be sure, it is a reminder of the brain and its determinateness, and it reminds us of other skulls with different formations, but it is not a reminder of any conscious animation, since neither a countenance nor a gesture is impressed on it, nor is there anything which would indicate that it came from a conscious act, for it is the kind of actuality which is supposed to put on view a different aspect in individuality. This other aspect would no longer be a being reflecting itself into itself; rather, it would be pure *immediate being*.
>
> 335. Furthermore, since the skull does not itself feel, it seems that perhaps a more determinate significance could be given to it. Through their proximity to the skull, certain determinate sensations would allow us to take cognizance of what the skull is supposed to mean, and if a conscious mode of spirit has its feeling in a determinate place on the skull, then perhaps this place on the skull will indicate by its shape that mode of spirit and its particularity. (Hegel, 1979, p. 201)

This long passage is important because it casts into relief what it is exactly that Hamlet is reacting to as he confronts the mindless vacuity in his hand, the fear in the handful of dust which he clutches. His 'This?' is so pregnant, as are the gravedigger's 'E'en that' and Horatio's doubly echoing 'E'en so' (V.1.189–91), because it is hard to accommodate the thought that this 'indifferent, unencumbered' thing, which is not 'an organ of activity' and lacks 'speaking movement' and 'agency' and 'conscious animation' even though it once housed 'a being reflecting itself into itself' and was 'the proper location of Spirit's outer existence', of 'being-for-self' and 'being within-self' (Hegel, 1979, p. 197) and of 'self-conscious individuality' (p. 200), is much less now than even 'an ossified property of Spirit' (p. 203). In process is Hamlet's accommodation to the idea that, in Hegel's words, *'the actuality and existence of man is his skull-bone'* (p. 200; emphasis in original), and our awakening to the idea that the posthuman may be nothing more than that, despite all the hope and faith that might be encountered in religion, in Dante's idea of *transumanar* in the first canto of *Paradiso*, in the idea of transhumanist re-engineering of the human. It is the same abjection glimpsed in Géricault's canvas.

The third point arises from the scene immediately following the one in the graveyard. Hamlet, who has just been contemplating a disembodied head once familiar to him, reveals to Horatio how Rosencrantz and Guildenstern had the method of his murder set out in 'their grand commission'. Claudius recommended

> That on the supervise, no leisure bated
> – No, not to stay the grinding of the axe! –
> My head should be struck off. (V.2.22–4)

It is time, then, to consider Hamlet beheaded.

Posthumanism and the graveyard scene in *Hamlet*

That Hamlet might have been killed by beheading is piquant. He has just been considering a skull, holding it close to his own head. We are called to attend to Hamlet's head often in the play: because of his madness (whether feigned or unfeigned) and also because he could have possibly lost it (in more ways than one). That loss is scarcely believable. 'Is't possible?', as Horatio, in a reaction seemingly less credulous than Hamlet's 'This?', says when Claudius's plot is revealed to him – but it could have happened. ('Is't possible?' is incidentally uttered by Hamlet too, but only in the First Folio, and in conversation with Rosencrantz and Guildenstern, who respond in that particular context that 'there has been much throwing about of brains'.)[16] Hamlet, in other words, could have been *de-headed*, a word I use here because it seems so much more exact than *beheaded*, which appears to rather presume – language can be funny like that – the bestowal rather than removal of a head.

But what does all this – character jugs, Vesalius, Géricault, Hegel, the graveyard scene, even – have to do with posthumanism? Why insist on faces and skulls, familiarity and misrecognition, defacement and disfiguration, cliché and catachresis in a posthumanist context, where questions concerning technology, digital culture, bioengineering and autopoieitic systems might appear more relevant? Why, indeed, figure in Shakespeare at all?[17] Certainly it is not because Shakespeare, unlike Nietzsche, never had a modem or because Hamlet is not yet on any holodecks that this essay focuses rather on the model of a 'posthumanism without technology' (cf. Graham, 2002; Murray, 1997; Herbrechter and Callus, 2007). No ingenious effort will be made at the close to forge some bizarre connection between the withdrawal of the 'The Shakespearean Collection' in 1991 and the republication in that same year of Donna Haraway's 'The Cyborg Manifesto', a foundational posthumanist text. Nor will any link be contrived with the affordances of Foucault's thoughts on technologies of the self (cf. Haraway, 1991; Martin, Gutman and Hutton, 1988). If, instead, the chapter insists on a more lettered rather than a meta/morphic posthumanism, and is not above porcelain knick-knacks and avowedly humanist histories, it is not because some other form of posthumanism might emerge there in opposition to more technocultural approaches. It is because it suspects that these alternatives demonstrate how the graveyard scene in *Hamlet* – the most recognizable staging of humanism and of humanity's confrontations with the 'biological substrate' of life when that is not yet re-engineered to a time after 'information lost its body' – bears rereading and demonstrates what might need to be remembered when this most familiar and (im)mortal of human(ist) episodes is revisited in our more posthumanist times (cf. Hayles, 1999, p. 2). And what emerges there has already been flagged, above, as not so much the redefinition of posthumanism as its readaptation to the process of the experience of the estrangement from what is most familiar to the human.

The thing, of course, is that even in a time of 'enhanced humanity' we still die. Indeed, as Hollywood shows, it is amazing how many people do when a cyborg – that herald and embodiment of the posthuman – comes visiting. Death outlives the promise of the posthuman, and when it manifests itself will estrange the human to itself by taking its form and challenging memory – as cyborg or skull, as spectral familiar, or in the image of dismembered limbs. And as, through Shakespeare, we have moved away in this chapter from clichéd representation of the posthuman as an inevitably technological redetermination of the human as it becomes 'seamlessly articulated with intelligent machines' (Hayles, 1999, p. 4), reasserting instead an arguably even more clichéd scene of unenhanced and mortal humanity, what remains is only as much time as is ever left to adapt to the (dis)estrangement from what had been most familiar.

Back, therefore or illogically, to the jug: ultimately, like man, not much more than 'a sophisticated piece of earthenware', as Margreta de Grazia, alive to 'the human/humus connection', puts it (2007, pp. 33, and 147). The Royal Doulton character jug of Hamlet has already been seen as scarcely recognizable as Hamlet. 'This?', we might well ask when we first see it, echoing Hamlet's own reaction to the skull. 'That?', we might ask when we see a new Hamlet on the stage or in the cinema, playing him back in our minds across all the Hamlets we have known. We keep putting new heads on Hamlet, constantly beheading (in the sense anticipated above) the character who came within a storm of being de-headed. Let us permit ourselves to read a little more into this, using the jug again. Paradoxically, jugs concentrate cultural associations and cultural memory, as well as meaning, within the process of truncation. The trunk itself, the body, appears nowhere or hardly. But the head is all too present, surrounded by several visual cues prompting us to recognize who it belongs to. Such over-accumulation of allusions makes it tempting to conclude that what is defaced in the iconography of the Hamlet character jug, with its crassly compressed references to the play's figuring in the popular imaginary, is more than our private picture of what the hero might have looked like (a picture that might well persist despite the unending procession of actors who have played him on stage and film). It is, rather, the replayed freshness of the play itself, which finds itself denominated in the currency of a collectible that is not so endowed with subtlety of design that it allays over-familiarity or resists a deadening of aesthetic and critical sense. The jug, then, makes cliché even more clichéd. As it does so we find that the familiar is oddly if not productively defamiliarized. This is scarcely Hamlet. It is not all that recognizably him. But we know it as him from the skull. The jug does not thereby allay the cliché on which it thrives, and it is further still from being a posthumanist artifact. But it prompts consideration of deeper processes of defamiliarization in the cultural history of *Hamlet* and in the posthumanist present and future of the play. For it can stand as the emblem of the relation of (dis)estrangement from what we have held most familiar. And as we move, below, to speculate on how rereading posthumanist cliché through a rereading of humanist cliché might work, and to how defamiliarizing what is familiar in both can reverse cliché and catachresis, we know in advance that we cannot refresh what was never new. The difficulty of that task is discouraging, especially as there is much in posthumanism that promises plenty that is new.

'Is't possible?', therefore? Not quite. It is certainly, in more ways than one, strange that it could be tried. It is also, in a sense, strange that posthumanism itself could be tried. The graveyard scene seems to predestine the reminder that as we move towards the posthuman death pulls us back. The posthuman is already death. To the extent that the most clichéd scene in Shakespeare reminds us of that, it is almost enough to allay posthumanism's fondest clichés and hopes. The '*Ecce homo*' / 'This?' moment in the episode with the skull (in effect, 'Here is/was (the) man' / 'e'en that') is precisely the kind of moment that posthuman (or, rather, transhuman) technological utopianism seeks to engineer forever away. Humanity will, indeed, be unrecognizable in the transhuman.[18] It will scarcely figure. And in the graveyard scene that is all too true, though not in the manner envisaged by transhumanism. The familiarity of death is what transhumanist posthumanism seeks to forget; it is, however, what the graveyard scene will not. The transhuman, then, must have its forgetting of death defamiliarized, lest 'purposes mistook' find themselves 'fallen on th'inventors' heads' (V.2.368–9). For its part, the human must have its curious consideration of death defamiliarized, until the two paradigms can be estranged from themselves in recognizing the other. And in the process of this strange dynamic, cliché must be undone, starting with defamiliarization of the dead(ening) figure of human mortality as it is staged in this most famous of scenes. Except, of course, that it cannot quite – for that, as we saw above, would require newness and, perhaps, firstness, not merely novelty.

For what does it mean to kill a cliché and a dead metaphor? It does not do to try to eliminate them, we know. Garrick tried that with the graveyard scene. Like terminating cyborgs, however, it kept coming back. Indeed, how can catachresis be refigured when it has already killed figure? The skull, we know, has always been a catachretic token of humanity's mortality. That did not need the graveyard scene. Its effectiveness arrives already deadened in Shakespeare, though he revives it by 'ne'er so well' expression. What that expression does is to recast what Paul de Man calls '[t]he specular moment that is part of all understanding', which 'reveals the tropological structure that underlies all cognitions, including knowledge of self', in the staging of a gaze between the human(ist) subject and a death's head (cf. de Man, 1984, p. 71). Consequently in the episode with the skull a determining figure is prosopopeia, 'the fiction of the voice-from-beyond-the-grave' that might have been recognized by Hamlet as Yorick's had the skull and its chaplessness not been as remote from revivification or elo-quence as the dead limbs, abjectly deheaded and trunkless, given figure by Géricault. It is a figure, we should also remember, the thought of which arises at all only from what is perhaps an imposture on the part of the gravedigger – 'Is't possible?' – and a figure, too, which in de Man's words is implicated in 'the giving and taking away of faces, with face and deface, *figure*, figuration and disfiguration' (de Man, 1984, pp. 76–7). Now specularity, we know from Lacan, depends on 'the *function of misrecognition* that characterizes the ego in all [its] defensive structures' (Lacan, 2006, p. 80). The point here must surely be that in the unrecip-rocated gaze with the skull Hamlet is being anything but defensive as he looks into the face of the Real as the very figure of death. Indeed, in the familiarity of the episode we perhaps forget that it is not usual for any human except for those whose work lies that way to hold a skull in their hands. The familiarity of this unfamiliar gesture is the result of the prosopopeiic and the specular and the curiously considered recognition of the Real having become clichéd. As a result, if we are to defamilarize the scene in any posthumanist (re)reading what must be taken away is its familiarity, its ciphering of the recognition of death as the place of the (post)human. One might as well attempt to sweep all of humanist heritage away.

Some forms of transhumanism might try that, of course. Their forward momentum, towards a posthuman that will estrange humanity from itself to the most complete of misrecognitions, so that enhanced humanity is no longer familiar – either in body or spectrally – is in denial of the 'dorsality', as David Wills has it, of 'retroversion', of 'what shifts of terrain might occur once we take the technological turn back to a place behind where we traditionally presume it to have taken place, turning back around it from the start' (Wills, 2008, p. 6). Taking posthumanism back to the graveyard scene in *Hamlet* is perhaps, then, not so perverse. Indeed, it is urgent. In another place – 'Had I but time' (V.2.320) – we might perhaps have figured how this dorsality does, in fact, look ahead, and become 'the name for that which, from behind, turns (it) into something technological, some technological thing' (Wills, 2008, p. 5). But that will be for another place.

So let us, in conclusion, go back, to the clichés to be found in endings. Foucault's conclusion to *The Order of Things* has often been cited in posthumanist circles to the point of cliché and in pointed confirmation of poststructuralism's relevance to posthumanist thought. Here, instead, mindful that poststructuralist thought, which in its own way has been very post-humanist, has been integral to this essay, I reword – with all the insouciance of a gravedigger who chucks cherished pasts about, and all the incongruity of reference to a character jug in Shakespearean criticism – one of Lacan's endings:

> Poststructuralism can accompany the posthumanist to the ecstatic limit of the '*Thou art that*', where the cipher of his (im)mortal destiny is revealed to him, but it is not in our sole power as poststructuralists to bring him to the point where the true journey begins.[19]

To that '*that*', '*This?*' is the only word that provides the adequately inadequate response.

Notes

1. 'Toby jugs', the jollier and more familiar term, is not quite accurate for the purposes of this chapter. Useful terminological sharpness is provided by Louise Irvine's introduction to Jean Dale (1997): 'The term "toby" is frequently used to describe all Royal Doulton jugs, but strictly speaking it should only be applied to jugs in the form of a full seated or standing figure. Although Royal Doulton began by producing toby jugs at their Burslem factory, they are better known for their character jugs, which feature only the head and shoulders' (p. x). The distinction, absent from the Catalogue's tenth and most recent edition of 2008, becomes significant in what follows, and exists at all because 'the character jug ... showed the head only' (see Lukins, 1994, p. iv).
2. Even the 'Shakespeare Characters' series (produced on vases, dishes and other settings between 1912 and 1938), or the scenes from the plays that the company dramatized in faience tiles and plaques between 1873 and 1914 or in porcelain between 1914 and the Second World War, are less busy. So are the statuettes of Shakespeare produced in 1994 and 2007 (HN3363 and HN5129). However, the former, with the Bard resting his hand on an eclectic pile of Shakespeareana that at the top has an escutcheon bearing his arms, bound volumes at the bottom and the masks of Comedy and Tragedy in between, remains less than austere.
3. See, for instance, the Noke 1892 and 1900 vellum examples recorded in Eyles, Irvine and Baynton (1994, p. 60), and the various other designs depicted on pp. 80–1.

4. All line references to the play are to Shakespeare (2006). This edition is based on the Second Quarto text (Q2), and follows Harold Jenkins, T. J. B. Spencer and before them J. Dover Wilson in choosing Q2 as their 'control text' over the First Quarto or the First Folio (see the volume's Appendix 2, p. 487).

5. The full quotation (ll. 297–8) is '*True Wit* is *Nature* to advantage drest / What oft was *Thought* but n'er so well exprest' (Pope, 1963, p. 153). I am grateful to Stuart Sillars for his comments on this and other points in this chapter.

6. See Derrida (1982) and Paul de Man's ongoing reference in his work to the figure of catachresis and the co-implication of prosopopeia, knowledge of which must for reasons of brevity be assumed rather than explored here (see, for instance, de Man 1982; and 1984), as well as 1978, pp. 13–14, and his 'Hypogram and Inscription' (de Man, 1986, pp. 27–53).

7. For a review of the cultural history of literature and art's representations of the vanity of human wishes, and of the recurrence of the image of the skull, see Tapié (2010).

8. 'Garrick's production of *Hamlet* omitting the comedy of the last act was not staged until 1772' (see Tomarken, 1983, p. 27).

9. The associations are atavistic too, for the human skull was in prehistoric ritual used as an object of worshipful contemplation, or as a prop in a dance, or – more pragmatically – as a receptacle in drinking (cf. Henschen, 1966; Gastaut, 1972).

10. My thanks to Gloria Lauri-Lucente for indicating the Dante passage.

11. Related motifs are found in Shakespeare himself – Othello mentions the anthropophagi in his wooing of Desdemona – and in Pliny the Elder's reference to the Blemmyae, people with mouth and eyes on their chests, in *Naturalis Historae*. Like Carroll's *Alice*, Washington Irving's *The Legend of Sleepy Hollow* (1820) also has a few games played with heads, though they are rather more sinister. See also Georges Bataille's use of acephalous motifs, in *Encyclopaedia Acephalica* (Georges Bataille et al., 1995), and Giorgio Agamben's essay thereon, 'Acephalous' (Agamben, 2004).

12. One performance that suggests more active doubt in Hamlet's mind is Rory Kinnear's as the Prince, in the National Theatre's 2010 staging of the play, directed by Nicholas Hytner.

13. A related keynote address was delivered to the American Shakespeare Center Bi-Annual Blackfriars Conference on 22 October 2009: 'Thinking with Skulls: Hamlet, Holbein, Vesalius, and Fuller'.

14. See Neill (1997, pp. 234–6), and Paster's further acknowledgement (Paster, 2009, p. 265), concerning the question of the uncertainty of the skull being Yorick's, of Bristol (1985, p. 192).

15. I am indebted to James Corby for the point developed here.

16. In the text established by Ann Thompson and Neil Taylor, this occurs in II.2.355–7 (Shakespeare, 2006, 244).

17. It is noteworthy, for instance, that Shakespeare is not mentioned in Cary Wolfe's influential *What Is Posthumanism?* (2010).

18. For handy representations of transhumanist envisaging, see the online journal *H+*, http://www.hplusmagazine.com.

19. The rephrasing is of the last sentence of 'The Mirror Stage' (Lacan, 2005, p. 81).

Works cited

Agamben, Giorgio (2004) 'Acephalous', *The Open: Man and Animal*, trans. Kevin Attell, Stanford: Stanford University Press.

Bataille, Georges et al. (eds) (1995) *Encyclopaedia Acephalica*, trans. Iain White et al., London: Atlas Press.

Belsey, Catherine (2001) *Shakespeare and the Loss of Eden: The Construction of Family Values in Early Modern Culture*, Basingstoke: Macmillan, now Palgrave Macmillan.

Belsey, Catherine (2002) 'Was Hamlet a Man or a Woman?: The Prince in the Graveyard', in Arthur Kinney (ed.), *Hamlet: New Critical Essays*, New York: Routledge, pp. 135–58.

Bloom, Harold (2003) *Hamlet: Poem Unlimited*, New York: Riverhead.

Braidotti, Rosi (2002) *Metamorphoses: Towards a Materialist Theory of Becoming*, Oxford: Polity.

Bristol, Michael D. (1985) *Carnival and Theater Plebeian Culture and the Structure of Authority in Renaissance England*, New York and London: Routledge.

Callus, Ivan, and Stefan Herbrechter (2007) 'Critical Posthumanism, or, The *Inventio* of a Posthumanism without Technology', *Subject Matters* 3.2/4.1, pp. 15–29.

Dale, Jean (1997) *The Charlton Standard Catalogue of Royal Doulton Beswick Jugs*, 4th edn, Toronto: Charlton.

Dale, Jean (2008) *Royal Doulton Jugs*, Toronto: Charlton Press.

De Grazia, Margreta (2007) *Hamlet without Hamlet*, Cambridge: Cambridge University Press.

De Man, Paul (1978) 'The Epistemology of Metaphor', *Critical Inquiry* 5.1, pp. 13–30.

De Man, Paul (1982) *Allegories of Reading: Figural Language in Rousseau, Nietzsche, Rilke and Proust*, New Haven: Yale University Press.

De Man, Paul (1984) *The Rhetoric of Romanticism*, New York: Columbia University Press.

De Man, Paul (1986) *The Resistance to Theory*, Minneapolis: University of Minnesota Press.

Derrida, Jacques (1982) 'White Mythology: Metaphor in the Text of Philosophy', *Margins of Philosophy*, London: Harvester Wheatsheaf, pp. 207–71.

Eyles, Desmond, Louise Irvine and Valerie Baynton (1994) *Royal Doulton Figures*, Shepton Beauchamp: Richard Dennis.

Fehrman, C. (1952) *Diktaren och döden*, Stockholm: Bonnier.

Frye, Roland Mushat (1979) 'Ladies, Gentlemen, and Skulls: *Hamlet* and the Iconographic Traditions', *Shakespeare Quarterly* 30.1, pp. 15–28.

Gastaut, H. (1972) *Le Crâne: objet de culte, objet d'art, Musée Cantini, Marseille, 13 mars–15 mai 1972*, Marseille: Musée Cantini.

Graham, Elaine (2002) 'Nietzsche Gets a Modem: Transhumanism and the Technological Sublime', *Literature and Technology* 16.1, pp. 65–80.

Hapgood, Robert (1999) *Hamlet*, Shakespeare in Production, Cambridge: Cambridge University Press.

Haraway, Donna (1991) 'The Cyborg Manifesto: Science, Technology, and Socialist-Feminism in the Late Twentieth Century (1985)', *Simians, Cyborgs and Women: The Reinvention of Nature*, New York: Routledge, pp. 149–81.

Hayles, N. Katherine (1999) *How We Became Posthuman: Virtual Bodies in Cybernetics, Literature, and Informatics*, Chicago: University of Chicago Press.

Hegel, G. W. F. (1979) *Phenomenology of Spirit*, trans. A. V. Miller, Oxford: Oxford University Press.

Henschen, Folke (1966) *The Human Skull: A Cultural History*, trans. Kenneth P. Oakley, London: Thames and Hudson.

Kerrigan, William (1994) *Hamlet's Perfection*, Baltimore: Johns Hopkins University Press.

Lacan, Jacques (1977) 'Desire and the Interpretation of Desire in *Hamlet*', ed. Jacques-Alain Miller, trans. James Hulbert, *Yale French Studies* 55/56 (*Literature and Psychoanalysis: The Question of Reading Otherwise*), pp. 11–52.

Lacan, Jacques (2005) 'The Mirror Stage as Formative of the *I* Function as Revealed in Psychoanalytic Experience', *Ecrits*, trans. Bruce Fink in collaboration with Héloise Fink and Russell Grigg, New York: Norton & Co.

Lukins, Jocelyn (1994) *Collecting Royal Doulton Character & Toby Jugs: The Diamond Jubilee 1934–1994, A Record of the First Sixty Years*, 3rd edn, London: Venta.

Martin, Luther H., Huck Gutman and Patrick H. Hutton (1988) *Technologies of the Self: A Seminar with Michel Foucault*, Amherst: University of Massachusetts Press.

Murray, Janet (1997) *Hamlet on the Holodeck: The Future of Narrative in Cyberspace*, New York: Free Press.

Neill, Michael (1997) *Issues of Death: Mortality and Identity in English Tragedy*, Oxford: Clarendon Press.

Nye, David E. (1994) *American Technological Sublime*, Cambridge, Massachusetts: MIT Press.

Paster, Gail Kern (2009) 'The Pith and Marrow of Our Attribute: Dialogue of Skin and Skull in *Hamlet* and Holbein's *The Ambassadors*', *Textual Practice* 23, pp. 247–65.

Pope, Alexander (1963) *An Essay on Criticism, The Poems of Alexander Pope*, ed. John Butt, London: Routledge.

Powell, Larssen (2008) *The Technological Unconscious in German Modernist Literature: Nature in Rilke, Benn, Brecht and Doeblin*, London: Camden House.

Rosenberg, Marvin (1992) *The Masks of Hamlet*, Cranbury, NJ: Associated University Presses.

Saunders, J. B. dec. M., and Charles D. O'Malley (1973) *The Illustrations from the Works of Andreas Vesalius of Brussels*, New York: Dover Publications.

Shakespeare, William (2006) *Hamlet*, The Arden Shakespeare, Third Series, ed. Ann Thompson and Neil Taylor, London: Thompson Learning.

Tapié, Alain (2010) *Vanité: Mort, que me veux-tu?* Paris: Editions de la Martinière.

Tomarken, Edward (1983) 'The Comedy of the Graveyard Scene in *Hamlet*: Samuel Johnson Mediates between the Eighteenth and Twentieth Centuries', *Eighteenth-Century Life* 8.3, pp. 26–34.

Whittecar, George, and Arron Rimpley (2002) *Royal Doulton: A Legacy of Excellence 1871–1945*, Atglen: Schiffer.

Wills, David (2008) *Dorsality: Thinking Back through Technology and Politics*, Minneapolis: University of Minnesota Press.

Wolfe, Cary (2010) *What Is Posthumanism?* Minneapolis: University of Minnesota Press.

Afterword

12
Post-Posthumanist Me – An Illiterate Reads Shakespeare

Adam Max Cohen and David B. King

In their introduction to *Posthumanist Shakespeares* Stefan Herbrechter and Ivan Callus discuss how posthumanism explores 'the implications of bio-, nano-, cogno-, and info-technologies on body, mind, culture, and epistomology.' They investigate 'what it means to be human' in an era 'of dramatic technological change' (p. 6). In my books *Shakespeare and Technology: Dramatizing Early Modern Technological Revolutions* (2006) and *Technology and the Early Modern Self* (2009) I explore how Shakespeare's own era of 'dramatic technological change' similarly redefines 'what it means to be human'. As historians of technology including Lynn White, Jr. (1978) and George Basalla (1988) have shown, in late medieval and early modern Europe mechanical inventions and technological revolutions spurred theoretical and philosophical breakthroughs. In fact the technological revolutions in the realms of print, navigation, optics, surveying and other fields in the fifteenth, sixteenth and early seventeenth centuries may have helped lay the groundwork for the rise of science in Europe in the second half of the seventeenth century. New technologies such as the printing press, the telescope and the microscope jarringly brought far things close and revealed them to be wildly different than we had assumed, much more like us or more different than we had dreamed, dislodging previous understandings of interior and exterior, safe and unsafe, good and evil. The disorientation they created was also a function of their novelty because users needed time to figure out what to make of these strange new machines. In the resulting confusion the self became unmoored from its assumptions, adrift in its world, and a process of self-redefinition became necessary. As Basalla puts it, 'Not until the Renaissance did European thinkers begin to draw parallels between the organic and the mechanical. This association of what had hitherto been thought to be disparate elements was the result of the appearance of a host of new technological contrivances and the emergence of modern science' (Basalla, 1998, p. 15). People begin to wonder, what impact do technologies have on us? Do the often powerful and sometimes mysterious tools, instruments and machines that we use on a regular basis reinforce pre-existing personality traits, or do they create us anew? These questions are important in any historical period but they seem particularly apt in relation to the Renaissance because the two major paradigms related to the period highlight the development of individualism on the one hand and revolutionary cultural shifts on the other.

Because artists are drawn to that which is undefinable reading their work can yield important insights about technological changes and their disorienting effects on the self. Such an artist certainly is Shakespeare and a close study of his work indeed indicates that the metaphorical or symbolic transformation of the human being into a technological implement was well underway in the early modern period. Consequently the technology metaphors in Shakespeare's plays are numerous, elaborate and striking. In his plays I continually find 'a developing general cultural ambiguity towards the machinic other' (Herbrechter and Callus, 2009, x) – a disturbing cyborgization or 'turning tech' where sudden dramatic technological advances loosen individuals from old meaning structures without providing viable replacements, creating a confusing dislocation. Old meaning paradigms are shredded and a moment opens up when new meanings can be created by and for the self. My books examine how Shakespeare's work reveals and untangles this disorienting process of self-redefinition during a time of great technological change. By locating ourselves within the experience of Shakespeare's characters at their most technologized – as they were 'turning tech' – and most disoriented we may better understand our current moment of identity confusion and upheaval.

In *Shakespeare and Technology* and *Technology and the Early Modern Self* I analyse this process in detail, looking specifically at how the influx of technologies created a new kind of continually evolving and often paradoxical self. While the generation of the self is *physis*, a sort of blooming, a self-revealing independent of any immediate exterior influences, the making of the self can rely on the combined influences of other people and other things. This observation reflects an important paradox at the heart of the *OED*'s definition of the *self*. On the one hand the self is 'permanent' but on the other hand it experiences 'successive and varying states of consciousness'. The conscious component of the self is diachronic. It changes over time. The *OED* deals more explicitly with the diachronicity of the self in sense 4.a.: 'What one is at a particular time or in a particular aspect or relation: one's nature, character, or (sometimes) physical constitution or appearance, considered as different at different times. Chiefly with qualifying adj. (*one's*) *old, former, later self.*' While relevant to the present study, this sense post-dates the Renaissance period, first appearing in 1697. Paradoxically the only individuating sense of the word *self* that was available in the sixteenth century indicates multiple personalities or at the very least a split personality: '4.b. An assemblage of characteristics and dispositions which may be conceived as constituting one of various conflicting personalities within a human being. *better self*: the better part of one's nature.' This definition is followed by a citation from Spenser's *Amoretti* (1595): 'And in my selfe, my inward selfe I meane, Most liuely lyke behold your semblant trew.' Clearly during Shakespeare's era the self was entering a state of flux.

To better understand how technology affected this newly emerging and ever changing self I looked closely at the relationship between identity and machinery in Shakespeare's work. Through a historically informed study of technological metaphors in Shakespeare's plays I found that characters frequently describe other characters and themselves in technological terms. While a great deal of emphasis has been placed recently on Turning Turk in the Renaissance, my work focuses on Turning Tech, by which I meant the description of the individual as a machine. In certain instances in Shakespeare's plays parts of the individual are described as machine parts, and in other instances the whole individual is described as a machine or the byproduct of a mechanical process. For example in *A Midsummer Night's Dream* Quince, Bottom and Snout are named for tools or implements that are required for their trades. While depictions of the Athenian craftsmen vary from patronizing to laudatory, the word *mechanical* retains a negative connotation in the plays. In *2 Henry IV* Pistol claims that Doll Tearsheet and Mistress Quickly have been dragged off to prison 'by most mechanical and dirty hand' (V.5.34), in *Henry V* Canterbury refers to 'poor mechanic porters crowding in / Their heavy burdens' at the gates of a hypothetical society of bees (I.2.200–1), and Cleopatra fears that she will be 'enc­encloudyed' by 'Mechanic slaves / With greasy aprons, rules, and hammers' (*Antony and Cleopatra*, V.2.205–8) if she is taken to Rome. Jeffrey Masten, Peter Stallybrass and Nancy J. Vickers have suggested that resistance to all things mechanical may date back to clerical suspicion about the body, the flesh and things of this world (1997, p. 2). Elizabeth Pittenger adds that Hugh of St Victor described the mechanical arts as 'adulterate', drawing his opinion from the derivation of the word *mechanical* from the Greek *moicos* and the Latin *moechus*, meaning *adulterer*. One of Dr Johnson's three definitions of *mechanick* is 'mean, servile, of mean occupation', while the *OED* defines *mechanick* as 'involving manual labor, even servile, vulgar' (Cohen, 2006, p. 16). In *Dream* Puck epitomizes aristocratic disdain for those who worked with their hands by calling the artisans 'rude mechanicals'.

That Shakespeare at times repeated stigmas associated with various technologies should not lead us to conclude that Shakespeare himself despised these technologies. On the contrary, I believe that the condition of the self-fashioning he observes is in flux and unsettled. Thus Prince Hamlet reveals a more promising – if equally disorienting – way of Turning Tech when he closes his love letter to Ophelia by describing himself as a *homo mechanicus*: 'Thine evermore, most dear lady, whilst this / machine is to him, / Hamlet' (II.2.123–5). This reflects a more benign view of technology equally present in Shakespeare's day. Again the issue was unsettled, perhaps because early modern men and women routinely viewed technology in religious terms. Augustine noted toward the end of *City of God* that the products of *techne* included clothing, architecture, navigation, theatre, engines of war, poetry, geometry and arithmetic. Augustine believed these constituted a 'compressed pile of blessings'. These blessings were God's way of mitigating the difficulties of postlapsarian existence. They were, in Augustine's words, 'the consolations of mankind under condemnation' (1984, 1072, 1075). This view was often repeated throughout the Renaissance. As David Noble notes in his book *The Religion of Technology*, 'technology came to be identified ... with both lost perfection and the possibility of renewed perfection ... not only as evidence of grace, but as a means of preparation for, and a sure sign of, imminent salvation' (1999, 12). People were not sure yet what to make of these new 'blessings' of the Renaissance, nor was Shakespeare. Dehumanizing? Violent? A chance for perfection on Earth? All views of technology are seen at times in Shakespeare's work.

Perhaps the most fascinating and emblematically contradictory example of these mechanical-human characters is Pistol. He is not only an Elizabethan version of the braggart soldier but also the personification of a particular type of Elizabethan weapon. That he would explode into a rage in each play in which we find him is inevitable given his name. Shakespeare never denies his audience members the excitement of seeing or hearing a charged piece fire. In II.1 of *Henry V* Pistol is only on the stage for eleven lines before he draws against Nim. Pistol threatens,

'For I can take, and Pistol's cock is up, / And flashing fire will follow' (II.1.46–7). Shakespeare's Pistol resembles an actual pistol in several ways. Sixteenth-century pistols made lots of noise but they rarely struck their targets. Because pistols were expensive they were used primarily by two very distinct groups: nobles on the one hand and thieves, criminals and poachers on the other. Since Falstaff is a titular nobleman and a lovable villain it is appropriate that he possesses Pistol as part of his entourage. Ford's brothers in *Merry Wives of Windsor* are the only other characters in Shakespeare's plays who have pistols, a sign of the Ford family's affluence. Pistol is thus a character manipulated by Shakespeare to make authorial points just as technology was manipulated in his time. Yet Pistol is also a living person beneath the externally originated machinations, someone both harmed and harming from within his fashioned portrayal. As with Shakespeare's view of technology the issue of who Pistol is and what he means remains in flux. Elizabethans and Jacobeans may have embraced certain tools with a quasi-religious fervour, but early modern English faith in revolutionary technologies, while ultimately quite durable, was certainly not an unexamined faith. Shakespeare's plays reflect the fact that Englishmen held a wide variety of views regarding revolutionary technologies ranging from enthusiastic embrace to grudging acceptance to occasional suspicion to the firm conviction that certain tools, inventions and machines were instruments of the devil. In an attempt to make sense of these strange new artifacts and practices authors like Shakespeare often depicted them in human terms, and they also described human beings themselves as technologies. Ambivalence regarding technology's impact on the self and society seems only to have intensified during the industrial revolution; it persists today in most societies; and it will probably continue as long as the invention and use of tools and machines remain integral to human existence.

In these ways and many more *Shakespeare and Technology* and *Technology and the Early Modern Self* carefully examine how technological advances during Shakespeare's era created a new, contradictory, unfinished, fluctuating self. However, though in these books I effectively *explained* how technological invasion spurred the collapse of old paradigms and incites dizzying identity redefinition until a new paradigm emerges, I did not actually *comprehend* it because I had not personally experienced this disorienting process with force or directness. I was seeing the process as scholars do from afar until an event of catastrophic bio- and techno-invasion plunged me into disorientation and radical self-redefinition much like that experienced in Shakespeare's era. My brain was invaded by a malignant tumour. And like individuals in Shakespeare's time I was invaded from without and within by strange technological forces that incited a sudden dizzying redefinition of myself and my place in my world. Inner–outer, safe–dangerous, self–other and biological-technological pairings were suddenly blended, dislodged and confused by this invasive change. Having now plunged into and through this terrifying process I have emerged with a new way of seeing and speaking Shakespeare and the process of self-redefinition he so effectively deconstructs. Blinded, I found sight. Made dumb, I found speech. Invaded, I constructed a self more enlivened and intact than ever. Out of techno-biological chaos and upheaval I found new information about the self and a post-posthumanist aspect of Shakespeare studies.

In early November 2008 after I attained tenure at the University of Massachusetts Dartmouth, and finishing the final draft of my second book *Technology and the Early Modern Self* I began to lose my ability to read. This was very frustrating. I tried but failed to read bedtime stories to my two-year-old daughter. My four-year-old daughter started to insist that my wife read because I could not read adequately. During the Thanksgiving break I saw my eye doctor who told me to take it easy. He said I was working too many hours on the final revision of *Technology and the Early Modern Self* and that the headaches and vision loss were the results of working too hard. I tried working less and playing with my girls more often during the evenings, but my daughters love to read so interacting with them meant suffering terrible frustration. For my classes I tried enlarging pages of Shakespeare's texts on the computer and using giant printed emails, but these attempts did not work either. The old technologies on which I had relied were ineffective and new ones were unusable. I began to feel a creeping terror and a dizzying sense of dislocation. What kind of scholar cannot read? I had become partially blind. How could I learn to read again?

When I went to my eye doctor the second time he recommended a study of my brain using a Magnetic Resonance Imaging, an MRI. It was a Wednesday, and I requested an immediate MRI testing so that I would not have to cancel my Thursday classes. The doctor's assistant contacted an MRI clinic 40 miles away in Brockton where I was told I could be seen that afternoon. I liked the timing because it gave me an hour to eat. I drove to a restaurant and did my best to order but did not get what I really wanted because I could not read the menu. After I ate I asked the servers to help me plan my drive to the MRI. They did their best but the normally 45-minute drive took me over an hour and a half because I had to drive slowly, stay in the right lane, and try to monitor the other cars with my impaired vision.

The technology on which I had so often relied – cars, the modern highway, my own sight – had become unusable and my relationship to roads and cars became dangerous and terrifying.

Somehow I found the MRI centre and was relieved to make it safely inside the building. But the technological invasions, dislocations and redefinitions had only begun. For 40 minutes I laid like Ophelia on her bier inside an enormous all-encompassing machine that weirdly whined, bellowed and hissed. I held my breath for long stretches so as not to mess up the x-ray. I was terrified regarding what this cyborg-like machine might find within me. After 40 minutes the radio turned off. These exams were not supposed to go this long. After an hour and fifteen minutes they took me out of the MRI machine and gave me a package containing copies of its images. Then they left me alone in another room. I opened the package containing the images and learned that I was suffering from a massive brain tumour and was probably about to die.

In psychic and emotional free fall I heard the phone in the room ring, answered it and listened as my father Dr. Max Harry Cohen, a cancer surgeon in Bethesda, MD, told me I needed to go immediately by ambulance to Brigham & Women's Hospital in Boston and that the family would fly to Boston that afternoon to meet me there. Dad also said that my father-in-law Dr. Stuart Bauer, a pediatric surgeon at Children's Hospital in Boston, had arranged a meeting for me at the hospital with the best brain surgeon in the area. After hanging up I was terribly concerned. I was alone with my horrific news, and I felt everything about me and my life collapsing, spinning, lost. I worried that I might soon die. I began to cry, not for myself but because I knew that if I did die I would never again see my daughters. It was such a shame that I would not see them grow up, go to school, fall in love or experience other forms of joy. I love my wife Debbie very much, but the possible loss of my two young daughters was my greatest sorrow. Everything that mattered most to my identity like my kids, wife and work seemed to be going, going, gone.

When I arrived at the hospital my doctor wanted to avoid a physically interactive surgery because my tumour was located in a terrible location. It was way too close to the middle of the brain. To try to remove the tumour would damage the brain's areas which enable sight, speech and comprehension. But as the evening progressed the tumour continued to spread. It was killing me. The doctors decided to try to cut parts of it out since the game was basically over and I had nearly lost. Miraculously the doctors managed to remove my tumour without destroying all the sensitive components of my brain. They saved my life and retained my gift of sight. I would no longer be partially blind, and I might even live a while to see my children grow up a little bit. What a relief it was for my family to see me survive that night.

Unfortunately more darkness was to come. After a few days of recovery from my surgery I began steroid therapy and chemotherapy that flooded my body with biotechnological invaders and radically altering my relationship with my world. For over 40 days I could not sleep at all, was often on edge, ate gigantic meals 6–8 times a day, and experienced vivid, terrifying nightmares. At the same time I commenced daily radiation treatments in which I was laid prone on a hard flat slab (like Juliet's) within a grid of lasers and told not to move as a mammoth, rotating, loudly humming mechanical beast whirled above me. The Shakespeare scholar who had sat comfortably at his computer ably directing it to do as he wished was now at another machine's mercy. Before, I had controlled my world. Now my world controlled me. Never had I felt so powerless and scared and less like myself. Unfortunately even worse experiences were yet to come.

I want to emphasize the desperation I felt when my doctors gave me radiation for my brain from 31 December 2008 until 11 February 2009. This treatment made me incapable of reading just as I had been unable to read before. Why did I have to lose my ability to read again? I was supposed to be a reader and a writer, a father, a doctor of philosophy and a Shakespeare professor! Who was I now? What had this invasive toxic cancer and the technologies thrust upon me to remove it done to me and my relationship to my world? I felt like Lear in the wilderness, Hamlet after his father's death, Caesar as Brutus plunges in the dagger, and so many other Shakespearean characters. I felt like a man whose relationship to his world had suddenly become unmoored. During both these periods of illiteracy I was continually terrified, furious and frustrated. What a drag illiteracy was! It made me so upset and terrified that I might never be able to read again. I cried every day in early March when I could not read. I felt terrible despair when I experienced illiteracy.

Not only did I lose my ability to read, I lost my ability to clearly express myself through speech. After my tumour treatments I could not remember simple terms. No longer the voluble, confident scholar, I was now an idiot incapable of using simple words to describe people, places and things. It is incredibly frustrating being incapable of saying words, and even now as I begin to improve I still struggle to express myself clearly. I often ask people to be patient with me as I try to describe things, but the speech attempt process sometimes does not work. I try to spell words but sometimes that does not work either. I try to draw a spatial image with my fingers to express words, but that often fails too. How can I be a teacher, I wondered, if I cannot even explain that I want a sandwich for lunch? The technologies and methodologies on which I usually relied were unusable, my place in my world lost. Like so many of Shakespeare's characters I had been yanked out of a life in which my place was certain and thrown into a maelstrom, an Arden Wood of the mind and spirit, a Prospero's island where I had no idea who I was or where I belonged.

A brain I had thought under my control was attacked by an internal enemy and temporarily overtaken by it. The tumour's cells were mine, but they were not my normally functioning self. My body was seized by a radical insider, a tumour that behaved like an outsider. It took over my brain and my brain could not combat it. I had to defeat and remove the tumour, but the tumour was me. Self-defence required an attack of the self. Inner–outer, self–other, safe–dangerous dichotomies all fell apart, merged and fell apart again as my whole sense of an intact self baffled me. I was experiencing interiority as exteriority and exteriority as interiority until my self was utterly deformed. With or without technology it became ridiculous to believe that my heart or mind could work in only one way.

Yet as happens with so many of Shakespeare's characters, I found within this dizzying series of reversals, redefinitions, assaults and losses powerful insights that propelled me to a fuller and more direct encounter with the process of Shakespeare's technologically driven meaning loss and redefinition. My descent brought me new insights and methodologies that actually strengthened my scholarship. As a result of a biotechnological invasion I was unable to read, speak, live and define myself as I always had, but after an agonizing period of disorientation I was forced to find new ways of doing work until a new paradigm for myself and my world emerged. Having done so brought me closer to my subject than ever, and substantially improved my work, yielding to me a new post-posthumanist perspective.

Let me next discuss how my 'disability' of illiteracy gave me the 'ability' to better read Shakespeare. I will begin with a discussion of what literacy did and did not mean in Shakespeare's age. During the English Renaissance powerful technological innovations in everyday life dramatically changed how people related to themselves, others, and their worlds. Perhaps the most radical of these technologies was the printing press developed by Gutenberg in the 1450s. Suddenly information that had only been delivered orally or visually and according to the presenters' agendas was available as text. One of the most important texts was a version of the Bible. Though we tend to think now of that moment as empowering, it was a very contradictory issue at the time. Faith was traditionally vested in a person or institution. The origins of printed texts, however, were far less trustworthy, and so engendered far more confusion and mistrust. Erasmus reportedly secured money from multiple patrons by inserting different dedication pages into printed copies of his new books and then distributing the dedicated copies to different patrons. Thomas Dekker's pamphlet *Lanthorn and Candlelight* (1608) describes a similar con-game in which a rogue misleads a gentleman into believing that a printed work has been dedicated exclusively to him. Texts could in these ways deceive in using techniques people could not. Of this Shakespeare was acutely aware, and he reveals a fluctuating attitude toward print in his plays.

One of the most humorous references to the unreliability of print technology in the plays occurs in *The Merry Wives of Windsor* after Falstaff sends identical love letters to Mistress Page (like Pistol, her very name connotes a new technology) and Mistress Ford. Mistress Page is shocked and outraged both by the letter that she receives and by its duplication:

> I warrant he hath a thousand of these letters, writ with blank space for different names – sure, more, and these are of the second edition. He will print them, out of doubt – for he cares not what he puts into the press when he would put us two. I had rather be a giantess, and lie under Mount Pelion. Well, I will find you twenty lascivious turtles ere one chaste man. (II.1.65–71)

In Mistress Page's claim that Falstaff has written a thousand of these love letters with blank spaces for different names she indicates anxiety regarding the abuse of print technology. Here the integrity of both the letter and its deliverer are in question. The true origins and aims of each letter are uncertain. The new technology has yielded disorientation that is here comic.

As always with the technologies of his age Shakespeare fluctuates in his view. Analogies between printing and procreating in his work did not always suggest infidelity or gender ambiguity. In fact printing terminology becomes a metaphor for marriage in *The Taming of the Shrew* when Biondello uses a somewhat obscure legal phrase to encourage Lucentio to ready himself to marry Bianca: 'Take you assurance of her *cum privilegio ad imprimendum solum'* (IV.5.17–18). This Latin phrase which means 'with the exclusive rights to print' or 'with the privilege of printing only' was the statement of a printer's copyright and it appeared on the title pages of many printed books.

How might Shakespeare and his contemporaries have benefited philosophically, psychologically or artistically from the print revolution? Perhaps access to multiple texts and multiple editions of individual texts permitted Europeans living during the first full century of the print revolution a certain *perspectival lightness* by which I mean a certain tolerance for contradiction or at least a tendency to accept as valid distinct viewpoints that might have previously seemed mutually exclusive. Elizabeth Eisenstein believes that in the age of print technology Europeans could 'come to terms with the coexistence of incompatible views and the persistence of contradictory movements without treating any as anomalous and without forcing them into over-simple grand designs' (1979, 440). This seems an excellent gloss of Shakespeare's creative genius. Shakespeare provides an array of characters with distinct and valid perspectives.

Certain characters have more lines to speak than others, and some are certainly more sympathetic than others, but rarely are characters given epistemological or ethical monopolies. 'O brave new world / That has such people in't!' says Miranda. ''Tis new to thee,' her father answers (V.1.186–8). The equipoise between different perspectives on the same reality may not have been *caused* by the tempest of texts that emanated from English and Continental printshops, but it mirrored the equipoise that developed coincidentally with the massive proliferation of printed materials. Miranda's mention of a 'brave new world' is usually read in a proto-colonial context, but it also resonates with recent work on early modern print culture. Several scholars have indicated that the explosion of printed materials that took place in the sixteenth century represented the creation of a New World of texts which may have been more important to literate European than the discovery of the previously unknown lands and peoples across the Atlantic. Rhodes and Sawday have asserted that a 'new world – a paperworld – had come into existence some fifty years before Columbus's encounter with the "New World" of the Americas', and the creation of this paperworld was 'the defining moment of the European Renaissance' (Rhodes and Sawday, 2000, 1). If Elizabethan and Jacobean Englishmen could not read a broadsheet, a pamphlet, a chapbook, an octavo, a quarto or a folio they could either examine the woodcuts and engravings that came with printed texts or listen to one or more individuals recite a proclamation, a song, a psalm, a traveller's tale or a play.

The technology of print was transforming not only Shakespeare's world but also his audience's relationship with his work. Many plays that he intended to be solely experienced visually and directly became available as written texts in the last years of the sixteenth century. Reading his work as text, which is how the vast majority of scholars have primarily approached it ever since, changed the experience of it fundamentally from what the author intended. But how do we know what it was like to experience his work only visually and directly? How can we experience Shakespeare's works as free from the 'pollution' of textual interpretation?

This is what happened when I lost my ability to read. My temporary illiteracy forced me and my students to engage only visually with the plays, exactly as Shakespeare intended. My 'disability' thus became an 'ability' because I could experience the play exactly and only as the author intended, different from most scholarly approaches. We saw film clips then talked about them, examining their strengths and weaknesses, exploring how they affected us. Watching Trevor Nunn's 1996 filmed production of *Twelfth Night*, for example, I found myself unable to rely on a printed text of the comedy or a printed critique of the play by a fellow scholar. This forced me to listen to and watch the DVD editions of the play with uniquely necessary intensity. I began to think about how many of the audience members for Shakespeare's plays were in fact illiterates, groundlings, similarly struggling to understand their place in an increasingly confusingly technological, mechanical, textualized world. From the ashes of my old posthumanist intellectual metacriticisms emerged flesh-and-blood people on stage in Shakespeare's time with whom my 'disability' allowed me to connect. This experience of illiteracy gave me a unique insight into how the technology of the printing press changed the perception of Shakespeare's work.

My illiteracy also enlightened me regarding a current technological disruption in our ability to experience Shakespeare's work. Unable to drive a car, I could not travel to a live Shakespeare performance. I was forced to experience his plays solely on DVD. The DVD provided the ability to connect more directly to and understand his characters' agonizing dislocations and redefinitions. Also the DVD revealed another way in which we are separated from the experience of the play intended by its author. On DVD one can skip through plays (or films) according to one's own agenda. Using technology I could reinterpret the filmed work, watching scenes to discover my own ideas about sub-plots, character arcs and thematic patterns.

How do my new insights relate to our own era of great technological change? I began work on *Technology and the Early Modern Self* in earnest in 1999, the end of a decade that had seen tremendous technological breakthroughs including the rapid development of the Internet and the Web. As high-tech industries of every conceivable stripe revolutionized the marketplace, my fellow Stanford graduates who opted to stay in Silicon Valley amassed tens of millions of dollars in stock options, a phenomenon I observed with a mixture of amazement and envy. At the same time, though, there was a steady stream of apocalyptic rhetoric related to the so-called Y2K or Year 2000 problem. The Millennium was approaching, and what it seemed to hold in store was the catastrophic collapse of our computer-based society. Planes could fall from the sky, bank accounts could be wiped out, and all home computers and personal electronics could be rendered useless.

In Jonathan Sawday's *Engines of the Imagination: Renaissance Culture and the Rise of the Machine* he points out that a similar combination of optimism and pessimism marked early modern attitudes toward technology. This dualism was true in our time as well. For example, as my work on my dissertation continued beyond the millennium year the poles of optimism and pessimism remained, but they were strangely reversed. The date, 1 January 2000, came and went without undue inconvenience. Programmers had managed to insert patches into countless lines of computer code that corrected their myopic error. The apocalypse had been averted. There was a collective sigh of relief, a sense that our technoculture was more durable and more versatile than we had feared. But in less than two years the nightmarish predictions made in the months leading up to 1 January 2000, proved strangely prophetic. Planes did indeed fall from the sky on September 11, 2001, taking skyscrapers and part of the Pentagon with them. At the same time the paper fortunes that so-called *dot commers* (a term that neatly conflated technology and identity) had amassed for themselves and their investors were quickly erased as the high-tech bubble burst. The technological, military and economic crises we have recently suffered will raise many new questions about Shakespeare's roles within our culture. Will Shakespeare help us gain new insights and stronger connections to what is most real and move forward to a better understanding of our culture? Only time will tell.

It seems worthwhile to consider briefly in closing what the future may hold for relationships between technology and the self. How will we cope with the present environmental crisis? Technologies which consume fossil fuels are part of the problem. Can other technologies provide the literal and figurative 'saving power'? How will we manage the weapons of mass destruction that nations have long sought both for their immediate destructive ability and for what they believe to be their potential to deter so-called conventional war? The key question for the future posed by the present studies is this: how will the technologies of the future influence who we are? If history is any guide they may instill discipline, enable ambition, encourage versatility, transform our perspectives on the world around us, provide us outlets for play, inspire artistic creations and remake us in countless other ways. Frequent or repeated use of a technology can make us forget its presence.

Like any habitual activity, technology use becomes *second nature*. Every now and then, though, particularly when technologies fail, we are reminded of our dependence on certain types of tools, instruments and machines. We may even occasionally stop to consider that we are constantly being remade by the tools and machines we use to remake the world around us like the laptop, the Internet, the cell phone and the car, to name just a few. Yet we rarely stop to consider precisely *how* the tools that we make come to remake us. I undertook these studies primarily to answer questions about the early modern period, and I have done my best to limit my analysis to that era. However, as historians of technology are quick to point out, tools designed for one purpose often have unanticipated ramifications. While my primary goal has been to help sort out the relationships between early modern technologies and their users, I hope that my work in this area also helps us to better understand the relationships between tools and the people who use them in our own time.

Fortunately my illiteracy has faded slightly in recent weeks. I can catch many words now. I can almost read. I cannot read a scene from a published Shakespeare play from start to finish yet, but I can read the occasional word, even the word Shakespeare. After losing my ability to read I felt stupid for weeks, but now I am starting to enjoy literacy again. What a thrill it is today, 19 March 2009, to begin to feel that I may soon be able to read again. My hope is that I will retain the insights gained from apprehending Shakespeare's works as he intended, merging these with insights gained from more traditional textual scholarship, and producing a uniquely accurate perspective on his works. Only when stripped of the ability to read does one learn the tremendous importance of experiencing a Shakespeare play in performance. Though my situation has been terribly frustrating and troubling it has also taught me fascinating information about how one experiences Shakespeare.

(Adam Max Cohen died on 2 January 2010, aged 38)

Works cited

Augustine, St (1984) *Concerning the City of God Against the Pagans*, trans. Henry Bettenson, Harmondsworth: Penguin Books.

Basalla, George (1988) *The Evolution of Technology*, Cambridge: Cambridge University Press.

Cohen, Adam Max (2006) *Shakespeare and Technology: Dramatizing Early Modern Technological Revolutions*, New York and Basingstoke: Palgrave Macmillan.

Cohen, Adam Max (2009) *Technology and the Early Modern Self*, New York and Basingstoke: Palgrave Macmillan.

Eisenstein, Elizabeth (1979) *The Printing Press as an Agent of Change*, Cambridge: Cambridge University Press.

Masten, Jeffrey, Peter Stallybrass and Nancy Vickers (eds) (1997) *Language Machines: Technologies of Literary and Cultural Production*, London and New York: Routledge.

Noble, David (1999) *The Religion of Technology: The Divinity of Man and the Spirit of Invention*, London: Penguin Books.

Pittenger, Elizabeth (1996) 'Explicit Ink', in Louis Fradenberg and Carla Freccero (eds), *Premodern Sexualities*, New York and London: Routledge, pp. 223–42.

Rhodes, Neil, and Jonathan Sawday (eds) (2000) *The Renaissance Computer: Knowledge Technology in the First Age of Print*, London: Routledge.

Sawday, Jonathan (2007) *Engines of the Imagination: Renaissance Culture and the Rise of the Machine*, London and New York: Routledge.

Shakespeare, William (1997) *The Norton Shakespeare based on the Oxford Edition*, ed. Stephen Greenblatt, Walter Cohen, Jean E. Howard and Katharine Eisaman Maus, New York: W. W. Norton & Company.

White, Lynn, Jr. (1978) *Medieval Religion and Technology: Collected Essays*, Berkeley: University of California Press.

Index

Names beginning with Mc are filed as if spelt Mac, for ease of reference.

Abraham, Nicolas   181, 188–90,
    191, 192
Adorno, Theodor   106
affect   10, 12, 25–39, 77, 98–9, 104,
    107, 110–12
Agamben, Giorgio   60, 126, 128, 129,
    223, 235
animal studies   16, 58–76, 77,
    161, 204, 209: see also human;
    Shakespeare, William, and animals
anthropocentrism   13–14, 42, 44, 45,
    52, 64, 77, 86, 98, 105, 109–11,
    119, 130, 143, 187, 218: see also
    posthumanism
anthropomorphism see
    anthropocentrism
Appelbaum, Robert   70
Ariosto, Lodovico   63
Aristophanes   156
Aristotle   32, 41, 61–2, 64, 100,
    122–3, 128, 171
Arnold, Matthew   6, 10
Ascham, Roger   137
Augustine of Hippo, Saint   41
autothanatography   226

Bacon, Francis   58
Badmington, Neil   43, 156, 157
Bakhtin, Mikhail   165
bare life see Agamben, Giorgio
Barthes, Roland   52
Basalla, George   241–2
Bataille, Georges   3, 235
Baudrillard, Jean   52, 107
Beattie, James   33, 39
beheading (defacement)   220–9, 231
Belsey, Catherine   4, 38, 42, 48–51,
    52, 54, 191, 217
Benjamin, Walter   125, 164
Bennington, Geoffrey   52, 174, 175
Bentham, Jeremy   60

Bergson, Henri   55
bêtise see animal studies; obstinacy
Bilgrami, Akeel   10
Blackmore, Susan   24
Blair, Hugh   24
Blanchot, Maurice   186, 187
Bliss, Lee   115–16, 130
Bloch, Ernst   164
Bloom, Harold   7, 14, 15, 35, 41–2,
    46–50, 161, 216, 220
Bodmer, Walter   23, 35, 39
body politic   114, 118–20, 122, 126,
    127, 129
Boehrer, Bruce   13, 16, 58
Boswell, James   72
Boyce, Benjamin   61
Bradley, Andrew Cecil   32, 33, 35, 103
Braidotti, Rosi   214
Brecht, Bertolt   61, 106, 122–3
Brewster, Scott   51
Burckhardt, Jacob   156
Burke, Edmund   37

Calderwood, James   123
Campbell, George   29, 33, 34
Capell, Edward   80
Carroll, Lewis   222, 235
Castiglione, Baldassare   151
catachreses   216–18, 223–4, 227,
    231–2, 234, 235
Cavell, Stanley   114
Cavendish, Margaret (Duchess of
    Newcastle)   25
Charnes, Linda   3, 5
Chaucer, Geoffery   61, 144, 146
Cicero   130
Cixous, Hélène   186, 199
clichés see catachreses
cognitive poetics   8, 107
Cohen, Adam Max   11, 15, 17: see
    also turning tech

Coleridge, Samuel Taylor 33, 59, 197
Copernicus, Nicolaus 78
Corballis, Michael 23
Corby, James 235
Corneille, Pierre 30, 33
Cottom, Daniel 55
Crane, Mary Thomas 12
Crowley, Martin 164
cyborgs 11, 16, 45, 46, 52, 114–32, 225, 230–1, 232, 241, 247: *see also* human; inhuman

Damasio, Antonio 77, 86
Danby, John 109
Dante Alighieri 41, 218, 229, 235
Darwin, Charles 52, 77, 78, 81, 86
Darwin, George Howard 79
Dawkins, Richard 82
De Grazia, Margreta 195–7, 198, 199, 204, 217, 231
De Man, Paul 216, 233, 235
De Waal, Frans 77, 92
dead metaphors *see* catachreses
defacement (beheading) 220–9, 231
Dekker, Thomas 250
Deleuze, Gilles 17, 52, 60, 194–7, 198, 201–11
Dennett, Daniel 78, 84, 92
Dennis, John 25
Derrida, Jacques 17, 49–50, 52, 55, 60, 114, 117–18, 124–6, 130, 164, 169–71, 175, 181–6, 187, 191, 194, 210, 216, 235
Descartes, René 46, 58, 60, 61, 64, 65, 77, 85, 124, 182
Diogenes Laertius 62, 74, 175
disembodiment *see* embodiment
Dixon, Thomas 27
Dollimore, Jonathan 42–3, 100–1, 161
Dr Who 38
Dumas, Alexandre 144
Dunbar, Robin 24, 35, 39

Eagleton, Terry 61, 101, 110
earth systems science 78, 79, 81, 82
ecocriticism 16, 92
Egan, Gabriel 13, 16

Eisenstein, Elizabeth 251
embodiment 77, 86, 112, 117–19, 125, 128, 135, 205, 230: *see also* cyborgs
emotion *see* affect
Engle, Lars 105
Enlightenment, Scottish
    Enlightenment 24, 26, 35, 36, 37
Erasmus of Rotterdam, Desiderius 137, 250
Erlich, Avi 186
Everyman 110

Felperin, Howard 157
Fenves, Peter 174, 175
Fernie, Ewan 168, 185–6
Fineman, Joel 161
Fisher, Philip 28
Fletcher, John 71
Fontaine, Jean de la 126
Forset, Edward 130
Foucault, Michel 26, 139, 161, 194, 230, 234
Fowler, Elizabeth 59, 63, 73
Fraenkel, Michael 209–10
Freeland, Cynthia 37–8
Freud, Sigmund 52, 110, 147, 156
Fudge, Erica 13, 45, 63–4
Fukuyama, Francis 36
futurism 3, 12: *see also* pastism; presentism

Gaia 78, 80, 81, 82, 85, 92
Galilei, Galileo 78
Garrick, David 217
Géricault, Théodore 221–2, 229, 230, 233
Gibson, James 102
Girard, René 63, 191
Globe Theatre 213
Goethe, Johann Wolfgang von 32, 59
Goldberg, Jonathan 161
Gower, John 133, 146
Graham, Elaine 43
Gray, Chris Hables 129
Greenblatt, Stephen 16, 42, 67, 109, 134–5, 199–200
Guattari, Félix 17, 52, 60, 194–7, 198, 201–11

Habermas, Jürgen 106
Hamlet 3, 15, 17, 30, 31, 33, 35, 41,
    59, 70, 91, 102, 105, 108, 110,
    134, 161, 181–237, 248
    the Ghost 204, 211, 227: *see also*
    hauntology; monster
    graveyard scene 207, 213–37
    the skull 214, 216–20, 222–33, 235
    spectre 181–6, 188–90, 191; *see
    also* out of joint; untimeliness
Hammond, Antony 82
Haraway, Donna 14, 45, 46, 230
Hardy, Thomas 102–3
hauntology 17, 184, 190: *see also
    Hamlet*, the ghost; monsters
Hawkes, Terence 42, 52, 184–5,
    190, 200
Hayles, N. Katherine 55, 85–6, 107,
    157, 230
Headlam Wells, Robin 8–9, 14
Hegel, Georg Willhelm
    Friedrich 228–9, 230
Heidegger, Martin 17, 122, 164, 171–3,
    175, 181–2, 185, 186, 187, 191, 205
Herder, Johann Gottfried 32
Heresbach, Conrad von 68, 71
Hillis Miller, J. 52
Hobbes, Thomas 117–19, 121–2,
    125–30
Hoby, Sir Thomas 137, 151
Holbein, Hans 110, 217, 225
Hölderlin, Friedrich 171–4, 175
Holderness, Graham 12
homeostasis 77–94
Homer 41, 122
homo sacer see Agamben, Giorgio
Horace 34
Horkheimer, Max 106
human
    and animal 45, 46, 117–18, 125:
    see also animal studies
    and machines 23, 38, 51, 129:
    see also cyborgs
    and nonhuman 58, 67, 118
    and plants 209
    and technology 52: *see also* cyborgs
    human nature 8–9, 10, 23, 24, 27,
    29–39, 44, 45, 77, 108
    see also humanism; inhuman;
    posthumanism

humanism 8, 201, 203, 208
    and humanist criticism 32, 42–4
    and the humanist subject 85–6,
    107, 119, 125, 233
    see also human; posthumanism
Hume, David 24, 26, 27, 58, 61
humours *see* affect
Hutcheson, Francis 26, 27

incest 86–91, 134, 147–8, 152,
    156, 206
inhuman 46, 51, 99, 129, 182, 188:
    see also human

John of Salisbury 130
Johnson, Barbara 174
Johnson, Dr Samuel 67–8, 72, 73,
    80, 244
Jonson, Ben 62–3, 70, 146
Jowett, John 82
Joyce, Richard 92
Jung, Carl Gustav 156–7

Kafka, Franz 160, 168, 170
Kames, Henry Home, Lord 15, 23,
    24–5, 26–32
Kamuf, Peggy 52
Kant, Immanuel 37–8, 41, 60, 73
Kearney, Richard 188, 191
Keats, John 33
Kepler, Johannes 78–9
Kermode, Frank 162, 174
Kierkegaard, Søren 191
Kinney, Arthur F. 11
Knights, Lionel Charles 59, 60
Knowles, Richard 204–5, 210
Kristeva, Julia 110
Kuhn, Thomas 63, 74
Kuzner, James 126, 128

Lacan, Jacques 52, 152–3, 157, 161,
    186, 188, 191, 216, 226, 234,
    235, 233
Lacoue-Labarthe, Philippe 187
Lamarck, Jean-Baptiste de 86
Laroche, Emmanuel 195
Latour, Bruno 3, 61, 73
Lauri-Lucente, Gloria 235
Leibniz, Gottfried Wilhelm 201
Levi, Primo 160

Levinas, Emmanuel 191
Locke, John 58, 61
Lodge, David 59, 61
Lovelock, James 78, 81, 85
Lunberry, Clark 123

Macchiavelli, Niccolò 99
McEwan, Ian 44
McLuskie, Kathleen 161
Marcus Aurelius 210
Marcuse, Herbert 164
Margulis, Lynn 78
Markham, Gervase 68–9, 71
Marlowe, Christopher 47, 167
Marshall, Cynthia 119, 161
Marx, Karl 143, 156, 175
Mason, John Monck 68
Menander 62
Miller, Henry 209–10
Milton, John 71
monsters 114, 119, 121, 128, 142,
    143, 163: *see also Hamlet*, the
    Ghost; hauntology
Montaigne, Michel de 63
More, Sir Thomas 137
Mousley, Andy 9–10, 11, 15, 16,
    52–3, 97
Murakami Haruki 130

Nancy, Jean-Luc 17, 164, 169
new historicism 109, 135
Newton, Sir Isaac 78
Nietzsche, Friedrich 52, 194, 203, 230
Norris, Christopher 52
Nutall, A. D. 161

obstinacy 114–15, 121–6
out of joint 221: *see also* hauntology;
    untimeliness

Parker, R. B. 116
passion *see* affect
Paster, Gail Kern 26, 225
Pasternak, Charles 23, 39
pastism 12: *see also* futurism;
    presentism
Patterson, Anabel 130
Paulin, Roger 32
Pechter, Edward 1
Pico della Mirandola 48, 137, 138–9

Plat, Gabriel 68–9
Plato 41, 156, 171, 173
Pliny the Elder 235
Plutarch 130
Pontormo, Jacopo 36
Pope, Alexander 25, 216, 227
postanthropocentrism 5, 13, 15, 16:
    see also posthumanism
posthuman 174, 181, 184, 187–90,
    192, 207: *see also* human;
    inhuman
posthumanism 6, 23, 31, 41, 53–5,
    73, 92, 97, 104–6, 111–12, 155,
    210, 241
    and alterity 46, 48, 135, 138
    and antihumanism 35, 48, 52, 97,
        137, 142
    and the care for the human 97–112
    critical posthumanism 5, 9, 15,
        16, 43–5, 51–2, 54, 97–9
    and death 160–77, 213–37
    and the deconstruction of
        humanism 44, 54, 60
    and information technology 108
    and misanthropy 16, 51–5,
        139, 142
    and philosophy 195
    and politics 17, 115
    and postanthropocentrism 54
    and the posthuman condition 85–6
    and the posthumanist subject 42–3,
        55, 85, 187
    posthumanities 43
    and posthumanization 45, 52
    and poststructuralism 234
    and the (proper) name 195–6
    and remediation 46
    and transhumanism 3–4, 11, 17,
        232–3, 235
    without technology 230
posthumous *see* posthuman
prehuman/prehumanist 58, 110
presentism 3, 9, 12: *see also*
    futurism; pastism
prosopopoeia 233, 235
prostheses 117–18, 122, 126, 127
Protagoras 171, 175

Quinones, Ricardo 184
Quintillian 33

Rabinow, Paul   52
Racine, Jean   30
Rancière, Jacques   17
Readings, Bill   2
Regan, Tom   60, 73
retrofitting   12, 13, 194
Rhodes, Neil   11, 12, 15, 46, 251
Richards, Ivor Armstrong   34
Richardson, William   33, 34
Riss, Arthur   119, 128
Robson, Mark   17
Rogers, Pat   32
romanticism   31, 32, 33, 35, 102,
    121, 133, 134
Roudinesco, Elisabeth   192
Roupnel, Gaston   184
Royle, Nicholas   163, 191
Ryan, Kieran   100–1, 164–5

Said, Edward   2, 5, 10, 15
Sanbonmatsu, John   53
Sartre, Jean-Paul   2
Saussure, Ferdinand de   52
Sawday, Jonathan   11, 12, 45–6,
    115–16, 251, 253
Schmitt, Carl   129
self-fashioning *see* Shakespeare,
    William, and Shakespearean
    character
self-regulation *see* homeostasis
Seneca   171
Shakespeare, William
  and alterity   135
  and animals   13, 58–76
  and early modern
      technology   241–6, 250–2
  and ecocriticism   13
  and humanism   6, 7–9, 45
  and humanity   65
  and the inhuman   41, 46–56
  and (the invention of) the
      (in)human   3, 6–7, 12–14
  Late Plays   90, 133–59
  and life   9–11
  and posthumanism   4, 13, 58,
      106, 134
  Romances   90
  and Shakespearean character   7–8,
      16, 30, 31, 32, 33, 41, 47–8,

58–76, 79, 99, 109, 114,
    133–59, 244
  soliloquies   30, 31: *see also* Hamlet
  and technology   11–12
  Tragedies   29, 103, 111, 161, 181
  works: *Antony and Cleopatra*   243;
      Coriolanus   16, 45, 55, 114–32,
      156; *Cymbeline*   90, 91; *Hamlet*
      see Hamlet; *Henry IV*   79,
      243; *Henry V*   167, 213, 243,
      244; *Julius Caesar*   248; *King
      Lear*   16, 26, 41, 65, 83–4, 86,
      97–113, 135, 248; *Macbeth*   33,
      41, 65, 84, 135, 213; *Measure
      for Measure*   17, 160–77;
      The Merchant of Venice   16,
      41–57, 65, 86, 147; *The Merry
      Wives of Windsor*   245, 250;
      *A Midsummer Night's
      Dream*   243, 244; *Othello*   24,
      26, 33, 135, 213, 235;
      Pericles   16, 86–92, 133–4,
      145–53, 155; *Richard II*   90, 208;
      Richard III   82, 84; *Romeo and
      Juliet*   161; *The Taming of the
      Shrew*   250; *The Tempest*
      53–4, 65, 135, 251; *Timon of
      Athens*   16, 133–4, 135–45, 146,
      149, 151–5; *Titus Andronicus*   58,
      66, 70, 72; *Twelfth Night*   252;
      Venus and Adonis   80; *The
      Winter's Tale*   84–5, 90, 91
Shrank, Cathy   130
Sicherman, Carol   123, 130
Sidney, Sir Philip   63
Sillers, Stuart   235
Simonides of Amorgos   62
Singer, Peter   60, 73
Socrates   156
Sophocles   32, 41
speciesism   13–14, 58: *see also* animal
    studies; posthumanism
Spenser, Edmund   79–80, 241
Stevens, Wallace   182
Stiegler, Bernard   118
strangeness   163, 165–6, 173–4
the sublime   37–8
Suddendorf, Thomas   23
Sypher, Wylie   184

Taylor, Gary 2
technological determinism 107
Tennenhouse, Leonard 161
Theophrastus 61–2, 74
Topsell, Edward 66–7, 69
Turner, Henry S. 72
turning tech 11, 243: *see also* Cohen,
  Adam Max
Tytler, Alexander Fraser 32–3, 39

untimeliness 181, 184–5, 187,
  188: see *also Hamlet*, the Ghost;
  hauntology; out of joint

Vesalius, Andreas 218, 220, 221,
  222, 230
Vickers, Brian 25, 42
Viola, Bill 36–8

Virgil 72
Voltaire 31, 32, 165, 194, 217

Watson, Robert 101–2, 162
Watt, Ian 61
Weber, Max 52, 106
Weismann, August 86
Wells, Robin Headlam 44
White Jr., Lynn 241
Whiten, Andrew 35, 39
Wilkins, George 146
Williams, Raymond 77
Wills, David 233
Wilson, Richard 161, 194, 200
Wilson, Scott 1, 2
Wolfe, Cary 235
Wordsworth, William 39
Wu, Duncan 39